BETWEEN
EAST AND WEST

BETWEEN
EAST AND WEST
THE ORIGINS OF MODERN RUSSIA: 862–1953

R. D. CHARQUES

PEGASUS BOOKS
NEW YORK LONDON

BETWEEN EAST AND WEST

Pegasus Books LLC
80 Broad Street, 5th Floor

Copyright © 1956 by R. D. Charques

First Pegasus Books trade paperback edition 2012

Library of Congress Cataloging-in-Publication Data is available.

ISBN: 978-1-60598-367-7

10 9 8 7 6 5 4 3 2 1

Printed in the United States of America
Distributed by W. W. Norton & Company, Inc.
www.pegasusbooks.us

CONTENTS

MAPS

PREFACE

Between East and West is addressed in the first place to the reader who does not know a great deal about the subject. Since the meaning of history is always in doubt, since the past is perhaps entirely without meaning save in the light of the experience of our own time, it is meant to offer some assistance in understanding the Russia of today.

If general histories are commonly deprecated nowadays, narrative history is suspect. The book takes the form of a chronological narrative for two reasons: first, because interest in the subject is likely to thrive best on a chronological narrative, next because so much writing in recent years on the Russian past has been expository and quasi-philosophical. How much is left of the substance of history after the interaction of persons and events has been abstracted from it I should hesitate to guess.

The book is essentially a work of vulgarization, though one beset by inexhaustible controversy. For the period up to the close of the eighteenth century I have gone to the classic Russian secondary sources, above all to Kliuchevsky, Platonov and Soloviev; to the heterodox (and sometimes pedantic) medieval studies of Presniakov, to the Marxist historian B. D. Grekov and the first three volumes by Professor Vernadsky in the Yale *History of Russia*; to Waliszewski and other biographers. I should also like to acknowledge the stimulus I have found in the brilliantly sustained and occasionally perverse work of Michael T. Florinsky, *Russia: a History and an Interpretation*. For the nineteenth century, which scarcely any Russian historian has tackled as a whole, and the subsequent period I have drawn upon the most diverse material, among which I would specially mention a work in English— Professor Hugh Seton-Watson's compact study of the period from 1855 to 1914, *The Decline of Imperial Russia*.

I have been uneasily aware all through of the perils of simplification. The history of the Russian national minorities receives scant attention in this volume, though Soviet text-books of history give almost as much space on occasion to events in Transcaucasia or in what are now the constituent republics of central Asia as to the progress of affairs in Russia proper. Although Russian objectives have continually oscillated between the lure of east and west and it may well prove in the end that the greatest significance of the Russian revolution has been in the east, I have had no choice but to concentrate on European Russia and the course of domestic

7

events; the account I have given of Russia's foreign relations is necessarily very condensed. Apart from describing the conditions of serfdom, the governing factor in the Russian economy before emancipation, there is little here in the way of economic history before the middle of the nineteenth century. And I have contented myself for epilogue with the broadest sketch of Russian history since the Bolshevik revolution.

In what sense the revolution was inevitable seems to me at this time of day matter for academic debate; though the predicted revolution, as someone has said, never arrives, history is what succeeds. But it should always be borne in mind that the Bolsheviks seized power by a *coup d'état* imposed upon a 'spontaneous' revolution, itself the culminating act in a long tradition of popular revolt. For the rest, though no doubt a view of history in which laws of causation are replaced by chance or accident is deservedly berated as philistinism, human destinies always come under the rule of Lecky's King Hazard or of what H. A. L. Fisher, in a famous passage, called the play of the contingent and the unforeseen.

All historiography is interpretation, but more especially a *Short History* such as this. I have attempted few arguments which are new; even in the writing of history our ancestors have stolen all our best ideas. But I have had three points of emphasis in mind throughout. The first is the formative part played at various periods of Russian history by the autocrat himself. The doctrines of economic determinism have no relevance here. Innovation in Russia, both before and after the revolution, has always been instituted from above, and the absolutism of the tsars gave to each reign a distinctive moral climate in which the opportunities for reform prospered or declined. From Peter the Great onward, except for the period of palace revolutions immediately afterwards, I have thought it best to devote a separate chapter to the reign of successive autocrats of all the Russias.

Next, since serfdom is the very fabric of Russian social history, I have tried to distinguish the successive phases of the 'peasant question'. Until yesterday the peasants were substantially the Russian people and Russian backwardness was more than all else the backwardness of the peasant masses. It is a commonplace that for a century before the revolution the condition-of-the-peasant problem, before and after emancipation, was the touchstone of Russian opinion. But it should also be borne in mind how often during the same period the peasant habit of resistance to authority determined domestic policy. It does so still.

It is this degree of continuity of the Russian present with the past which is the third and chief point of interpretation I have wished to make. The idea is more familiar to us to-day than it was a few years ago. The harvest of revolution was prodigious. In no part of the world and at no period of history has change been so rapid or so far-reaching as in Russia during the past decades. Much of the old life was broken up and the promise of a new world glowed with revolutionary faith and courage. Yet through all the convulsions of Russian society and the whole vast process of transformation the threads of continuity with the past remained unbroken.

In an obvious sense history is continuous and the past indestructible. It survives in geography, its monuments are not so much institutions as mental habit and tradition. In recognition of this truism the makers of the new Russia have aimed at nothing less than transforming both nature and Russian human nature. But in setting out to create a classless socialist society they reversed what for them were the universal laws of historical materialism; they proceeded, that is, from proletarian revolution to industrial revolution, not the other way round. It was thus more than ever necessary to adapt universal laws to Russian historical conditions. In this process the Bolshevik leaders encountered the same conditioning factors which had governed the experience of previous rulers of Russia—her size, her multi-national character, the disparate cultural levels of her population, the force of peasant psychology. In grappling with them as revolutionaries Lenin and his followers found themselves obliged to resort to historic Russian methods.

It could scarcely have been otherwise. The revolutionary idealism of 1917 was both utopian and practical, but when the utopianism had faded the impulse that was left resolved itself into the sacrificial ardours of a belated industrial revolution. Except for the empirical originality of a planned economy, what has happened in Russia since 1917 has in many respects less to do with Marxist ideology than with the inheritance from the past of material and moral backwardness. This the Communist rulers of Russia attempted to overcome by force. And the harder they tried to exorcize the ghosts of the past the more insidious was the legacy of Russian history under the tsars. As creators of a new society they found themselves committed to a revolution from above which required for its execution the extreme centralization of power effected by Ivan the Terrible, the principle of compulsion in universal service adopted by Peter the Great, the bureaucratic police state of Nicholas I. This, in sum, was what the mechanics of the dictatorship of the proletariat proved to be. If the Marxist formula, which governed statements of policy, was a new and powerful leaven, the dough was historic Russian dough.

Moral judgments, it is argued with some point, have no place in the writing of history. But in relating the regime variously described as Soviet or Communist or Bolshevik to its Russian origins it is impossible to ignore the moral claims it advances. Nor, perhaps, is there any reason to despair of a more liberal Soviet dispensation.

A concluding note on dates and the spelling of Russian names is obligatory. Complete consistency in the transliteration of Russian names is not to be looked for. I have sometimes followed familiar spellings even when they are questionable, have varied in one or two small ways what is more or less standard academic usage (for instance, – *sky* not – *ski*; *ia* after a consonant, *ya* after a vowel) and have similarly followed the current practice of Englishing Christian names like Ekaterina and Nikolay but not others like Vasily or Yury. As for dates, Russia did not abandon the old or Julian calendar for the Gregorian or new calendar (which is our own) until 1918. I have generally given the dates in new style, but on red-letter occasions I have given them in both old and new. The old is eleven days behind in the eighteenth century, twelve days behind in the nineteenth and thirteen days behind in the twentieth.

CHAPTER I

THE EURASIAN
BACKGROUND AND THE SLAVS

AN AREA OF NINE million square miles, almost a sixth of the earth's land surface, and a population of appreciably more than two hundred million of whom three-quarters are Slav but who comprise some sixty different nationalities and more than twice as many ethnic groups of smaller size: such was the mighty Union of Soviet Socialist Republics at its apex. How did it come into being?

Look at the map. Geography, which moulds the life of nations, has been a constant determinant of Russian history. In one sense, it still is.

Look at the three basic maps of the physical geography of Russia: the continuous, all but illimitable plain, or series of adjoining plains, the distribution of soil and vegetation, the rivers of western Russia. On these maps are written the commonplaces of eleven centuries of the historical development of the Russian state.

First, the vast level land stretching from the Baltic and the Carpathians across Siberia to the Pacific. East and south on the far rim of the plain are high mountain ranges, but, except for the narrow chain of the Urals running across it from north to south, within all that immensity of space the land is scarcely anywhere more than a few hundred feet above sea level. This is the unbroken mass of Russia in Europe and Russia in Asia. The Ural Mountains, which in the atlas still serve to divide Europe from Asia, are in no sense a natural barrier, since from gradual foothills they rise to a mean altitude of no more than 1,500 feet. Nor, apart from greater extremes of winter cold and storm in the east, does the atlas division mark any natural difference. On either side of the Urals the distinguishing features of soil and vegetation are identical. And through the wide southern passage between the Urals and the Caspian Sea, in historical and pre-historical witness to the geographical unity of the plain, the waves of migration from Asia have flowed westwards across those treeless expanses known as the steppes, their distant horizon evoking in other than landlocked eyes an irresistible image of the expanses of the ocean.

From this absence of any significant natural barrier to stem the tide of internal migration springs the motive force of the Russian past. The history of the Russian people derives in the first place from a continuous and still uncompleted process of colonization. Wanderers in vast and all but empty lands, they extended the boundaries of settlement with what can only be called the sanction of geography. It is this sanction which makes them wanderers still. Where other nations expanded oversea the Russian empire grew by migration into endlessly contiguous territories. The price of empire-building on so vast a scale was eventually paid in the main-tenance of autocracy and serfdom—in the ultimate reckoning, in the Russian revolution—but in historical retrospect the whole evolutionary process wears a simple and fateful logic.

Not unlike the United States, Russia has evolved, through still wider spaces and over a larger stretch of time, from an advancing frontier. Northward to the Arctic Circle and beyond to the ice of the ocean, reaching in the easternmost corner the tongue of land separated by only seventy miles of the Bering straits from the American continent; southward to the Black Sea and the Caspian and the Caucasus between; eastward to the Sea of Japan and the border regions of China and India, the frontiers were pushed forward almost entirely by settlement and only in the last resort secured by war. In the west alone, where expansion met the east-ward drive of other peoples, was the frontier for so long unsettled— a condition reflecting the age-long problem of the cultural boundary between Russia and Europe.

Next, across the whole of the Eurasian land mass, there is the regular latitudinal succession of distinctive zones of vegetation: tundra, forest, fertile steppe, desert steppe. The zones expand or shrink in depth between the eastern and western extremities and often overlap. In the west, below the forest region which presents to the foreign traveller's eyes the characteristic Russian landscape of pine, fir and birch, the central deciduous forest meets arable steppe in a wide belt of wooded open country which is the vital scene of political growth in Russian history; in the east, the desola-tion of the tundra merges into the impenetrable northern stretches of the Siberian taiga. But over the whole land the same succession of vegetation zones prevails, with the great stretch of *chernozem*, the famous black earth, at the agricultural heart of the steppe. This natural scheme has dominated the course of internal Russian development through the centuries.

From the monotony of the infinite plain and its severities of climate came the endurance of the Russian people. And more than all else from the short season between seed-time and harvest came economic backwardness.

The tundra of the northern zone is vast and all but empty still.

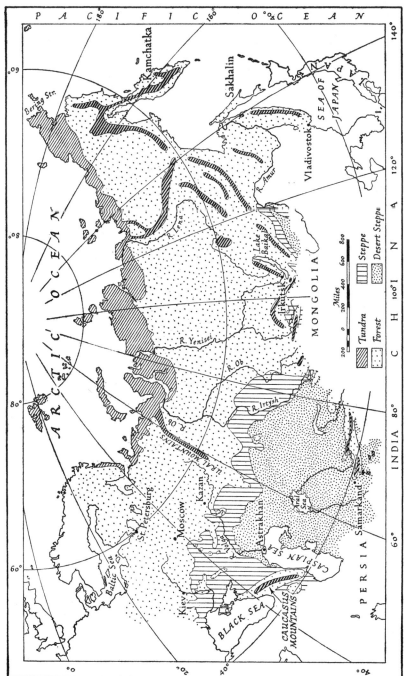

Vegetation Zones of Russia

A wilderness of frozen marsh, over which move the reindeer herds, it has played little part in the march of Russian civilization. Soviet development in the Arctic for strategic ends, however, appears to have brought with it here and there dramatic hints of a transformed scene.

The zone of arid steppe in the east and south-east, equally vast, includes the regions of many ancient cultures of central Asia, destroyed by barbarian war and conquest. Here modern technique has most sharply modified the old complex of geographical factors. Soviet development in these salt wastes, following on tsarist attempts to sow the desert, seems to prefigure a process of radical transformation. In the swift rise of industry, the growth of communications and the promise of ambitious works of irrigation the present appears to be joining hands with the remote past. For it was from these plains that the pastoral culture of the nomads reached across the fertile steppe to the agricultural settlements and commercial centres at the forest edge of the nascent Russian state, leaving in their passage to and fro enduring marks upon the whole order of Russian society.

Forest and steppe; steppe and forest. It is the shifting of the seat of power between them which points the logic of Russian political development. The original line of demarcation, which in the west reached from Kiev to just south of Moscow and thence to Kazan, near the junction of the Volga with the Kama, has long been obliterated in the creation of a single tract of agriculture. But it represents the axis upon which internal growth revolved. For long centuries forest and steppe constantly collided in war and as constantly met in commerce. They contributed twin and mutually conflicting impulses to the evolution of a migrant society. The Russia of the forest lived in constant peril from the Russia of the steppe, and the political institutions originating in the one were shaped by struggle with the menace from the other. Yet at the same time it was out of the exchanges between them that, first, Kievan Rus, the earliest but abortive Russian state, and then Muscovy, its successor, proceeded to develop a social habit and tradition of their own. In the formative phases of the unification of the east Slavs the nomads alone served as a link between the widely separated centres of an embryonic Russian civilization.

Between them the relative security of the forest and the nomadic freedom of the steppe established a pattern of cohesion and anarchy in the national life. The task of centuries was to unify forest and steppe in a stable political order. Although immense steppe areas were conquered earlier, not until the middle of the eighteenth century was the task of integrating them in a unified scheme of administration effectively begun. It has not yet been completed.

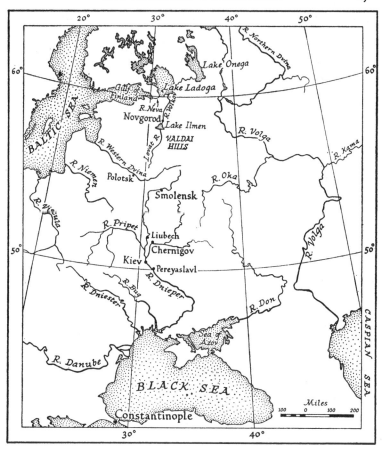

The River Roads of Western Russia

Finally, there are the great rivers of Russia in Europe, broad and slow, their tributaries too numerous to be shown on the map, flowing through forest and steppe in all directions but none issuing into a truly open sea. Russia, its endless distances for so long traversed by this single means of communication, has always been, and still is, a land of countless river roads. Along the dense forest and marshland reaches of these roads in the west, a barrier against the incursions of the nomads in possession of the steppes, the early tide of Slav settlement advanced. Linked by easy portages, the great river system originating in the Valdai hills signposts the trail of Russian colonization: the upper and middle reaches of the Dnieper flowing southwards into the Black Sea, the upper Volga farther

east, and the whole system of the Western Dvina and the Volkhov
flowing northwards into the Baltic, formed a close network of
waterways, along which the east Slav tribes spread out across the
plain.

Frozen for a third of the year or more, their steppe reaches
perilous, the greatest of them, the Volga, discharging its waters
into the landlocked Caspian, the rivers in the west were the prime
agent of unity among the migrating east Slav tribes. Kievan Russia
itself originated as a loosely unified state in 'the road from the
Varangians to the Greeks', the river road from the Gulf of Finland
to the Black Sea.

The history of Russia is ordinarily taken to begin in the ninth
century with 'the coming of the Varangians', a wave of the
astonishing tidal flow of Viking exploration and conquest which
swept over Europe and the Mediterranean. But there were
Scandinavian outposts of piracy and trade along the river roads of
Russian some two centuries or more before, and it is to the still
earlier centuries of the movement of the Slav tribes in ancient
Russia that we must look for the rudimentary beginnings of a
Russian state.

The Slavs make their earliest recognizable appearance in history
in the northern Carpathians and on the Vistula, in the fifth century,
as subjects of the Huns, the most predatory of the nomadic invaders
from Asia. But by then the recurring pattern of invasion of the Slav
tribal lands had already been established. Russian pre-history
echoes with the onrush across the steppe of the mounted nomads.
Archaeological, linguistic and other studies within the past sixty
or seventy years have filled in a remarkable picture of the earliest
civilizations on Russian soil, above all in the Black Sea region,
where a cluster of Greek colonies fringed the camping and trading
ground of the Iranian tribes known to Herodotus in the fifth
century B.C. as Scythians. Its most striking feature—a key to
Russian historical continuity—is the evidence of the interchange
between the desert and the sown, between the economy of the
pastoral steppe and the developing agriculture and handicrafts of
the settled or half-settled areas.

From the Scythians and their successors, the Sarmatians, through
the Goths who descended from the north in the third century and
the Huns from the Mongolian desert at the end of the fourth, to
the Mongol invaders in the thirteenth century, the Russian steppelands experienced a succession of great waves of migration. It was
the collapse of the Hun power after the death of Attila that set in
motion all the peoples under that barbarian sway, the Slav world
among them. From this wide dispersion came the eventual division
into east Slavs, west Slavs and south Slavs. Assimilated in time

to the culture of the west were the Slav tribes who became Poles, Czechs and Slovaks; into the pattern of disparate cultures in the Balkans were drawn the south Slavs—Serbs, Croats, Slovenes, Bulgarians. The east Slavs became Russians, the largest of the Slavonic family of Indo-European peoples.

Towards the middle of the seventh century empire over an immense area of the Russian land, stretching from the Urals to the Dnieper, was firmly held by the Khazars, in whom were probably mixed Hun elements and Caucasian tribes. Theirs was the first real attempt to unify steppe and forest. The Khazars cultivated the land, engaged in cattle-breeding and fishing, but remained essentially nomadic. Their empire was above all a trading empire, in which the exchange of horses, cattle, hides and wool for grain and handicrafts of metal and leather extended to Byzantium and to Arab and eastern lands. The east Slavs were an integral factor in this trade. The rule of the Khazar khan—who, according to legend, had adopted the religion of Judaism—was mild, even beneficent, and was marked by exemplary religious tolerance; the pagan Slav tribes were in a sense allies rather than Khazar subjects. But Arab encroachments in the south of the empire culminated in a disastrous military defeat of the Khazar host in 737, in which great numbers of Slavs were taken prisoner. It was evidently in these circumstances of growing insecurity that the Slav tribal leaders turned to the Northmen—the Varangians—for aid and protection.

No less intrepid as explorers and warriors than the Vikings in England, France or Sicily, their fellow Northmen in Russia had already penetrated from the Baltic into the region of the upper Volga and then moved westwards and to the south. Some had reached as far afield as the Sea of Azov. Pirates, traders and mercenaries, they soon came to share power in the trading towns on the banks of the Dnieper with the Slav merchants there. At the time the Khazar power was at its height they were concentrated along that great river road to the Black Sea and the rich markets of Byzantium. The Varangians levied tribute, fought and plundered, gave armed support to Slav trading expeditions and mounted trading expeditions of their own. A Varangian military company or companionship—the *druzhina* of the princes of the Kiev era—usually guarded merchandise in transit.

With the progressive weakening of the Khazar power Varangian leadership grew steadily along the river road from Novgorod on the Volkhov in the north to Kiev on the Dnieper in the south. The Northmen pressed hard upon the Khazars as the organizers of commerce with Byzantium. To meet the challenge, the Khazar khan fortified the lower reaches of the rivers of the steppe to bar the trade routes to the Black Sea. It was to re-open these trade

B

routes that a Varangian expedition in some strength crossed the Baltic either in the year 862 or some years earlier. This is the origin of the legend, dramatically commemorated in the ancient Russian chronicles, of Rurik, the founder of the ruling dynasty of Kievan Russia.

The story tells of a Slav revolt against the Northmen in the service of Novgorod and of popular dissensions and disorder after they were driven out. The decision was then taken to invite a prince to govern Novgorod and to dispense justice. 'Our land,' went the appeal, 'is great and rich, but there is no order in it. Come and rule over us.' Here, in an evident rationalization of history, is the chronicler's version of things.

In the event, an expeditionary force set sail under the leadership of Rurik, ruler of south Jutland. After spying out the land from the region of Lake Ladoga, he re-established order in Novgorod, without himself attempting to penetrate farther south. It was a partly Slav force led by two Varangian adventurers in his following, Askold and Dir, which advanced towards the edge of the southern steppe and possessed itself of Kiev. In 878 or thereabouts Rurik's successor, Oleg, took the river road south, captured Smolensk on the way, and in turn seized Kiev from its Varangian overlords.

Oleg was the real founder of the primacy of Kiev in the Russian land. 'The mother of Russian cities', it was to unite under its power the principal Slav tribes scattered along the great river road of the plain and so bring into being the loosely organized state of Kievan Rus.

Rus was the ancient name of what became known popularly as Russia only in the late seventeenth century. Its origins have been endlessly debated and are still problematical. Was it, as scholars on the whole are inclined to think, the name of either a Scandinavian tribe or military retinue, or of the place near Kiev where the Northmen first settled? The whole notion of a foreign derivation for Rus is strongly distasteful to the temper of Russian nationalism to-day. But one thing is certain: the use of the name spread from the Varangian-Slav heart of Kiev to all the lands conquered or assimilated to their cause by the princes of Kiev.

CHAPTER II

THE ERA OF KIEV

MORE THAN THREE and a half centuries passed between the coming of the Varangians and the Mongol conquest of Russia. The period, for which 'Kievan' is a convenient rather than accurate description, bristles with problems of interpretation. Brilliantly lit by legend, it has a glow of enchantment for Russian scholars and has always excited in them a peculiar poetic pride.

The era of Kiev brought to birth, if not a Russian national consciousness at least a unifying sense among the tribes of a common Slav inheritance. It wrought, within narrow limits, a profound cultural transformation through the introduction of Christianity and of a literary language. It produced the first flowering of Russo-Byzantine art. For all the savagery endured at the hands of the nomadic invader and the internecine strife of their own princes these were centuries of fruitful growth in the life of the Russian people. In some ways Kievan Russia reached an appreciably higher level of civilization than was attained in these centuries in the west. And yet the historical significance of Kiev is not at all what this record of achievement would suggest.

For the true beginnings of the imperial Russia of the tsars were elsewhere. They must be looked for not on the Dnieper but on the Volga. The classic nineteenth-century view that there was no line of evolution from Kiev to its successor state has been heavily discounted, more particularly by Presniakov, who lays elaborate emphasis on an organic link between them. The fact remains that Kiev proved, in effect, a false start. The primacy of its grand-princes was brought to a close three-quarters of a century or more before the Mongols overran the land, and at no time had they achieved real unification of the territories over which they claimed suzerain rights. Where the ruler in Kiev led the princes of the other Russian lands often followed; it was Kiev, above all, which in its period of effective power offered a measure of security against the incursions of the nomads of the steppe. The city itself, which in the eleventh and twelfth centuries was apparently larger than any contemporary city of the west, shone with the splendour and pride of its new stone churches; while as a great commercial metropolis it drew the other Slav trading towns like a magnet. But, unlike Moscow long before the Muscovite state took coherent shape, it was never in any sense a national centre.

Even to describe Kiev in this period, as since Kliuchevsky it has so often been described, as the cradle of Russian nationality is in some degree to echo the nationalist (and anti-Polish) exaggeration of nineteenth-century Russian historiography*. The Varangians, it is true, who were relatively few in number, in the end proved only a potent and dramatic stimulus; they were at no higher level of cultural development than the Slavs, and then, as afterwards, it was Russian numbers which counted. For the rest, though the ancient chronicles bear eloquent witness to a deepening sentiment for the *russkaya zemlia*, the Russian land, the sense of unity in the Kievan era was still too weak and uncertain to permit the rise of a political order radiating from a single centre. The peculiar dynastic principle of Kievan rule, moreover, ran counter to any form of centralized government. The suzerain prince, or grand-prince (*veliki kniaz*), of Kiev stood at the head of the line of descendants from Rurik, and ruled as such—not in his own person but as senior representative of the princely dynasty. Though he drew regular tribute and taxes from the territories absorbed under his titular rule, the other members of the princely line installed there were seldom slow to dispute his authority. Only a common interest in foreign trade and defence, indeed, united the Russian city-states of the period of Kiev, much of whose history, after all, consists of civil war. In what from the beginning took the form of a loose and precarious federation of independent riparian territories rather than a single state, Kiev enjoyed an ascendancy that always fell short of implicit overlordship.

The degree of unity attained through the power of the grand-princes of Kiev could not have been won without the support of the Greek Orthodox Church. Here the initial commonplaces on the role of Orthodoxy in Russian history need to be borne in mind. With Christianity, which Russia took from Byzantium, there came not only Byzantine canon and civil law but also the Byzantine conception of the sanctified state. The spiritual content of Greek Orthodoxy in Russia, as distinct from its complex ceremonial, made little immediate impression upon either rulers or the people as a whole; even the ritual of Orthodoxy, in point of fact, was assimilated by the rude majority only centuries after it was introduced to Russia. But from the beginning the Church was the instrument by which Byzantine secular doctrine pervaded the land. The doctrine which, even in conditions of Russian disunity, impressed

* The Polish claim to recognize in Kiev an original centre of Polish culture has, of course, never made sense for any Russian historian.

itself most deeply, and which in the course of time was so powerfully strengthened by the example of the Mongol khans, proclaimed the divine right of the sovereign ruler. Against the old pagan custom of recognizing the rule of the military leader, the Church set the Byzantine principle of the anointed and absolute prince. Thus the attempted unification of the Russian lands by the princes of Kiev always had behind it the authority of the Church. Greek Orthodoxy in Russia, from the first a central prop of the state, was in later years the keystone of the arch of imperial autocracy. Save only in its brief trial of strength with the state in the seventeenth century, the Church recognized in the ruler of Russia God's supreme representative on earth.

It was the close-knit trading relations between Kiev and Byzantium which lent strong support to the adoption of Greek Orthodoxy. Before the official conversion of Russia to Christianity in 988 several expeditions were launched from Kiev against Tsargrad (Constantinople) which were designed to protect the rights of Russian traders in Byzantium. Every spring a flotilla of trading vessels assembled at Kiev to be escorted by the prince and his *druzhina* down the Dnieper to the Black Sea. The produce of the Russian forests, honey, wax, tar and, above all, furs—sable, marten, fox, beaver, otter—which were collected by the merchant-princes of Novgorod and elsewhere, partly as tribute to the prince of Kiev, were exchanged against Byzantine silks, spices, wine and gold. But more valuable than Russian furs were the cargoes of slaves destined for the slave-markets of Constantinople and the Islamic east. There the prince of Kiev was famed as a slave-dealer.

Until recent years, before Marxist historians had fully elaborated their theories of Russian feudalism, it was customary to point a contrast with western feudalism by discovering in slavery the whole basis of Kievan Russia's economy. This was to ignore the growing importance of her trade in foreign markets to the west and also the development in the forest areas even at this early period of agriculture. But it is clear that slave-trading gained a lively impetus from the feuds of the Russian princes. The captive in war and the victim of raid or reprisal might always be sold into slavery together with the defaulting debtor. The Church was a humanizing influence here, setting its face against slavery though all too often tolerating it on the Church's own lands.

There had been some infiltration of Christian ideas into the pagan society of Kiev in the ninth century. But further progress was slow. Eclectic and formless, Slav paganism had a pantheon of deities representing the forces of nature but no very clearly marked ceremonial rites. Yet its appeal to so backward a people long survived the conversion of Russia, as indeed pagan belief and practice long survived the introduction of Christianity in the west. The formal act of conversion took place some thirty years after the celebrated pilgrimage to Constantinople of Olga, mother of Sviatoslav, one of the great heroes of the early Kievan period. Not all the energy of Olga's proselytism availed her with the princes of Rus. The task of officially instituting Christianity as the religion of the land fell to her grandson Vladimir—Vladimir the Saint, as he became centuries afterwards—who renounced the old beliefs on behalf of his subjects, in familiar fashion enforced a general baptism and then married a sister of the Byzantine emperor.

Our knowledge of Kievan Russia is still largely conjectural. The ancient chronicles, which are our chief source, are not, strictly speaking, contemporary documents. They were compiled, for the most part in churches and monasteries, in the fifteenth and sixteenth centuries, and reproduce, together with local-historical supplements, a 'fundamental' chronicle of Kievan beginnings originally composed in the early twelfth century which was itself based upon an earlier and lost collection of existing records and of oral tradition. Their ecclesiastical bias is very evident. Yet they reflect clearly enough the civilizing mission of the Church. Though its direct influence was for long restricted to a thin crust of the population, the Church stood for the civilizing values common to the Christian world: it was a school of letters, it softened barbarous custom, it upheld to some extent the rule of law. Through Church Slavonic, which was based upon a Bulgarian dialect and which was brought into use throughout Orthodox Slavdom by 'the apostles of the Slavs', the Greek brothers Cyril and Methodius, Russia received its translations from the Greek scriptures and liturgies and evolved a native literature, sacred and secular, of its own.

This, however, was achieved at a price. Church Slavonic closed the door in Russia upon Greek classical culture. Its perpetuation as a literary language narrowed intellectual horizons. It struck few roots in popular speech. And with all this the adoption of Eastern Christianity marked the initial stage in the separation of Russia from Europe. Byzantium, the gilded heir of Rome, which attained its greatest brilliance in the tenth century, admittedly preserved and diffused the riches of western civilization at the time of the conversion of Russia. But the widening breach between the Roman and Greek Churches, to which formal effect was given in 1054, could not but precipitate division between Russia and the west. That ominous division, which was to be completed by the Mongol conquest and which neither Peter the Great nor any of his successors could repair, was of supreme and lasting historical significance.

The Russian Church did not become, at least in title, a national Church until the fifteenth century. Until then it remained a metropolitan district of the patriarchate of Constantinople. Its head, the metropolitan of Kiev, was appointed by Constantinople and for centuries was almost always a Greek; probably most of the bishops under him, like the lower clergy as a whole, were Russian. The ignorance of the mass of the lower clergy in Russia has always been notorious, the abundance of churches a cause of wonder. The earliest of the churches adapted in style from Byzantine models were the cathedral of the Holy Wisdom (St Sophia) in Kiev and in Novgorod, both begun in the middle years of the eleventh century. The famous Pechersky monastery (the monastery of the Caves), founded by the hermits Anthony and Theodosius, came into existence near Kiev at the same time. This was to prove the most notable centre of Kievan ecclesiastical culture and the heart of early medieval Russian piety.

For the Christian ideal in Russia for many centuries, and perhaps until the very last, was essentially monastic. Beyond monastery walls the pomp and formalism of Orthodoxy left little room for spiritual fervour. It was from the 'black' clergy in the monasteries, as distinguished from the 'white' and married clergy who ministered to the world outside, that Orthodoxy drew not only its bishops but power and purpose. The monasteries in the later period of Kiev reflected all that was most aspiring in the polity of the Church. Yet at the same time, of course, as in the medieval west, they sheltered gross corruption, or were mere places of refuge in a barbarous land, in which not the Christian revelation alone summoned men to withdraw from the world. The monasteries in the towns, still more those which in later years sprang from rude hermitages in the forest, reaped a harvest of great possessions from the attractions of their mode of life.

The accumulation of wealth was pursued more deliberately by the early grand-princes of Kiev through the conquest of wider domains and the consequent extension of their sources of tribute. A campaign of expansion on the most ambitious scale, harking back to Oleg's attempt to possess himself of the whole of the southern lands and of Constantinople itself, was waged by Sviatoslav (964-972), the earliest ruler of Kiev to bear a Slavonic name but almost certainly a Varangian warrior. Sviatoslav fought the Khazars and captured their urban centres on the steppe, warred against Byzantium and held brief sway over an empire that stretched in the south from the Volga to the Danube. His power was shattered by the recurring waves of violence of the nomadic Pechenegs, a name which in Russia ever afterwards came to stand for deeds of peculiar savagery. Taken by surprise in a Pecheneg raid and killed in battle near the Dnieper rapids, his skull, we are told, was fashioned into a drinking cup for the princely victor.

During the next two and a half centuries the Russian power advanced and retreated across the land. Supremacy now went to the princes of the forest regions or of the steppe borderlands, now to the nomads beyond. In the west, towards the close of the period, when the internecine struggle of the princes was at its height, new enemies appeared on the scene to threaten the integrity of the settled Russian lands.

The most successful of the suzerain princes of Kiev was Yaroslav —Yaroslav the Wise (1019–1054)—the son of Vladimir the Saint. It was he who came nearest to establishing undivided control of the whole system of princely territories. Yaroslav, who disposed finally of the Pecheneg menace, made of Kievan Russia not only a more coherent state than it was to be for many generations afterwards but also a considerable power in Europe. War and dynastic marriages both made their contribution. Yaroslav himself was married to a Swedish princess; his sister was married to the Polish king; three daughters were married to the kings of France, Hungary and Norway respectively; a son married into the Greek imperial family of the Monomachus. At the end of prolonged hostilities with Byzantium Kiev once more established relations with the city of Constantine, and these bore fruit in the building of great churches and the progress of learning. It was during the period of Yaroslav's rule that the preparation of the first code of Russian laws, the *Russkaya Pravda*, was begun. Though the code—which was largely concerned to regulate commerce—permitted resort to private vengeance, the enforcement of a scale of penalties for the different sorts of crime known to the law marked a considerable step forward in that untutored time.

With the death of Yaroslav the tentative growth of a centralized state ruled from Kiev comes to an end. Though individual suzerain princes show foresight and resolution, though a common dynastic loyalty asserts itself from time to time among the contending territorial princes, the land is given up to feuds and rivalries, the corrosion of civil war and the onslaught of the invading nomads. Much historical controversy has raged round the principle of dynastic succession during these events. It is known that Yaroslav divided rule of the territories of Kiev between his five sons, enjoining upon them a fraternal unity. But whether in fact there was a new and strange law of succession, not from father to son but from brother to brother, with a general post of the princes in order of seniority to subsidiary domains and titles, remains doubtful. What is certain is that the princely line of Rurik swelled in numbers, disputes multiplied, and almost everywhere the opportunity occurred for a prince to claim hereditary rights of possession to the land his father held. This is the origin of the so-called appanage system, the system of small patrimonial principalities within the dynastic order of a suzerain prince, which first developed in the early part of the thirteenth century.

Into the earliest phase of this process of disintegration there entered the Cumans, or Polovtsi, of the southern steppes. An even fiercer and more bloodthirsty tribe than the Pechenegs, they carried fire and slaughter into the land, destroying towns and villages and massacring their populations or carrying them off into slavery. Their fearful raids, the first of which had occurred in 1061, continued at yearly intervals during the next 150 years, almost right up to the appearance of the Mongols. The princes built forts and entrenchments, enclosed settlements within walls, but all to little purpose. It was the lands bordering the steppe, including Kiev, which necessarily suffered most, and there civil war raged most recklessly. So envenomed were the quarrels of the princes in the south that almost every one of them resorted at some time to Cuman or Polish aid in waging war upon a neighbour. There was no enduring leadership on the Russian side, no apparent hope of united resistance. Foreign trade languished with the Cuman possession of the southern river roads. The Russian retreat into vast empty spaces, above all into the depths of the forest, which was precipitated in the first place by the threat of slavery, was resumed.

The final attempt under the leadership of Kiev to rally the princes in a united front against the invader was made by Vladimir Monomakh (from the Greek imperial name Monomachus). A virile warrior and statesman, who at the age of sixty was chosen to rule as grand-prince, Monomakh had already led successful expeditions against the Cumans and restored temporary order. But his rule only lasted twelve years, and at his death in 1125 the old dissensions were resumed more violently and the Cuman terror once again distressed the land. Once more there were appeals for unity; from time to time an attempt was made to carry the war into the enemy's country. Such was the disastrous campaign of 1185 led by a prince of Chernigov which is nobly recorded in *The Song of the Host of Igor**. Here the prevailing note is one of genuine national sentiment and of bitter reproach against the princes for their divisions in face of the Russian land's mortal peril.

The grand-princedom of Kiev declined. Its central support, the great river road stretching from the Gulf of Finland, by way of the Neva, the Volkhov, the Lovat, the Western Dvina and the Dnieper, to the Black Sea, collapsed in the southern border regions with the decay of foreign trade. The scale of movement away from

---

* Although the authenticity of this poem or prose-poem has been strenuously contested, it is still generally accepted as the masterpiece of early Russian literature.

the domains of Kiev mounted rapidly. Migration was in three directions—north-west, north-east and south-west.

In the far north-west stood Novgorod, the city built on both banks of the Volkhov from which the trade in furs and the produce of the primeval Russian forests reached in all directions. The highest period of Novgorod's power—the greatness of *Gospodin Veliki Novgorod*, Lord Novgorod the Great—was still to come, but already the city exercised dominion over a vast commercial empire stretching to the White Sea, the Arctic and east of the Urals. It offered opportunity and wealth to the newcomer adventuring across great tracts of marsh and forest from the despoiled south. It also offered, though as yet still uncertainly, the rewards of a developing tradition of republican liberty.

Novgorod had originally paid tribute to Kiev, but from an early date it won virtual though not unchallenged independence. By the beginning of the thirteenth century the city had built securely upon the foundations of great wealth and republican custom. Its princes, as indeed was the case with the princes of other territories, were not infrequently 'shown the way out'—that is, deposed; power was concentrated in the hands of a *posadnik* (mayor) and a ruling council. The institution of the *veche*, the city popular assembly, was common to all the principalities of the Kievan era and, where it flourished, preserved a rude basis of urban democracy; but nowhere did it attain the authority it reached in Novgorod.

A gathering of the adult male population, the *veche* in Novgorod was ordinarily summoned by the great bell of St Sophia to the open space before the cathedral in order to register its opinion, which it did by shouts of approval or disapproval. The shouting, like the subsequent fighting, when the required unanimity was not reached, between rival bodies of opinion, was a token of civil liberty. The *veche*—it was never a representative body—grew to maturity in Novgorod only after the Mongol conquest, which brought a further great influx of population to the north, but the republican tradition it served spread deepening roots all through the period of Kiev's decline. The prospects of freedom in Rus, indeed of freedom throughout the domains which widened into Muscovy, were centred upon Novgorod.

It was the migration north-eastwards, towards the historic region between the river Oka and the upper Volga in which Muscovy originated, that was to have the most fruitful consequences. Movement into the river valleys of these forest areas, from which the indigenous Finns retreated or where the two races intermingled, favoured the growth of the existing small principalities there and stimulated the rise of new political centres. These were the circumstances in which the power of the prince of Suzdal, within whose territories lay the negligible settlement of Moscow, emerged as a rival to Kiev. Its founder, a grandson of Monomakh, Andrey Bogoliubsky, rapidly extended his authority and removed his capital to the newly created city of Vladimir, on the Kliazma. Vladimir was a portent of change throughout the Russian lands. Of fierce and formidable temperament, the earliest exemplar of Muscovite autocracy, Andrey challenged the sovereignty of the grand-prince and in 1169, in a rage of massacre and pillage which Kiev had never before experienced at Russian hands, laid waste the city. This done, he returned to his throne in Vladimir. He died in 1174, murdered, like later Russian autocrats, by members of his personal following.

Thereafter Vladimir-Suzdal, whose princes maintained a large military retinue, held what was in effect a dominant position in Rus while apparently sharing titular honours with Kiev. But the one, sheltered from invasion, waxed in strength, while the other continued to be exposed to the marauding violence of the steppe. Its prestige fatally shaken, its trade all but vanished, Kiev suffered an irreparable blow from the capture of Constantinople in 1204 in the Fourth Crusade and the establishment of the Latin empire. This brought Kiev the final loss of its privileged connexions with Byzantium. Impoverished and greatly diminished in population, the mother of Russian cities was to go down in ruin at the Mongol conquest and then to be drawn into the rising power of Lithuania and of Catholic Poland. Not until the latter part of the seventeenth century was it finally restored to the empire of the tsars of Muscovy.

Before the light of Kiev faded, however, its heritage passed to the princes of the south-west. Out of the Russian migration to the lands west of the Dnieper, to the marshlands of the Pripet basin and the upper valley of the Niemen, and to the land between this region and the Carpathians, sprang the domination of the princes of Volynia and Galicia. From this removal to a new border-land (for which the Russian word is *ukrain*) sprang also the sub-division of the Russian people, characterized by differences of language and culture, into Great Russians, Little Russians (Ukrainians)* and White Russians. The power of Volynia-Galicia seemed likely for a time to flow back towards the river road; its princes contested supremacy in Rus with Vladimir-Suzdal. But the political map in the west was undergoing swift change. There, while the Cumans were still uncontained in the south and south-east, new enemies of a dispersed Rus made their appearance in the shape of the warlike Lithuanians, themselves under Teuton pressure farther west. The Livonian Order of Sword-Bearers, an

* Polish historians, it should be repeated, give a very different interpretation of the ethnic origins of the Ukraine.

off-shoot of the Crusading orders, advanced eastwards from Riga; the Teutonic Order of Knights, which was to become the spearhead of Prussia, spread out between the Niemen and the Vistula. Powerless to resist the German tide, the Lithuanian tribes drove eastwards on to Russian soil.

The more enveloping and more mortal threat had still to come. The dreaded name of the Tatars first became known in Russia in 1223. 'No one knows for certain,' says the chronicler, 'who they are, or from where they come, or what their language is, or race, or faith, but they are called Tatars.' The Cumans on the south-east steppe fled at the approach of a Mongol host and looked for the means of common defence to the princes of Russia. Russian and Cuman forces were joined: it was resolved not to await the enemy's further advance but to go out and give battle on the steppe.

The armies met on the river Kalka, near the Sea of Azov. Experienced in military leadership, proved in battle, the Mongol horsemen wreaked hideous slaughter. The prince of Kiev was crushed to death under the boards on which the Tatar victors' feast was spread.

But the invaders, after having reached the line of the Dnieper, did not penetrate further into the land. They turned back, their reconnaissance completed, and the people of Russia were incredulous of their deliverance and fearful of what was to follow. For fifteen years they knew no more of 'the evil Tatars', 'the accursed godless strangers'. Only then did the Mongols sweep forward once more from the alien steppe and press on like a devouring sea over the Russian land.

CHAPTER III

THE MONGOL POWER

IN THE WEST, conquering armies in earlier ages of history have generally imposed their system of government and law upon the conquered. In the east, the conquered have often assimilated the conquerors. Situated between east and west and belonging to neither, Russia under the Mongol power suffered both experiences.

Out of the nomadic clans dispersed in the Mongolian desert a chieftain named Temuchin, who became known as Genghis Khan, had forged an instrument of war both disciplined and savage and with it built a vast empire in Asia which extended westwards as far as the Transcaucasian lands. This was a first step only. The goal of Mongol power was nothing less than world conquest.

Genghis Khan died in 1227. It was under his grandson Batu, whose armies were led by the redoubtable Subutai, that the plans for a further great movement of migration across the Russian plain were put into effect. In 1237 a mounted host, in its train a moving encampment of women, children, horses, cattle, camels, felt-roofed tents and primitive siege artillery, swept over the Siberian steppe, crushed the Bulgar tribes east of the Volga and crossed the river. Extended in 'decimal' organization, their advance covered by intelligence and scouting parties, the host stormed the divided principalities of the Russian land.

The Mongols, although as a military power they comprised great numbers of Turkish and other elements, continued to be known to the Russian people as Tatars. Their method of conquest everywhere was to demand money tribute and to punish resistance with fire and sword. First the principality of Riazan, which was so often to take the initial shock of Tatar invasion, was devastated: the towns and settlements were burned, captives were slaughtered, tribute was exacted. Then came the turn of the territories of Vladimir: Kolomna was laid waste, Moscow was burned down, the city of Vladimir itself and its cathedral razed by fire. Ruin and massacre followed everywhere in the path of the invader in the north-eastern lands. In the spring the horde struck out for Novgorod, but, protected by its hinterland of marsh, which the weather made impassable, the city was spared. The Tatars withdrew southeastwards, to the country of the lower Volga and the Don, only to return a year later. After ravaging the remaining centres of the north-eastern principalities, they pressed south into the regions bordering the steppe, Pereyaslavl and Chernigov, and, notwithstanding desperate resistance, which was passionately commemorated in oral legend, captured and sacked Kiev itself. The devastation was prodigal even by Tatar standards; for years afterwards, it appears, the deserted city was strewn with the bones of the dead.

The invaders now advanced further west. Volynia and Galicia were subdued and the restless horde crossed the Carpathians. Separate armies overran Hungary and Poland. The Mongol power had spread from Peking to the gates of Vienna and the Adriatic when it was halted by united resistance in Bohemia. Batu, simultaneously disturbed by news of the great khan's death and of dissensions in Mongolia, retired through a conquered Russia to the lower Volga, where the fertile steppe joins the edge of the Caspian desert. In the city and encampment called Sarai, which at first was located near the mouth of the river and was afterwards moved higher up, not far from what is to-day Stalingrad, the Golden Horde—the westerly *ulus* or division of the Mongol empire—set up its capital.

The Tatar yoke endured in all for two and a half centuries, though with undiminished pressure only during the first century. While the Golden Horde preserved internal stability and military cohesion Russia lay prostrate. The rule of Sarai was tyrannous and absolute. The strictest order in the land was essential not only for the punctual payment of tribute but also for the protection of foreign trade, in which the Mongol khans were as interested as their Khazar predecessors centuries earlier. Tribute was heavy. In the earlier phase of domination there were Mongol officials in all the Russian principalities to assist in the task of collection. More than anything else it was the burden of these regular payments which provoked Russian revolt and disturbance during the period of Tatar supremacy. Revolt was put down by the conquerors with extreme ferocity, not seldom through the agency of Russian princes or with some degree of Russian aid. For a further task of the Mongol officials was to recruit Russians for service with the Mongol armies. A Russian force fought in China under Kublai Khan.

Though the steady movement of population continued towards the north-east and north-west, the people of the devastated southern borderlands largely remained where they were after the conquest. There was no alienation of the princely lands; as cattle-breeders and horse-breeders the Mongols were content to encamp on the pastures of the steppe, and even as cultivators they found on the steppe fertile land enough and to spare. But in all the principalities the heir to the princely title was required to establish his claim to the succession by paying homage in person to the khan of the Golden Horde in Sarai. From him—or, sometimes, in the earlier and supreme period of Mongol power, from the great khan himself in Mongolia or in China—the Russian princes received their *yarlyk*, the seal of their investiture. This favoured the rise in various parts of the land of new suzerain princes, each with his own appanage system of patrimonial lands. The system continued to breed violent dispute, but in the last resort all quarrels were now resolved in Sarai.

Kiev had gone down in ruin and the light of a new Russia focused upon Vladimir had seemingly been extinguished by the Mongol conquest. How then did Moscow, a small and obscure provincial centre, rise to ascendancy over its rivals in the Russian land and become the heart and capital of a Russian nation? The familiar question—the familiar form of the question—which is the root and substance of medieval Russian historiography, projects a central pattern in the history of the Russian state.

The first mention of Moscow—the name, Moskva, is Finnish, not Slavonic—in the ancient chronicles goes back to the year 1147: Moscow is then only the site of a rude resort in a clearing in the woods on the river bank built by Yury Dolgoruki (Long-Arm), the son of Vladimir Monomakh. Nine years later the wooden walls erected round the building and its adjacent settlement enclosed the original fortress or Kremlin, which served as a seat for a succession of minor princes of the Vladimir line.

Moscow emerges into the full light of history in the latter part of the thirteenth century, when it is ruled by the youngest son of Alexander Nevolty, Daniel, on whom at least a gleam of his father's fame descended. Alexander is one of the holy names of medieval Russia—he was indeed canonized by the Church—and before and during the second world war was the most heroic of ancient names in Soviet hagiography. Prince of Novgorod, it was he who, having defeated the Swedes in 1240 on the Neva (hence his title), two years later won the legendary and decisive victory over the German knights on the ice of Lake Peipus. In that same year, 1242, Alexander paid his homage to the Golden Horde and returned with the title of grand-prince of Vladimir. Not for nothing had it been conferred upon him. Ambitious and prudent, always conscious of the danger from the Teuton west, Alexander had chosen the road to fortune through complete submission to the Mongol power. Even under alien domination Vladimir aspired to follow in the footsteps of Kiev and establish its power over rival principalities. The goal of unity in Rus, in brief, was unchanged; it was the method of pursuing unity which had of necessity been transformed. Alexander—who enforced the strict collection of tribute to Sarai—made no fewer than four journeys to the Golden Horde and died just after his return from the last of them in 1263. He had lived and died, says the somewhat flattering chronicler, for the Russian land and the Orthodox faith, and with his death the sun of the Russian land had set.

Under Daniel, his son, the small principality of Moscow was enlarged by the seizure of Kolomna. Under Yury, Daniel's successor, the stealthy acquisition of fresh territories, including Mozhaisk, continued. Since all roads to power led to Sarai, due return for these gains was made to the Golden Horde. Prince of Moscow from 1303, Yury was recognized at Sarai in 1318, against the rival claims of the prince of Tver,* as grand-prince of Vladimir. At his death in 1322 he was succeeded by his brother, Ivan, known

* Now Kalinin.

as Ivan Kalita (Ivan Moneybags). And from then onwards, until
the extinction of Ivan Kalita's line in 1598, the title of sovereign
prince in Russia, which was to flower into tsar and autocrat, was
held by the princes of Moscow.

The pre-eminence which they won and retained is not to be
explained by an absolute logic of events. Like so many other forms
of historic greatness, the achievement of Moscow appears in large
part fortuitous. But certain contributory factors are plain. First,
there was, once more, geography. The river Moskva, a key water-
way in the system of north-eastern waterways, gives easy con-
nexion between the valleys of the upper Volga and the middle Oka,
along which moved a growing volume of commercial traffic, more
particularly from and to Novgorod. Moscow itself was at the
junction of a number of land routes leading north, south and south-
east. As a metropolis for internal trade during the period of Tatar
rule it was almost as well placed as Kiev had been for the purposes
of foreign trade.

But geography alone is not an adequate explanation. If it were,
as has frequently been observed, the capital of a new Russia should
have been Nizhny-Novgorod,* at the junction of the Volga and
the Oka. What favoured Moscow as much as all else, it is agreed,
was the character of its princes, uniformly greedy, resourceful,
unscrupulous and undeviating of purpose. Kliuchevsky, the
greatest of Russian historians, who brilliantly analysed their
character, also found the princes commonplace. But their conduct
in the struggle for supremacy over their rivals rather suggests a
considered political strategy. Apparently unmoved by other
passions, the princes of Moscow set themselves to acquire, at
whatever cost, more land and larger money chests. Their last will
and testament, as Kliuchevsky was at pains to illustrate, was
always an inventory of possessions. By the power of wealth and
diplomacy, by the seizure of princely appanages and the settlement
of virgin forest lands, the grand-princedom constantly extended
its scattered possessions. And all this was paid for by absolute
submission to the Golden Horde. It was as the humblest vassal of
the Mongol khan that the prince of Moscow prospered. No other
prince in the land made the journey to Sarai more frequently or
brought with him for the occasion richer offerings, none laid
heavier contributions on his subjects for tribute to the Horde, and
none was so ready to do the khan's bidding in visiting the latter's
punishment upon a neighbouring prince. In this ruthless policy
of subservience to the conqueror the occupant of the throne of
Vladimir had the firm support of the Church.

The decisive event for both Church and state occurred at the

* Now Gorky.

beginning of the reign of Ivan Kalita. From the time of the final decay of Kiev, through the continued shock and confusion of the domination of the Golden Horde, the need had grown to establish a new seat for the metropolitan of the Church. The move from Kiev to the city of Vladimir at the beginning of the fourteenth century was significant; the further move, in 1326, from Vladimir to Moscow, was much more so. The two sources of effective authority in the land—Sarai on the one hand, the Church on the other—had thus recognized the paramountcy of the princes of Moscow. Two years later the grand-prince of Vladimir-Moscow was made responsible for the collection of tribute over a wide area of Russian territory. Here, in the hands of Ivan Kalita and his successors, was a potent means of extending their influence, of claiming rights of financial supervision of appanage territories and of maintaining law and order there. It was, in truth, an instrument of the domination of Moscow and of Russian unification.

Under Kalita's immediate successors, Simeon the Proud (1341–53) and Ivan the Red (1353–59), Moscow continued to grow in wealth and authority. New areas of forest and swamp were cleared and settled; adventurous or malcontent princelings from elsewhere entered the service of Moscow, bringing with them their armed following; individual boyars—nobles descended perhaps from a *druzhina* personality of the Kievan age, though the origin of the word 'boyar' is obscure—similarly took service with Moscow; merchants brought trade and riches; even Tatar princes, seeking their fortune amid sudden shifts of power at Sarai or farther east, came over to serve the grand-prince of Vladimir-Moscow. Ivan the Red was a weak ruler and Dmitry, his son, who became Dmitry Donskoy, at his accession was still a minor; but power in Moscow was firmly exercised by the metropolitan Alexis and by the monk Sergius, founder of the famed monastery of the Trinity in the forest north-east of Moscow, who as St Sergius of Radonezh is the supreme name in the Russian calendar of saints. The prospect of complete unity of the Russian lands was still remote, but the hope, centred upon Moscow, of throwing off the Tatar yoke, was a beckoning light in the darkness.

In the event it was a century and a half of almost unceasing struggle for power within the Golden Horde itself which contributed most to the liberation of Russia; the efforts of the Russian princes themselves were subsidiary to that process of internal decay. After the death of Genghis Khan only an unstable degree of Mongol imperial unity had been preserved. The violent clashes of ambition in the virtually self-contained western *ulus* from the middle of the fourteenth century onwards trace a familiar pattern of imperial disintegration.

C

This, however, is to anticipate. It is necessary at the point reached so far to turn from the east to the west, from the Mongol decline to the rise of Lithuanian power. Far from receding, danger from the west had drawn ever nearer since the Mongols had established their dominion. To the pressure of the Teutonic Knights had succeeded the ambition and voracity of Lithuania, the last pagan power in Europe, and then of Catholic Lithuania and Poland in alliance. The ground for what was in some measure a war of religion in eastern Europe was already well prepared in the fourteenth century.

In the years after the Mongol invasion it was the ruler of the principality of Galicia in the south-west who had assumed primacy in the waste land of Kiev and the south. Daniel of Galicia, who was contemporary with Alexander Nevsky, waged prolonged war against the bordering Russian principalities in order to establish his claim to paramountcy in Rus. But, unlike Alexander, in face of dual pressure from east and west he chose to resist the current of Mongol domination. The choice had historic consequences only a degree less momentous than Alexander's. Daniel looked in vain for aid from the Pope of Christendom, and, when this hope failed, turned to the neighbouring Lithuanian tribes. He found in them not an ally but an implacable rival.

The early history of the Lithuanians, an Indo-European but not Slavonic people, is still obscure. United in their Baltic lands under the rule of a chieftain named Mindovg, they proved a formidable hostile power in spite of successive defeats in battle at Russian hands and rapidly overflowed into Russian territory. Civil war between the tribes followed the death of Mindovg in 1263, the year of Alexander Nevsky's death, and lasted for more than half a century. But in 1316 the prince Gedimin restored order, and the great era of Lithuanian conquest and expansion opened.

Bled by Mongol exactions and gripped by constant disorder, the adjoining Russian lands were now an easy prey. Great slices of the west and south-west of Russia were cut off by Gedimin, from Polotsk in the north to Kiev and beyond in the south. 'The grand-princedom of Lithuania and Russia', as the new ascendant power was called, had its capital in Vilna, but its population always included more Russians than Lithuanians; for two centuries, indeed, Lithuania was, in substance, the foremost Russian state, larger and stronger by far than its rival centred on Moscow. The threat to the very heart of the grand-princedom of Vladimir-Moscow was intensified after Gedimin's death, when the Lithuanian throne was divided between his two sons, Olgerd and Jagiello, of whom the first, to whom fell the conquered Russian territories, became the architect of a still vaster Russian-Lithuanian empire.

Olgerd possessed himself of the greater part of Little Russia, extinguishing Mongol overlordship there, seized part of the western territories of Novgorod, even established himself for a time in the Crimea, and was thus master of the great distances between the Baltic and the Black Sea. In 1370 his advance eastwards brought him as far as Moscow, to which he laid siege and which was narrowly saved from capture by the stone walls that had been built round the Kremlin a few years earlier. Only the continuing pressure of the Teutonic Knights stood in the way of further Lithuanian absorption of the Russian land and people.

It was now that divisions in the Horde brought new opportunity to Moscow and its grand-prince Dmitry. Power in Sarai was seized by Mamai, who in 1378 sent a punitive force against his unruly Russian subjects. The Tatars invaded Riazan and Nizhny-Novgorod and made for Moscow. The ensuing Russian victory on the Vozha river registered no decisive gain, but it was an unmistakable challenge. Mamai assembled his forces, reached out for allies and concluded an agreement with Jagiello of Lithuania by which they would strike jointly in the late summer of 1380. Dmitry also took stock of all potential sources of aid among the princes of Russia. But the legend of Tatar invincibility and the dread of Tatar vengeance were still potent. Most of the other princes of Russia recoiled from the charge laid upon them. Riazan struck a bargain with the Horde; Tver, Suzdal and Nizhny-Novgorod temporized; the civil rulers of Novgorod—which enjoyed contractual immunity from any such call to arms—delayed; and only its own junior princes and a handful elsewhere rallied to Moscow. Nevertheless Dmitry mustered his resources and went out to meet Mamai on the steppe, as the Russian princes had done in the fatal battle on the Kalka a century and a half earlier, before the Tatars could effect a junction with the Lithuanians.

The Russian triumph in 1380 on the field of Kulikovo, near the right bank of the upper Don, was a great event in Russian history, though it was not the political achievement that patriotic sentiment alone has made of it. Won after bitter exertions, at a heavy cost in life, and with the tide turning in Moscow's favour only when the battle appeared already lost, it boldly asserted at one and the same time the Russian claim to independence and the right of the prince of Moscow to pursue the claim in his own person.

But Kulikovo was far from being the end. Dmitry Donskoy, as his new title went—Dmitry of the Don—had won an epic victory, but the might of the Horde was not yet broken. Only two years later, indeed, after Mamai had given way to Tokhtamysh, a lieutenant of Timur the Lame, or Tamerlane, the Tatars surged forward again across the steppe. Again the Russian cities of the north-east suffered a cruel ordeal. Moscow, its Kremlin betrayed to the enemy, was sacked and burned, so that Dmitry on his return to the city wept at the spectacle. The whole principality was plundered, captives were carried off in great numbers, and Dmitry was obliged to resume the payment of tribute and to give his son in hostage to Sarai. The full weight of the yoke fell upon Russia once more. The sole gain to Moscow at this point was Mongol aid in resistance to the Lithuanian conqueror. It was the crushing defeat by the Tatars of the Lithuanian army on the river Vorskla in 1399 which for the time being freed the western marches of the grand-principality of Vladimir-Moscow from the threat of invasion on that side.

For the time being only, however. The period from 1377 to 1434, which is known as the age of the Jagiellos, marked the peak of Lithuanian power. Through the 'personal union' effected by the marriage in 1386 of their respective sovereigns and at the price of conversion, together with the conversion of all his Lithuanian subjects, to Roman Catholicism, Jagiello became King Wladyslaw of Poland while remaining grand-prince of Lithuania. But the cause he thus served was more Polish than Lithuanian, and in 1392 he was compelled to accept the formidable Vitovt as grand-prince of Lithuania and his nominal vassal. Under Vitovt, only a few years after the defeat on the Vorskla, the Lithuanian drive eastwards was resumed; in 1404 the ancient Russian city of Smolensk on the Dnieper was incorporated into his territories, and still the Lithuanian appetite grew. Though Galicia had been ceded to Poland, virtually the whole of White Russia and the right bank of the Dnieper were brought under Lithuanian rule.

A rival Russian empire in this form could not but pose acute internal problems. Religion, or the secular passions which are masked by religion, brought Lithuanian policy to the test. Vitovt's Orthodox Russian subjects, though they had been willing enough to be liberated from the Tatars, were less willing to endorse the Catholic policy to which he was impelled by his need for Polish support. Poles, Lithuanians and Russians could combine in the famous victory in 1410 over the Germans at Tannenberg, the scene of an equally famous Russian disaster in 1914; but otherwise the Russian population of Lithuania were not easily to be assimilated to the religious and cultural enemy in their midst. Almost unwillingly, they saw in the Orthodox grand-prince of Vladimir-Moscow their protector.

Dmitry Donskoy died in 1389 at the age of 39 and was succeeded by his eldest son, Vasily. In the west and east alike Moscow was hard pressed. The incursions of Tamerlane, in whom was reborn Genghis Khan's dream of conquest, halted at the Riazan border, but a Tatar army under the fearsome Edigei, though it vainly laid siege in 1408 to Moscow, ravaged the surrounding country and imposed fresh tribute. Peace on almost any terms with Lithuania was essential. Married to a daughter of Vitovt, Vasily was able to effect a half-hearted truce by recognizing the existing frontier in the west.

The long reign of his successor, Vasily II—Vasily the Dark (1425–62)—was specially turbulent and threatening, yet at the same time it brought renewed hope. For it was now, after the violent ebb and flow of Tatar strength, that the Golden Horde succumbed to the fearful injuries inflicted upon it by Tamerlane. The collapse of the centralized system of Mongol authority in the west was illustrated by the formation of a separate khanate of Kazan, on the Volga. This originated in the secession from Sarai of a Tatar force, whose khan established himself in a newly built encampment on the upper Volga and from there launched repeated raids in the direction of Moscow. Though Vasily's military venture against these Tatars in 1445 was a failure, he was nevertheless able to impress some of the khan's followers into his own service. An independent khanate of the Crimea was proclaimed four years later which was destined to be the more long-lived and dangerous. Significant, too, was the creation later still of the small Tatar principality of Kasimov, on the Oka, as a dependency of Moscow and an auxiliary against the designs of the Kazan khan.

Though final deliverance still waited, these events foretold the end of Tatar domination. Even token payments of tribute had now ceased. Vasily himself, whose method of ensuring by special favours the loyalty of his Tatar followers had provoked extreme jealousy in his own camp, was struck down by his enemies in Moscow and blinded, though he reigned for another fifteen years afterwards. The task he bequeathed to his successor, Ivan the Great, of formally shaking off the Tatar yoke, was in truth three parts a formality.

It has seemed desirable to describe the Mongol period of Russian history at relative length because of its bearing on the course of events during the succeeding centuries. Earlier generations of historians have differed acutely on the subject of the effects of the Mongol conquest; the most authoritative nineteenth-century scholars, on the whole, either appeared to evade the issue or else were inclined to minimize the consequences. A later writer like Miakotin has strongly denied that the Mongol power left its imprint on Russian institutions, though it seems as unreasonable to question the Mongol inspiration of the seclusion of women in Russia, for instance, as the Mongol derivation of so many Russian household words. To-day, in the light of fuller study, there is a growing measure of agreement on the range and depth of the Mongol impact and the enduring influence of the conquest long after the period of domination was over.

Not that it has been necessary to wait upon contemporary scholarship to recognize, for instance, in the burning question of the Ukraine in Russian-Polish relations the legacy of the conquest. In hardening the division of the Russian people into an eastern Russia and a western Russia, the eastern part, in which the forms of the state originated, being subject to the influences of Asia, while the western part formed an enclave in a European environment and was cut off from the main stream of Russian political life, the Mongol power sowed the seed of centuries of embittered nationalist conflict.

These influences of Asia lie at the heart of the matter. Although in the past the use of the epithets 'Asiatic' and 'Tatar' for the darker aspects of Russian life and civilization was often crude and unconsidered, in one respect at least it erred on the right side of history. Many of the distinctive forms of despotism in government and civil and military administration in the Muscovy of the tsars came to her from the Mongols. Weakened by the long years of the Tatar yoke, medieval Russia absorbed the habit of the conqueror.

The actual destruction wrought by the Mongols in the Russian lands is immeasurable. The losses in life and property through massacre, plunder, the burning of cities and the hauls of captives sold into slavery were on a prodigious scale. Together with the payment of tribute, they represented a fearful impoverishment of the land and people. But the destruction also went deeper. Though the political structure of Kievan Rus had crumbled before the conquest, it was the continuing order of civilization growing from Kiev that was now cut off at the roots. The destruction of the towns was an irreparable disaster. It extinguished industry and commerce, converting Russia into a wholly agrarian economy, and it stifled everywhere except in the north the *veche* and the popular liberties it served. Only Novgorod and its enterprising 'younger brother', the city of Pskov, retained the free institutions of the Kievan age throughout the Mongol occupation, and even this was not accomplished without resort to Lithuanian aid in resisting the princes of Moscow. Even so, both cities remained so vulnerable to this pressure that in the end their liberties were to go down before it. Both the level of Kievan civilization and the democracy of the *veche* are perhaps commonly romanticized, but from the eclipse of the active life of the cities as much as from all else sprang the historic and artificial cause of Russian backwardness in the medieval period. The continued isolation from the western world of the dominant north-east region centred in Moscow, completing as it did the process of cultural alienation from Europe begun through Byzantium, helped to make Russian backwardness peculiar and lasting. This, indeed, is perhaps the chief reason why Russian historians have so often dwelt on Russia's service to Europe in maintaining the full burden of the centuries of Asiatic invasion.

The profoundest consequences of all were the rise of Russian autocracy and the accelerating impulse given to serfdom. The contagion of Mongol political ideas spread first of all from the remote but pervasive example of the great khan. The Asiatic absolutism of the Mongol state, which was founded upon the principle of universal service and the total submission of classes and persons to a supreme ruling will, served as a model for Moscow. There is a considerable Mongolian-Turkish admixture in the Great Russian stock, dating for the most part, it is true, from the period after the break-up of the Golden Horde, but originating in the marriages of the medieval princes and boyars. It was while the Russian principalities were coming to life again after a century of unqualified Mongol despotism, and when the hope of deliverance centred upon Moscow, that the rule of its princes acquired the habit of absolutism. Beelzebub alone could cast out Satan, and military necessity was invoked to justify the absolute will of Moscow. Serfdom, in its legal as distinct from its economic aspect, originated in the same principle of universal service, taken over from the Mongol conqueror, on which was raised the structure of Muscovite autocracy. Not for nothing did the Russian radical idealist of the nineteenth century equate 'Muscovite' with 'Tatar'.

It remains to note the effect of the Mongol conquest upon the Church and the most significant event in the history of the relations of Church and state in Russia. Like earlier nomad conquerors, the Tatars, even after they had embraced Islam in the earlier part of the fourteenth century, were tolerant in matters of religion; there was an Orthodox bishop in Sarai, where even proselytism was permitted. The metropolitan of 'Kiev and all Russia', like the senior princes, received his seal of investiture from Mongol hands and acknowledged no other temporal authority; while the entire body of the clergy was exempt from taxation. Thus favoured, the Church—and particularly, as in the west, the monasteries—grew ever richer and more powerful. Within little more than a half-century after its foundation the Trinity monastery of St Sergius had become the greatest of all Russian landowners. Monastic asceticism seldom survived these conditions, in which there were no monastic orders as in the west to diffuse the graces of piety.

Its prestige and authority at the side of the developing state thus assured, the Greek Orthodox Church in medieval Russia was never in any danger of emulating the medieval Church in the west in resistance to the claims of the temporal power. By the beginning of the fifteenth century its position of dependence as a metropolitan district of the patriarchate in Constantinople had become dangerously exposed, since Constantinople itself was threatened by the Turks. The reunion under Rome of the Eastern and Western Churches proclaimed in 1439 as a means of saving Constantinople by the Council of Florence, an assembly of Orthodox and Catholic clergy, was anathema to the Orthodox faithful in Russia. The Russian metropolitan—a Greek—who had approved reunion on terms of the supremacy of the Pope, was deposed, and in his place in 1448 the bishops of the Russian Church themselves appointed one of their number, bishop Iona of Riazan, as metropolitan. What independence the latter office had retained through appointment at the hands of the patriarch in Constantinople now vanished. With the fall of Constantinople five years later the Russian Church emerged as in every respect a national Church, the pure fountain of Holy Orthodoxy in the sole surviving state ruled by an Orthodox sovereign.

CHAPTER IV

THE GROWTH OF MUSCOVY

WHEN IN 1486, twenty-four years after he had ascended the grand-princely throne of Vladimir-Moscow, Ivan III, the son of Vasily the Dark, was offered the title of king by the Habsburg Holy Roman Emperor, he took leave to decline in challenging terms. 'We have been sovereign in our land,' he replied, 'from our earliest forefathers, and our sovereignty we hold from God.' This reply voiced the national ambitions and the hieratic pretensions of the new rulers of Muscovy. Ivan had already, in fact, though with some caution, begun to adopt the sanctified title of tsar. It was his son, Vasily III, who habitually appended to state documents the signature of 'tsar and autocrat by the grace of God of all Russia'.

All Russia: the designation was pregnant with meaning. It had served in the fourteenth century to denote the embracing jurisdiction of the metropolitan of the Church and the claim to titular

leadership among the Russian princes of the ruler of Moscow, but
no temporal ruler had as yet formally adopted it in this context of
unqualified sovereignty. 'Tsar', of course, is Caesar, the Caesar of
Byzantium. But it was also the term used in Russia both for the
Mongol great khan and for the khan of the Golden Horde.
'Autocrat'—*samoderzhets*—was similarly translated from the
Greek, though the Russian word at first signified only a ruler
independent of any foreign power (in this case of Mongol power)
rather than the absolutist monarch to which it was imperceptibly
stretched. Three specific factors, extending the logic of the earlier
expansion of Moscow, entered into the claims advanced by Ivan III
and his successor. These were the great sweep of the 'gathering-in'
of Russian lands; Ivan's marriage into the family of the last of the
Byzantine emperors; and the extinction of the remnants of power
of the Golden Horde

Ivan (1462–1505), known as Ivan the Great, had no need to
vary in any significant way the methods pursued by the earlier
princes of Moscow. But in the arts of power, as of so much else,
nothing succeeds like success. In the circumstances of Moscow's
growing strength the continued fragmentation of the Russian
land, in which suzerain princes ruled in Tver, Riazan, Rostov*
and Yaroslavl, each with its own crop of appanage princelings, gave
him one signal advantage over his predecessors. Each fresh territorial acquisition he made won popular support for what was in
effect a movement of national unification.

By war and diplomacy the extent of Ivan's domains was trebled
during the forty-three years of his reign. Since he had propounded
the doctrine that all Russia was his patrimony, he chose to take
into his own hands the appanages of his brothers and the lands
which would otherwise have passed to his sons. Yaroslavl was
ceded to him; the last prince of Riazan, a nephew, ruled only as a
vassal; what remained of the possessions of Rostov was possibly
acquired by purchase; and Tver, which for so long had eluded the
grasp of the princes of Moscow, finally surrendered without a
fight. No independent prince in the immediate neighbourhood of
the former principality of Vladimir remained to challenge Ivan's
power. Nor had Novgorod itself withstood his claim to all-Russian
sovereignty.

It was Novgorod and its empire on which Ivan's eyes were fixed
most hungrily at the outset of his reign. Left relatively undisturbed
throughout the Mongol conquest, Novgorod had prospered greatly.
The range of its trading operations had constantly widened through
the daring and resource of colonizing ventures in the wake of the

* Near Moscow; not, of course, Rostov-on-Don, which was founded only in the
eighteenth century.

monastic communities pushing out ever farther into the 'wilderness'. The independence it had won from Kiev had grown more ambiguous in relation to Vladimir; in relation to Moscow it was more ambiguous still. Partly because the resources of food in the north were always inadequate and the city ordinarily depended upon Moscow for the safe transport of grain, partly in recognition of Moscow's supremacy in the land, Novgorod had paid tribute to the grand-prince while jealously asserting sovereign rights. These it had sought to maintain against the growing pretensions of Moscow by drawing close to Lithuania whenever the threat grew critical. Yet its independence had in increasing measure been worn away; in 1456 the city had pledged itself not to harbour the (Lithuanian) enemies of Moscow and had been obliged to render further tribute to the grand-prince. Now, crowning the colonial rivalry in the north-eastern lands which Moscow had pursued for a generation, came a demand for complete submission. It came while the city-state, which after the fashion of city-states had declined to the rule of an oligarchy, found itself in turmoil. Civil disorder in republican Novgorod had indeed become endemic; the friction set up by commercial rivalries had given a reckless violence to the meetings of the *veche*, the poor were in revolt, republican virtue had decayed. Ivan's claims split the merchant aristocracy of Novgorod into hostile factions, one of which in 1471 favoured open alliance with Lithuania in order to resist further encroachments from Moscow.

The proposed alliance gave Ivan the pretext he sought. He condemned it as treason against his person and against the fraternity of the Russian Orthodox lands, and directed his army northwards. The opposing forces were unequally matched; the military strength of Novgorod had wasted away in the city's heyday of wealth and security, its levies were both raw and ungovernable, and the Lithuanians did not stir. Novgorod capitulated, swore loyalty to Moscow and paid a large indemnity.

But the pride and independence of Lord Novgorod the Great could not be extinguished, as Ivan himself recognized, at a single blow. It required several years of methodical attrition to complete the subjection of the city. The appeal of Ivan's own supporters there to put down faction was met early in 1478 by a renewed demand on his part for total surrender, and in the event Ivan was able to establish order on his own terms and in his own way. Though there was revolt still to come, the glories of Novgorod's independence were over. The *veche* bell was removed to Moscow—'there shall be no *veche* and no bell in our own land of Novgorod', Ivan had proclaimed—the ruling families of the city suffered execution or exile and their lands were distributed among newcomers from the Muscovite capital. Pskov, Novgorod's younger brother and even more truly a free republic, although for a time the *veche* was permitted to survive there, had not long to wait before it met a similar end. The incorporation of the vast imperial territories of Novgorod into Muscovy was swift and thorough; Perm* had acknowledged Ivan as early as 1472, Viatka† in the remote north-east made final submission in 1489. Advancing eastwards beyond the ethnographically Russian boundaries of the plain, Moscow entered upon a new phase of its history as the capital of a multi-national state, an empire of many different races and peoples.

In the west the gathering-in of the Russian lands proceeded more slowly. The forward drive of Lithuania-Poland was contained, though the eastern frontiers of Lithuania remained perilously close to the nerve centres of Muscovy. Ivan continued to press his claims to those Russian territories in the keeping of the Lithuanian princes and boyars since the time of Gedimin, and some of the greatest of them, including members of Rurik's line, did in fact transfer their allegiance to Moscow during his reign. But not until its closing years did he feel strong enough to press his claims by war. Some territory in White Russia was thus regained, and Ivan's possession of it was conceded in the truce agreed in 1503, but continued war in the west was as yet beyond Moscow's resources.

Ivan's marriage to the orphan niece of the last Byzantine emperor was a more resounding triumph. With it the odour of sanctity which the sovereign princes of Russia had originally acquired from Byzantium returned in a heightened form. Ivan's first wife, a princess of Tver, had died in 1467. Zoe Paleologus, whom he married in 1472, was a ward of the Pope, who had suggested the marriage in the hope of reviving the project of Church union of the Council of Florence. The hope vanished with Ivan's prompt assumption of the sacerdotal graces of the Caesars of Constantinople. The visible signs of grandeur surrounding the grand-prince were multiplied. To the orb and sceptre and other insignia of the Russian heir to Byzantium, including the cap or crown of Vladimir Monomakh, was added the Byzantine double-headed eagle; access to the sovereign being within the Kremlin walls was invested with an elaborate ritual; the whole ceremonial of the court, thickly overlaid with Byzantine custom, took on a fantastic pomp. Foreign envoys to the court of Vasily III noted with astonishment the atmosphere of oriental majesty around the throne. Here was the beginning of the servility and intrigue which marked the personal entourage of the tsars.

* Now Molotov.
† Now Kirov.

From the Church at this time came the conception of Moscow as 'the third Rome', the final and lasting successor to the Latin and Greek capitals of the Christian world. It was a monk of Pskov who wrote to Vasily II: 'Two Romes have fallen, a third stands, and a fourth shall not be'. This doctrine of the third Rome never became state doctrine, so to speak, in Russia, as it is still all too customary to imply; the whole conception was originally governed by rivalry with the re-created metropolitanate of Kiev in Lithuanian territory, which was dependent on the patriarch of Constantinople, and was always rooted in ecclesiastical bigotry. But it certainly drew some support from the lingering dualism of Church and state in Russia, which similarly inspired the attempt at this time to trace the origins of the Russian Church from the Apostles themselves.

It was in Ivan's reign, in the year 1502, after intermittent warfare between the three existing Tatar khanates, that the khanate of Astrakhan, the relic of the Golden Horde, was finally crushed by the Crimean Tatars. The khanate of Kazan, too, was for the time being reduced to an enforced passivity. But for almost three centuries more the Crimean Tatars, who in 1475 had become tributary to the Ottoman empire, continued to be a scourge to Russia. In the next reign their raids several times reached as far as the walls of Moscow. Vasily bought the khan off from time to time, but was also obliged to garrison the southern boundaries every summer.

Vasily, who reigned from 1505 until 1533, was very much his father's son and continued Ivan's unwearying labours. It was he who finally suppressed the liberties of Pskov, removing its *veche* bell to Moscow, exiling leading families and replacing them on their estates by servitors of his own. More than all else he attempted to win the Russian princes of Lithuania to his allegiance. This twice involved him in war; on the first occasion with little profit, on the second and more persistent attempt with the important but still only temporary gain of Smolensk.

It was in the reign of Ivan III that the machinery of government in a widening Muscovy took ordered form. The principal executive instrument of Muscovite power was the *boyarskaya duma*—the boyars' council—which towards the end of the reign lent to government decrees the obligatory and slightly ambiguous formula: 'The tsar has decreed and the boyars have decided, etc.' Only established custom, dating from the formative period of power of the suzerain princes of Moscow, not any form of constitutional right, gave the boyars' council its standing. True, the prescriptive claims to share in the task of government of the great boyars, descendants of the line of Rurik or Gedimin, were tacitly recognized. They themselves, now reduced from sovereign princes in

Rus to subjects of the Muscovite tsar, retained through all their feuds a lively sense of hereditary privilege as a governing class. But the other members of the council, consisting of lesser boyars, representatives of a newer nobility, and learned clerks (recruited largely from the sons of priests) at the head of the *prikazi* (government offices), could claim no such prescriptive right. It was thus from both aristocratic tradition and bureaucratic convenience that the boyars' council derived its authority.

The system worked well enough under Ivan III. Up to a point it continued to function smoothly in the circumstances of widening responsibility under Vasily III. But the consolidation of Muscovite autocracy in an expanding empire could not fail to threaten the existing balance of administrative power. Within the boyars' council the great boyars were no longer always supreme; new personalities and new centralizing principles were at work. Whatever the office or responsibility that fell to an individual, as a class the ancient families saw themselves being excluded from the centre of government, their political birthright ignored or slighted. So began, long after the feudal nobility in the west had yielded to the claims of monarchical absolutism, the protracted struggle between the Muscovite tsar and the hereditary princes of the land. From the long festering of the great boyars' grievances came the poison that eventually destroyed them as a class and at the same time all but destroyed the Russian state which had been in the making since the overthrow of the Mongol power.

From it, too, there developed in the early part of the sixteenth century the fantastic system of official ranking among the highest families which was known as *mestnichestvo* (from *mesto*, place). The system, evolving from embittered disputes over precedence, was designed to establish a hierarchy at court and in the uppermost grades of service to the state which accorded with the claims of genealogy. The principles governing the whole portentous code were inflexible. Briefly, no boyar could be obliged to discharge an official duty which was inferior to the duty which had been discharged at any time by a member of his family, and none could be required to accept an appointment in which he was junior to a member of a family to which his own family was senior. Not order but anarchy followed from all this; to endless dispute was now added paralyzing delay and obstruction, above all in military operations. The boyars kept the system going, however, in support of their own ineradicable rivalries.

During the period of seventy years in which the scheme of Muscovite government and administration ripened the complementary pattern of serfdom unfolded. Serfdom was not recognized in law until the early part of the seventeenth century, and was indeed never to be formally and specifically defined in other than negative terms. But in a great variety of forms regulated by custom the practical condition of serfdom was widespread in the fifteenth century or even earlier. The precise character of Russian feudalism in medieval society is a subject of recondite argument, most of which can be waived in this narrative; but there are two principal clues to the development of serf labour before the formal introduction of serf law. One is the growing burden of indebtedness among the agricultural population. The other is the principle of state taxation that derived from the Mongol-inspired claim to universal service.

While the Russian land was still divided into contending principalities service to the prince had been for the most part voluntary. Leading boyars had commonly established an hereditary title to land of their own through the labour of their slaves upon it; but, these fruits of slave ownership apart, estates were commonly granted to the prince's followers in return for serving him. Such service could always be transferred to another prince, in which case possession of the land might or might not be retained; in theory the estate was held in perpetuity, in practice it was perhaps more often than not given up or confiscated. In theory, the same liberty of contract prevailed among the rest of the free population settled on the prince's or Church's domains or on a boyar's estate.

There were different degrees and conditions of slavery, the differences becoming more marked as military or household slaves were increasingly diverted in the fifteenth century to agriculture. But originally there was an absolute and clear distinction between the bondsmen of one kind or another and those settled on the prince's land who as free tenants paid taxes to him. At what stage, and for what purpose other than the payment of taxes, the peasant cultivator was organized in a collective unit known as the *mir* or *obshchina*—the commune—is uncertain. But it is probable enough that common arrangements existed at an early date for regulating the economic relationship of landlord and peasant. At any rate, so long as dues or taxes were paid regularly the appanage prince of the time of Vasily the Dark, for instance, did not concern himself with the individual peasant's movements. In theory, the latter enjoyed complete freedom to come or go.

In point of fact, such freedom was all too often illusory. In Kliuchevsky's phrase, it was a juridical fiction. Almost everywhere in what were now the central regions of Muscovy the peasant freeholder had incurred a load of debt or other obligations which helped to keep him in the same place. Even after he had repaid whatever loan for the purchase of implements, stock or seed he had originally required or had discharged the terms of his contract with a landlord, a peasant who had been settled for any length of time in one place had virtually renounced the right of moving on elsewhere. Nominally he was still free; in reality, he was half-free and half-bound.

It was this ambiguity of status which was sharpened by the claims of the ruler of Muscovy. With the assertion of the sovereign rights of the tsar in Moscow all the domains of the princes had passed under his rule and all the freemen settled on them had become the tsar's subjects. The transfer of land or service from one proprietor to another was now unlawful; there was, in fact, only one proprietor, and all tenure of land carried with it the obligation to render state dues or service to him. Thus on both the widening state lands and the hereditary private estates the peasant's freedom of movement became progressively more restricted by a new feudal relationship. Not only that. from the time of Ivan III, when the needs of war grew more exacting, new grants of state land were made in ever increasing number which were strictly military fiefs. On every such *pomestie*, as it was called in distinction to the *otchina*, the hereditary estate, the prime need of the *pomeshchik*, the land-owner, was to prevent his peasants from moving elsewhere.

These were the early phases in the historic process, almost universally completed in Russia long before it was recognized in law, by which the peasant was bound in perpetuity to the soil and to the master he served.

One further aspect of land ownership in these years of the growth of Muscovy deserves mention. The accumulation of vast landed wealth by the monasteries had produced a crop of familiar evils and much unspiritual grossness in monastic life. Voices in the Church were raised in protest, recalling those who had taken monastic vows to the service of God and even condemning the subservience of the spiritual power to the temporal. A particularly eloquent voice was that of the abbot Nil Sorsky, who in the closing years of the reign of Ivan III argued in vain against a ruling section of the hierarchy for the renunciation of the wealth of the Church. The debate continued for some years and the first tentative proposals were indeed now made for the secularization of Church property, but in the meantime the princes of the Church could do no less than continue to support the unbounded claims of the autocrat of all Russia.

It has been said often enough that the developing personal autocracy of Ivan III and Vasily III was entirely in the national interest. The centralization of government in the person of a despot was essential to Russian growth; without it there could have been no gradual substitution of Russia (*Rossiya*) for Rus, a change almost casually introduced in the reign of Vasily but not fully endorsed by popular usage until the close of the seventeenth century. Yet the paradox of the Muscovite state after Vasily is that centralization of government was rendered increasingly ineffective by the peculiar forms of tsarist despotism.

The period of Ivan and Vasily was the high noon of the Renaissance. The Muscovy of those years was gross and uncultivated, its people almost entirely illiterate, its horizons narrow and unchanging. But both sovereigns were concerned to enlarge and enrich the Moscow Kremlin. The former built the crenellated walls and bizarre towers which stand to-day and imported, among a group of Greek and Italian artists, the superb Fioraventi, who designed on the site of the earlier church of that name the Uspensky cathedral (the cathedral of the Assumption) in which the tsars were to be crowned. Vasily for his part continued to import artists and craftsmen from the west and established somewhat perfunctory diplomatic relations with various European powers. He died in his sixtieth year, leaving two children by his second wife, of whom the elder, aged three, was to pass into history under the title of Ivan the Terrible.

CHAPTER V

IVAN THE TERRIBLE

THE DECISIVE EVENTS of the reign of Ivan *Grozny*, the Terrible, who deserves the more correct style of Ivan the Dread, burned deep scars upon later Russian history. Their balance of good and evil, like the character of Ivan himself, has been variously assessed. They bear a strange likeness to some of the shaping events in the history of Bolshevik Russia. For that reason no figure has been the subject of more anxious solicitude in the Bolshevik reinterpretation of the past.

Ivan's character cannot be dissociated from the events of his reign for the simple reason that the personal absolutism he practised was unlimited. That, in a sense, was his supreme achievement: he established the full measure of autocracy in Russia. By weakening beyond hope of lasting recovery the power of the only potential opposition to him in sixteenth-century Muscovy, the hereditary boyar aristocracy, and putting in their place a new service class of landowners wholly dependent upon him, he was able to extend political despotism to the logical extremes of caprice and madness. The instrument he used for this purpose was terror. And, as a footnote, so to speak, to his reading of the rights of autocracy, he all but encompassed the Russian land after his death in total ruin.

Though against these achievements must be set the conquest by war and colonization during his lifetime of vast new territories to the east and south-east of Muscovy and a bid to enlist the technical aid of the west which makes him in some sort a forerunner of Peter the Great, it might well seem that the balance of catastrophe is not in doubt. This, however, is to ignore the argument originally advanced by historians like Kavelin and given special emphasis in the Soviet revaluation of the past. The case for Ivan is made to-day not by playing down the sinister fantasy of his reign of terror (which outside Russia has long constituted the most familiar of all the lurid chapters of the Russian past) but by building up a heroic portrait of the founding father of the truly centralized Russian state and empire. This was the prize won by war against the anarchic boyars; this, not his despotic excesses, is the measure of what he accomplished; and this, runs the implication, is as necessary to Russia's salvation now as it was then. The contemporary name for it is democratic centralism.

The case, no doubt, is sound up to a point: amid the continued throes of Russian expansion the centralization of authority was bound to assume increasingly rigid forms. But the argument can scarcely rest there. Then as now, half-measures in Russia were ruled out, and Ivan's policy of centralization produced, as a French philosopher foretold in another context, apoplexy at the centre and paralysis at the extremities. The chief agent of history in these circumstances was the sovereign's personality.

Ivan was, in a psychotic way, a man of parts; he had great dialectical ability and what would nowadays be called acute political flair. There were currents of intellectual change in Russia beneath the surface of his innovations, a purposeful ambition behind their melodrama. Until the thirst for cruelty possessed him in his later years almost to the exclusion of all else, there was undoubted method in his perversities of statecraft. Certainly he showed in his preliminary phase of rule a touch of the enlightened despot of a later age. But there was no consistency in him, no compelling idea or emotion, it seems, other than a voluptuous rage of self-assertion. He struck out against his enemies in Church and state, real or

D

imaginary, with paranoiac cunning; even his orgies of blasphemy and lust were possibly designed as mockery of all authority other than his own. Steeped in the Bible and in the lives of the Fathers of the Church, he pitched the cruelties and persecutions of his reign on a note of divine reasoning. Few documents of the sixteenth century hold stranger psychological interest than the record of Ivan's correspondence with Prince Kurbsky, a favourite who deserted him—a correspondence which provides one of the few existing first-hand sources for the historian of the reign.

In setting out in the first place to humble the pride of the great boyar families Ivan was avenging, in something of the same spirit as Louis XIV after him, the humiliations of his childhood and youth. His minority had given the great boyars their opportunity after more than two generations of retreat. They had seen the grand-prince, who in lineage was in no way superior to themselves, engross in his pretensions the rights they claimed by heredity and custom. Ivan's mother, who had exercised jealous power in his name, died in 1538, possibly through poisoning at their hands. There was no question of formally appointing a regent: the boy Ivan reigned, the great boyars ruled. Of the two families who stood at their head the Shuiskys were descended from Rurik, the Belskys from Gedimin. Theirs was now the power for all that they formally bowed before the throne; theirs was also an unremitting rivalry in greed and spoliation. Nobody in the land was spared in the course of this rivalry, least of all the youthful prince on his father's throne. From the insult and injury he endured in these years there sprang, it would appear, a deep-seated insecurity of mind and something of his tyrant's appetite. From them, too, he evidently learned the arts of dissimulation he exercised so adroitly in later life.

Cruelty and a love of torture became marked in him during his unbridled years of adolescence. In 1547, at the age of sixteen, when he had already begun to assert a violent will and to pay off old scores, he announced his intention of ruling in person and also of marrying. His bride was a boyar's daughter, Anastasia, of the Romanov family, originating in Lithuanian Russia but long settled in Moscow. Ivan the Terrible was the first of the sovereign princes of Russia to be crowned tsar, in a ceremony which re-established the awful splendour of the crowning of the Byzantine emperors.

The earliest signs were seemingly propitious. Ivan chose as advisers two figures of whom little is known. One was the priest Silvester, the author of a famous and formidable little manual, the *Domostroy (Home Management)*, which illuminates all that was most severe and patriarchal in Russian family custom in the century; the other was the young and zealous Adashev. With their support he summoned a meeting of notables to recommend measures for reforming the administration of justice and of the Church's affairs. Those bidden to attend consisted for the most part of the boyars' council, among them the chief dignitaries of the Church and the heads of the government offices, together with representatives of the merchant guilds and other bodies in the capital. This was the first *zemsky sobor*, or assembly of the land, an institution which in the next century briefly assumed a likeness to an elected legislature and then decayed, and whose potentialities as a reforming states-general were so ardently and unrealistically canvassed in the nineteenth century. The assembly of 1550, however, was merely an extension of the existing pattern of central government.

Its deliberations produced a new legal code, which brought greater flexibility into the administration of justice; a more centralized administration of local government, designed to remedy such abuses as the flagrant extortion which went with the licensed 'feeding' of local satraps by the peasantry; and, more indirectly, an instalment of Church reform in the shape of the *Stoglav (Hundred Chapters)*, a document which, though it shelved the issue of the monastic lands, laid down moral and educational precepts for the clergy. To this initial period of Ivan's conduct of affairs belong also military reforms of some consequence, among them the establishment of artillery companies and the creation of a body of regular infantry, equipped with muskets, who took the name of *Streltsy* (literally, archers). Much more was to be heard of the *Streltsy* in succeeding years.

These military reforms were undertaken with an eye upon the traditional foes of Muscovy. The reclamation of all the Russian or half-Russian lands in foreign possession was a missionary task to be completed, but it was also from this time that access to the Baltic from the land-locked heart of Muscovy became an obligatory Russian ambition. To the east and south stood the Tatar khanates; immediately to the west the lands and lives of the Orthodox faithful were ruled by an alien Lithuanian or Lithuanian-Polish gentry in the grip of a proselytizing Jesuit mission; to the north-west the Swedes and the Germans barred the way to the Baltic. The easiest and, for the time being, the richest prize was the khanate of Kazan, fanatically Moslem but by this time politically weakened through its former dealings with Moscow.

The reduction of Kazan, now within sight of the Russian line of settlement on the upper Volga, was begun in 1551 by the building of a fort on the western bank of the river at that point. Next year an army of 150,000 besieged the Tatar city, using powder for the first time in Russian history against enemy fortifications. Kazan held out, its hopes pinned upon the Crimean Tatars advancing from the south upon Moscow. But when these were flung back at

Tula, on the entrenched line which marked the effective Russian frontier in the south, the Muscovite army pressed its siege, stormed and plundered Kazan and, after wreaking great slaughter, razed it by fire. The khan was captured and baptized, the khanate dissolved, and a new and Russian Kazan came into existence on the site of the destroyed Tatar city.

The conquest of Kazan, which was swiftly consolidated by the construction in the vast area subject to the khan of a ring of Russian fortresses, reaching as far east as Ufa, in the territory of the Bashkirs, was of major historical importance. The events which stemmed from it turned the eyes of the Russian people towards Asia and moulded the shape and character of the Russian empire. The conquest immediately opened to a flood-tide of colonization great stretches of fertile land on the middle Volga and the Kama and beyond. Four years after Kazan had fallen came the capture of Astrakhan, at the Volga mouth, the capital of the insecure Nogai khanate raised on the ashes of the Golden Horde. The entire length of the Volga, mistress of the fortunes of Muscovy, was now in Russian keeping, and on its banks in the years that followed rose the cities of Samara,* Saratov and Tsaritsyn†. The line of new settlement reached the Urals, and the migrant Russian people stood on the threshold of the illimitable spaces of Siberia.

The absorption of these territories into the Muscovite empire did not bring with it prompt assimilation of their non-Russian peoples. The way of empire was often rough and perilous; it was no light task to reduce to complete submission the aboriginal Mordvin, Chuvash, Cheremis, Votiak and Bashkir tribes. Their names echo ominously throughout the history of subsequent anarchy and revolt in the Volga lands.

The glory of the conquest of Kazan resounds in the *byliny*, the oral heroic songs of Russia, in which the figure of Ivan himself, the martial leader of a warrior nation, shines with sacrosanct splendour. He was, in fact, no hero, though he marched to Kazan with the cross of Dmitry Donskoy on his breast. It was to commemorate the victory that Ivan built in the Red Square in Moscow the astonishing cathedral of St Basil (Vasily), whose fantastic bulbous domes have stupefied and delighted foreign eyes ever since.

The menace of the Tatars of the Crimea remained. They were to destroy by fire the whole of Moscow, save for the Kremlin, later in the reign, and more than once in subsequent years they came near to undoing the Russian labour of generations. Among those close to the tsar there were some who urged even then the

* Now Kuibyshev.
† Now Stalingrad.

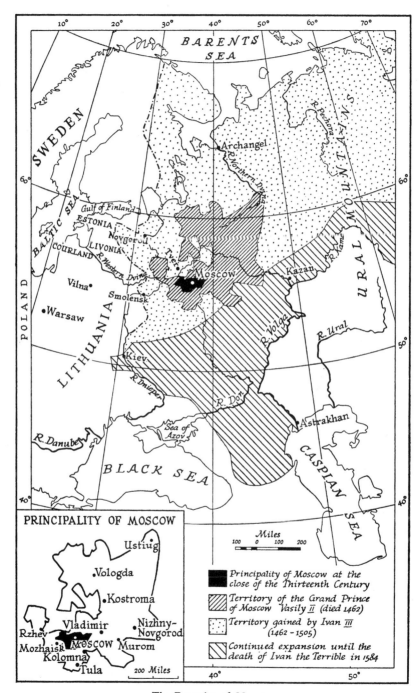

The Expansion of Muscovy

task of conquest across the wide southern steppes which a century later defeated all the efforts of Peter the Great. But Ivan's eyes, more far-seeing for all that he proved wrong in this instance, were fixed upon the Baltic and communication with Europe. Imperial expansion into the Baltic provinces of Livonia was desirable in itself, but beyond it was the prospect of ending the Livonian monopoly of Russia's foreign trade through the ports of Riga and Reval, and beyond that was contact with the west. So, in 1558, began Muscovy's vain war of twenty-five years for access to the Baltic seaboard. With the simultaneous collapse of the German knightly power in Livonia this meant war with Lithuania-Poland in the first place and secondarily with Sweden. The Russian failure was unrelieved, though here at any rate the strategic lesson was mastered later on by Peter the Great.

The easy successes of the preliminary phase of the Livonian war gave no inkling of the long drawn-out struggle to come. But they were almost hidden from sight in the riddle of domestic events in Muscovy. The time of reckoning had come for which Ivan the Terrible had apparently been preparing himself.

There had been indications years earlier of the ungovernable passions and the secret distrust by which the tsar was driven. In 1553, when he was aged twenty-three, he had been taken ill and had been visited by presentiments of death. His testament prepared, he had asked the members of the boyars' council to take the oath of allegiance to his infant son Dmitry. Was it an enlightened sense of duty which caused some of the boyars, who urged the better claims of a cousin of Ivan's, to hesitate or even to decline? All took the oath in the end, and the tsar recovered. But suspicion had done its work and Ivan chose not to forget. The changed attitude of the tsar towards his advisers was as yet veiled, but the veil dropped four years later, after the sudden death of his wife, who is believed to have been a good influence upon him. Now came the break with his former advisers and the swift violences of despotic power. Silvester and Adashev, whom, in Ivan's own words, he had 'raised from the dunghill to a place among princes', were fortunate, the one being confined to the remote Solovetsky monastery in the White Sea, the other finding death as a commander in Livonia. But for the less favoured there was punishment in its most ruthless forms.

Four years later still, in the thick of the Livonian war, Ivan staged the opening act of his reign of terror. He was in the grip, it is supposed, of some sort of psychological crisis. If so, its cause remains a mystery, though it seems probable that the storm was precipitated by the unexpected desertion of Kurbsky, a leading figure in the war, to the enemy.

In the last days of 1564 Ivan secretly abandoned Moscow and took himself, with his family, his retainers and treasure chests, to the village of Alexandrov, not far from the Trinity monastery of St Sergius. From there, after several weeks had passed in bewilderment and anxiety, he addressed two proclamations to the capital, one to the metropolitan and the other to his subjects in Moscow. He accused the princely boyars, the Church, the great in the land generally; he bore no ill will, he explained, towards the people, but he had stepped down from the throne because the robber boyars had betrayed both tsar and people. The shock administered by this simulated act of abdication was shrewdly devised. From the capital a mission of ecclesiastical and lay figures set out for Alexandrov to implore the tsar to return and to take the burden of government into his own hands. Ivan consented—on his own terms, which included as yet unspecified punishments.

In this way a remarkable apparatus of policy came into being under the name of the *Oprichnina* which worked havoc upon the traditional order of state. In the past, in the period of appanages, the term *oprichnina* had indicated a widow's portion—the grant of land set aside for the widow of a minor prince of the ruling dynasty. Now it came to stand for the idea of a wholly separate civil and military establishment for the tsar, resting on domains specially set aside for the maintenance of himself and his personal following. Within all was order and loyalty; outside treasonable winds blew. With grim deliberation Ivan proceeded to divide the Russian realm—'as with an axe', it was said at the time—into two halves. For himself he chose cities and lands from all parts of Russia to form the *Oprichnina*, carefully adding to them over the years until he had effected something like an equal division. The *Oprichnina* had its own court, its own government offices; the Kremlin was abandoned and Moscow itself was divided in order that an entire district might accommodate the Oprichniks, the members of the tsar's new following, in separate headquarters. The other half of the realm—the suspect and tainted half—formed the *Zemshchina* (from *zemlia*, the land), in which the ostensible responsibility for government and the defence of the country as a whole fell in the first place to the boyars' council. At a relatively late stage of the whole astonishing process Ivan went so far as to invest the *Zemshchina* with a tsar of its own in the person of a Tatar favourite converted to Orthodoxy, to whom he mockingly paid homage.

The calculation behind this seemingly insensate division of Russia was tortuous but also bold. The function of the *Oprichnina* was to concentrate government into the hands of a political security force directly controlled by the autocrat himself. The Oprichniks, originally one thousand in number but afterwards enlarged to several times that figure, were charged not merely with guarding the person of the tsar and executing vengeance upon his enemies. It was their task to destroy the tsar's enemies as a power in the state. For Ivan was resolved at all costs to crush the opposition of the great boyars. With the example before his eyes of Poland, where the territorial magnates and the gentry between them had reduced the crown almost to impotence, he pressed his attack at the most vulnerable point. It was above all the cities and patrimonial lands of the great boyar-princes which he took for himself, establishing his Oprichniks there to collect revenue and exiling from them, more often than not to the new frontier regions, those whom he had most cause to suspect. It was by murdering his enemies whenever possible and by dispossessing them of their hereditary lands—or, at the very least, by dispersing their estates more widely over Muscovite territory—that Ivan assured himself of the full prerogatives of autocracy.

The atrocities and the demoniac excesses he practised beggar nice description: decapitation, his favourite form of execution, was commonly preceded by gruesome torture. There is no means of knowing for certain the total number of his victims. The black-robed Oprichniks—members of the princely families among them —roaming the country on black horses and carrying at their saddle a dog's head and an emblematic broom, swept into their net not merely boyars and their servants but many more of all classes who might be plundered under the pretext of rooting out sedition and treachery. For himself Ivan methodically kept a complete list of his victims, frequently charging the monasteries he visited between one punitive tour and the next with the duty of offering prayers for the peace of their souls.

For religion of a kind entered into Ivan's mounting obsession. He enjoyed theological dispute and set much store by the doctrine of the third Rome. His retreat at Alexandrov was transformed into a parody of a monastery, with himself as abbot, in which bell-ringing and prayers at any hour of the day or night would be interrupted by orgies of drunkenness, lust and torture, with more bell-ringing and prayers to follow. Religion in this form, with the abbot's brows bleeding from violent prostrations, could not but be an intoxicant, constantly inciting the devotee to new extremes. When Ivan had tired of the usual run of victims, or when no other suspects were at hand, he looked for them among the most zealous Oprichniks. For protesting against the tsar's excesses the metropolitan of Moscow was deposed, exiled to a monastery and there strangled by the most notorious of Ivan's followers. The most barbarous, and the most lunatic, punishment inflicted by the tsar fell upon the city of Novgorod, which was subjected, on grounds of tell-tale suspicion, to attack by a regular armed force led by Ivan in person. Large parts of the city were destroyed, the richest quarters were ruthlessly pillaged and there were daily executions and tortures over a period of weeks; the Volkhov, it is said, over-flowed its banks with the number of corpses thrown into it. Novgorod, a more ancient city than Kiev, never recovered from this visitation.

Ivan's political purpose, it would seem, was not recognized at the time. The mass of the population were not greatly affected by his enormities of behaviour; like his debaucheries and his succession of wives, of whom there were probably seven, his cruelty appears to have excited only an uncritical wonder. The ways of the throne were mysterious; but, far from being thought insane, the tsar was held to possess altogether superior powers of mind. Yet ordinary reason in the end plainly deserted Ivan, who lost sight of his political aim in satisfying half-crazed passions. At no time does he appear to have envisaged an alternative machinery of administra-tion to the boyars' council. For that reason he did not finally shatter the power of the boyar-princes as a class, but only inflicted, through indiscriminate assaults upon individuals, disastrous injuries in the ranks of the great families. The sequel proved how fatal was his error.

Nevertheless, what was effected through the *Oprichnina* amounted in the last resort to a radical modification of the social structure of government. The older order of patrimonial lands and estates was largely dissolved and its place was taken by an extended system of land ownership in strict dependence on service to the crown. The *pomestie* became, as it were, a unit in the local apparatus of the autocratic state, the *pomeshchik* a hereditary steward of the autocrat. For by imperceptible stages he, too, established hereditary rights of possession, and, translated into a *dvorianin*, a member of the court (*dvor*), merged with the survivors of the old nobility and took over the title and function of a ruling class. In Ivan's reign the *dvorianstvo* were as yet too diverse, too unequal in wealth and status, to form a coherent body of gentry, but it was eventually in their interests that the condition of serfdom was formally laid upon the peasant population of Russia.

The legal enactment of serfdom was hastened by one further consequence of the campaign against the boyar notables. Migration to the territories thrown open by the conquest of Kazan broadened into a flood with the enforced removal to these new border areas of princely landowners from the central regions of Muscovy, and was still further swelled by the heavy exactions of their Oprichnik successors. In the result the central regions, the vital military prop of the realm, were rapidly depopulated. Both the service landowners there and the course of military operations in the west were gravely imperilled by this peasant exodus.

The Livonian war had settled down into an indeterminate and exhausting war of attrition. After the initial successes of the first two years, during which the invading Russian forces had devastated the Baltic countryside but failed to reach the sea, both Poland and Sweden had inevitably entered the struggle. The one had made of the province of Courland a tributary possession, the other had established a protectorate over the province of Estonia. The obstinacy with which the war was continued on the Muscovite side was attended by a policy of waiting upon events in Lithuania. Hopes ran high after the capture of Polotsk in 1563 and the subsequent advance into Lithuanian territory almost as far as Vilna, the capital. At this point, when Lithuania put forward peace proposals, Ivan summoned an assembly of the land for the second time. This was a more varied body than its predecessor, with representatives chosen more widely from the non-boyar ranks. The assembly pronounced in favour of resuming the war and Moscow's army made further headway. The Lithuanian reply, prepared by a joint meeting of the diets of Lithuania and Poland in Lublin in the closing days of 1568, took the form in the following summer of the complete political unification, under a single crown and a single parliament, of the two countries.

The consequences of the Union of Lublin were far-reaching. It immediately transformed the Livonian war into an open trial of strength between Moscow and Warsaw. It brought under the rule of the Catholic Polish gentry those wide borderlands of Little Russia which Moscow had long claimed as its own. It extended to them and to all the other predominantly Russian lands held by Lithuania the law of serfdom established in Poland. And it eventually delivered the destiny of Little Russia, and indeed of Russian-Polish relations, into the hands of the Cossacks of the Dnieper, the nucleus of the Russian Cossack world.

Heirs to the tribal liberties of Kievan Rus, the Cossacks represented the continuing challenge of the steppe to an evolving order, Muscovite or any other; of political freedom to state necessity. It is one of the commonplace ironies of Russian history that the Cossacks, who originally restored a lost tradition of freedom to the Russian people, became the notoriously punitive instrument of tsarist autocracy in decline.

The word 'Cossack' appears to be of Tatar provenance and originally signified a migrant or day labourer. In time it came to distinguish a mode of community life of the frontiersmen of the southern steppes. Such men, who were of diverse stock, lived on the margin of the steppe as adventurers and freebooters, hunting and fishing, fighting and plundering in much the same way as the Crimean Tatars; many, indeed, were themselves Tatars. They fought, in turn, and with equal unconcern, Tatar and Russian; now they raided the cities of the tsar and robbed and killed his messengers, now they accepted payment from Muscovy as border guards and auxiliaries. It was through the shift of population from the central provinces that their ranks began to swell with an inflow of roving and fugitive peasants and of the discontented and the lawless. Cossack bands alternately merged and clashed with the detachments sent from Moscow to garrison the fortified towns, linked by a chain of military posts, which served for the protection of the southern frontier. In time independent communities of 'free' Cossacks, submitting to no authority other than that of their own elected *ataman* (military commander), were established along the two great rivers of the western steppe, the Dnieper and the Don.* The history of the Dnieper Cossacks, the most powerful in the reign of Ivan the Terrible and for a couple of generations afterwards, belongs equally to Poland and to Russia.

The glare of war and predatory adventure that falls on the Cossacks of the Dnieper is softened by the romance of their permanent camp on an island in the river 'beyond the cataracts' (*za porog*)—hence the title Zaporozhian Cossacks. This was a purely military settlement, organized on fraternal principles, with property held in common and with no women admitted to it; the Cossack domestic settlements were on other river islands or elsewhere in the Dnieper valley. To all the other reasons for the growth of Cossackdom was now added, in the case of the Zaporozhian Cossacks, the incorporation of the western Dnieper lands into an alien Polish order of religion and society. New and complex factors thus entered into the security of the exposed south of a greater Poland.

In Muscovy the menace of the Tatars of the Crimea was countered but not as yet seriously reduced by the slow advance of the semi-fortified line behind which Russian agriculture encroached upon the black-earth steppe. All through the uncertain gains and intervals of truce of the long Livonian war the khan of the Crimea pointed a weapon at the heart of Muscovy. In 1571 the blow was directed at Moscow itself; only the Kremlin escaped destruction by fire and Russian losses included some 150,000 captives sold into slavery in Moslem lands. It was the prospect of a repetition of this disaster in the following year which persuaded the tsar to disband, at least in formal guise, the Oprichnik corps

* The Cossack communities of the other river valleys of the steppe—the Volga' he Terek, the Yaik (re-named in the eighteenth century the Ural)—were of later date.

and to restore to some of the princely boyars their former lands. Only in this way could he muster sufficient strength to throw back the Tatar incursion next summer almost on the line of the Oka.

In the west fortune still appeared to favour him until in 1575 the Hungarian Stephen Batory, one of the great military figures of the age, ascended the Polish throne, the first of a new line of elected kings. The tide of battle now turned swiftly, probably aided in no small degree by the gaps which Ivan's vengeance had made in the ranks of his military commanders. Batory's first signal victory was the recapture of Polotsk, after which he carried the war deep into Muscovite territory, seizing fortresses and burning cities, until the whole of the ancient Russian lands of the north-west were threatened. Only the heroic defence by its garrison of the fortress-city of Pskov—a famous feat of Russian arms—saved Muscovy from disaster. In 1582, two years before his death, Ivan accepted the mediation of the Papal nuncio. By the terms of peace he renounced all the Lithuanian territories he had won and all claims to Livonia. A year later the Swedes in turn seized their opportunity, recaptured the narrow strip of territory which Muscovy had succeeded in winning on the shores of the Gulf of Finland and formally possessed themselves of Estonia. The attempted Russian advance to the Baltic had been ruinously frustrated.

Yet there was ample compensation in the east, which was in fact the direction in which the boldest energies of the Russian people were turned. The land on the banks of the Kama granted by Ivan in 1558 to the Stroganovs, a merchant family of Novgorod, had almost overnight become the nucleus of a private commercial empire of enormous extent. Novgorod enterprise in an earlier period had created a sparse pattern of trade and settlement as far east as the river Ob. Now a more powerful current of adventure carried Russian colonization forward irresistibly. The new lands under cultivation, the fur-trading stations, the salt-mines, the iron deposits of the Stroganov empire stretched beyond the Urals into the Tatar khanate of Sibir. This was the last political obstacle to be surmounted in the Russian advance across the endless forests and plains of Siberia. In 1582 an expedition of some eight hundred Cossacks under their *ataman* Yermak drove its way forward into the khan's territory. The rout of the Tatar forces on the river Irtysh, largely accomplished through the secret weapon which the Cossacks possessed in the shape of firearms, signified the virtual conquest of Siberia. The Russian path had been cleared to the Pacific.

One further aspect of the reign of Ivan the Terrible remains to be recorded. Ivan had sought an outlet to the Baltic in order to make contact with western Europe after centuries of all but total isolation. At the beginning of his reign the very existence of a Russian kingdom east of the Lithuanian and Polish lands was almost unknown in the west. It was the backwardness fostered by isolation which made Muscovy weak; it was weakness which kept her from regaining the Russian lands in the west and so perpetuated her isolation. For her own ends Muscovy needed Europe—her knowledge, her skills, the secret of her strength. An imperfect substitute for victory in the Livonian war was provided by the fruits of English navigation. When the English, in search of a northern sea passage to India, opened a route to the fabled lands of Muscovy by way of the Arctic and the White Sea, more than all else it was the prospect of borrowing strength from the west that made them welcome. It was on those terms, and as a rule on those terms only, that the foreigner was made welcome in Russia ever afterwards.

Richard Chancellor, at any rate, who in 1553 reached the mouth of the Northern Dvina, where the English laid the commercial foundations of what was to become the port of Archangel, was received in Moscow with unwonted warmth. The English Muscovy Company proved the medium not only of lively trade exchanges but of English exports to Russia of gunners, shipwrights, engineers and masons. For his own part Ivan would have chosen additional and more intimate relations. In his correspondence with Elizabeth of England he urged the advantage of a military alliance and the cessation of English trade with Poland, and pledged himself, on condition of a similar pledge in return, to extend asylum to her in the event of her deposition. Elizabeth delicately evaded the offer of an alliance by her dear brother and good friend, but did not escape Ivan's mocking rage that she was evidently no ruler but was herself ruled by a nation of traders. Having released that historic shaft, he proceeded to alarm Lady Mary Hastings, who was related to the queen, by a proposal of marriage.

The balance-sheet of the reign is not easily drawn and judgment on Ivan himself halts at many obscure passages. Worn and diseased in his last years, he let the instrument of statecraft slip from his hands and finally destroyed at a blow the governing aim he had pursued through nightmare extravagances. He had two surviving sons by Anastasia Romanov, of whom the elder, Ivan, raised high expectations as heir to the throne; the younger, Fedor, was simple-minded. Less than two years before his death the tsar, in an access of rage, struck Ivan on the head with the pointed iron staff he habitually carried and killed him. The celebrated but somewhat facile painting of the scene by the Russian artist Repin, which hangs in the Hermitage in Leningrad, depicts the horror and remorse which have popularly been attributed to Ivan the Terrible. Whatever the feelings that in fact lay behind the tsar's hysteria and religiosity after the event, it seems clear that he knew he had achieved the destruction of the dynasty and the restoration, however temporary, of the boyars' power. What he could scarcely have foreseen was the true measure of the ordeal which he had bequeathed to his people. Then, as now, the centralization of government in a single person is apt to run to a tragic vulnerability at the centre.

CHAPTER VI

THE TIME OF TROUBLES

THERE IS NO absolute of misfortune in Russian history, but perhaps the early years of the seventeenth century come nearest to it. All that was most fantastic and destructive in the reign of Ivan the Terrible was easily surpassed by the fantasy and destructiveness of 'the confused time' (*smutnoe vremia*), or the Time of Troubles as it is generally called. This is the name given to the nine years of catastrophe, filled with a startling succession of pretenders to the throne of Moscow and progressing through social anarchy to civil war and foreign intervention, which ended in 1613 with the election as tsar of Michael Romanov; more loosely, to the period from the extinction of the line of Ivan Kalita in 1598 until 1613; more loosely still, to the whole melodramatic sequence of events during the twenty-nine years between the death of Ivan the Terrible and the establishment of the Romanov dynasty.

These events, which pose unsolved mysteries of identity and riddles of psychology, have been the theme of endless debate and conjecture. They set their stamp upon a great deal of later history. Their immediate cause was the break, or the impending break, in the genealogical continuity of the sovereign princes of Russia. But in substance they bore witness to a revolutionary ferment in all classes of the population. The relentless process of imposing cohesion upon the fluid Russian state had bred deep unrest everywhere. From every section of the Russian people came a surge of disaffection, each wave of violence or intrigue directed to different ends but all characterized by the same fearful Russian immoderation, against the system of society and government in the making. Amid the doubt or suspicion cast upon the person of God's representative on earth, total anarchy was loosed upon Russia.

Ivan the Terrible, after the murder of the son he himself had designated as successor, left two sons by different mothers: Fedor, the child of his first wife, Anastasia Romanov, and the infant Dmitry, the child of his dubious seventh marriage with another boyar's daughter, Maria Nagoy. The assembly of the land which was summoned after Ivan's death confirmed Fedor's succession. But at the age of twenty-seven Fedor was sickly in body and feeble in mind, devoted above all else to the pieties of bell-ringing and the lavish spectacle of the rites of Orthodoxy From the beginning it was plain that the sovereign tasks of government would fall upon a power behind the throne.

Pride of place among the great boyar families belonged to the Shuiskys, who had the support of the metropolitan and of a large part of the population of the capital. Of inferior lineage were the Romanovs, whose head, Nikita Romanov, was the tsar's uncle by marriage, and Boris Godunov, of Tatar origin, who had stood closest to Ivan the Terrible in the latter's closing years and whose sister Irina was married to Fedor. In the rivalry for the authority of effective regent all the advantages were with the tsar's relatives by marriage. Power was firmly concentrated in the hands of the elderly Nikita Romanov for the few remaining months of his active life, and then passed to Boris Godunov.

More than one Russian ruler has deserved to be called enigmatic; Boris Godunov is less an enigma, perhaps, than a fascinating unfinished portrait. We know too little of him for certain. Russian novelists and dramatists, with Pushkin in his superb drama dazzling all who came afterwards, have spun from Boris's character webs of intricate psychology, though still leaving crucial questions unanswered. On the central episode in his progress towards the throne of the tsars, the weight of opinion endorses popular belief at the time and makes of him a blood-stained usurper. But a great scholar like Platonov has argued a strong case for his innocence and claimed for him heroic virtue as well. Boris's contemporaries conceded not his statesmanship only but the humane purpose which mingled in him with the inhumanity of power; while the admiring tribute of foreign observers to his ruler's quality of mind carries a pointed suggestion of the tragic in his history.

Ambitious and quick-witted, with more love of learning than learning itself, married to a daughter of the most sinister figure among the Oprichniks but himself apparently free of the dark

Oprichnik taint, Boris had evidently exercised commanding gifts of personality in retaining the trust of Ivan the Terrible. As regent he assumed the full responsibility and much of the ceremony of the throne. He conducted direct correspondence with foreign sovereigns, among them Elizabeth of England; to the English he was known as Lord Protector of Muscovy. In recognizing Russia's need of technical aid and instruction from the west he also may claim the title of a precursor of Peter the Great. He had purpose and ability, even in some sort a conscience. What he unmistakably lacked is what almost all usurpers or suspected usurpers have lacked: a habit of self-confidence. And from that psychological disability, as so often, sprang the further and fatal lack of the gift of popularity. However well he meant, and even in his increasing want of scruple he appears to have meant well, Boris remained suspect. His demonstrable successes brought him little credit, mischance followed him, rumour of treason or murder fastened on him at every turn.

It was in this atmosphere of popular distrust, which was darkened by the plots and stratagems of rivals, that Boris fell back on the example of Ivan the Terrible. The severity of his punishments may have matched the age; but, even more faithfully than the *Oprichnina*, the system of espionage and delation with which he tried to secure his position foreshadows the police state of a later age. The practice, at any rate, of planting secret agents in the households of known or potential enemies reached an early and notorious perfection in Russia under Boris Godunov.

At the accession of Fedor the infant Dmitry, together with his mother and the Nagoy family, had been withdrawn from Moscow to the not very distant small town of Uglich, on the Volga—a normal enough proceeding in the circumstances, since the district was designated the widow's appanage—and suspected boyars had been banished from the capital. Firmer measures followed the boyar plot, hatched with the support of the metropolitan Dionysius, to persuade Fedor to divorce the childless Irina and marry again. Boris sent the ringleaders into exile under stringent conditions and compelled Dionysius to retire in favour of the archbishop Job. From then onwards the Church was his close ally.

Its loyalty to him was more fully assured by a bold stroke of diplomacy, the creation of the Moscow patriarchate. The hierarchy of the Russian Church had long been fretted by ambition. By comparison with the patriarchates of Jerusalem or Antioch or Alexandria, indeed of Constantinople itself, all under the infidel sway of the Turkish sultan, the metropolitanate of Moscow was a humiliating anomaly. Moscow, the truly sovereign and independent capital of Orthodoxy, required nothing less than its own patriarch. It was this triumph that Boris secured by his patient and astute handling of the patriarch of Constantinople on the occasion of the latter's visit to Moscow. Job was consecrated patriarch at the beginning of 1589 and in that capacity was able to assist some years later in Boris's election as tsar.

The establishment of the patriarchate, peace with Sweden and Poland, the creation of new townships in the steppe country, the development of colonization in western Siberia—these were tasks to which Boris bent his energies successfully. But the intractable problem that confronted him sprang from the deteriorating conditions of the great body of the peasantry. Over the whole landscape of government and law at the turn of the century hung the darkening cloud of serfdom.

In law, it must be repeated, the majority of the peasants on the private estates at this time were still free, still normally entitled to come and go after the autumn harvest, during the week before St George's Day (November 26) and the week after. But almost everywhere in the older areas of cultivation freedom in law had been dissolved in economic obligation. Through indebtedness to their landlord the peasants had been largely assimilated to the condition of the personal or domestic slaves now engaged in agriculture. As bondsmen, over and above whatever payment as rent they were required to make in kind they owed labour dues to the owner of the estate. This principle of obligatory labour (*barshchina*), the *corvée* of western feudalism, was the crux of Russian serfdom. Even where the peasant's right of departure might be conceded, removal elsewhere, except to the freedom of the frontier, could mean no more the exchange of an old economic servitude for a new, of labour bondage to one master for similar bondage to another.

In point of fact, however, such migration had already been beset by legal restrictions. Through all the continuing denudation of the central regions of Muscovy the dearth of labour had pressed hard upon the new class of service landowners. It was to them that the government looked in time of war, and it was from the labour of the peasants on their land that they in turn drew their means of support. Their *pomestia* were often small, the peasants settled on them few in number; many *pomeshchiki* were themselves not far removed from peasants. Almost of necessity the exodus from the central regions had been accompanied by a competitive bid for labour between the landowners, more particularly between the large estates and the small. The former—the great boyar and monastic properties—enjoyed all the advantages of bigger resources. Peasants were enticed, bribed, abducted by force from the small estates to the large; quarrels, lawsuits, even small pitched battles followed. And all the time the flight to the Cossack frontier continued. It

E

was in these circumstances that Ivan the Terrible, in an attempt to remedy the plight of the military-service landowner, had instituted the practice of forbidding the movement of peasants from one estate to another during a given year. His purpose had been to stay illegal flight and abduction, not to suspend the legal right of departure. Since 1581, however, the first of these 'prohibited' years, there had been several repetitions of the ban.

Of lasting significance from the point of view of law, since it marked the earliest stage of formal enserfment, the ban had had little practical effect, least of all upon the imperilled small estates, some indeed totally abandoned by now. To Boris Godunov fell the necessity of retrieving in some degree the position of *pomeshchik* and peasant alike, of attempting, in Platonov's phrase, to reconcile the irreconcilable. In a series of decrees from 1592 onwards he forbade the large landowners, lay and monastic, to procure the labour of the peasants on the small estates and introduced a new system of peasant registers on the service lands which could serve as documentary title in the recovery of illegally absconding or abducted peasants. A special decree in 1597 established—for claims made in that year, and in that year only—a period of five years for their recovery. Though the decree, in point of fact, wrought no change in the legal position of the peasantry, it long earned for Boris the undeserved reputation of having formally instituted serfdom.

Fedor died in the first days of 1598 and the line of sovereign princes of Moscow since 1322 was extinguished. It was left to the patriarch to summon an assembly of the land to elect a successor. Boris's only serious rival was Fedor Romanov, the eldest of the five sons of Nikita Romanov. But both the patriarch and Boris's secret agents, it is clear, had been actively at work; the choice was more apparent than real, the whole procedure was possibly rigged. Boris twice refused the proffered throne, then yielded to the entreaties of the leaders of the Church. His was the common dilemma of the intruder in a system of hereditary power; he must needs make his succession appear not only legitimate but sanctioned by the dead. In delaying his coronation Boris invoked the death-bed injunctions of Fedor, even a charge laid upon him by Ivan the Terrible. Duly crowned, he attended to his enemies. Within a year or two the Romanovs had all been sent into distant exile, Fedor Romanov himself having been translated into a monk under the name of Philaret.

Long foreseen, the break in dynastic continuity in itself effected no change in the condition of Muscovy. But it touched off every specific cause of discontent in the land, and in so doing demonstrated the historic function of the divine right of the tsars. In the absence of an undisputed tsar all reasons of state were open to dispute; the whole foundation of order was in the appointed sanctity of the throne. This was the reason why even the hollowest claim during Boris's reign to legitimacy in the succession earned for the pretender some measure of popular support, why indeed the appearance of pretenders was endemic in Russia for the next two centuries. What darkens the whole issue of people and tsar in the Time of Troubles is the wide divergencies of aim between the great boyars, the service landowners, the townsfolk, the Cossacks, the peasants, and the foreign princes and armies who lent the pseudo-Dmitry and later pretenders their support.

The pseudo-Dmitry; for Dmitry, an epileptic, had died in Uglich in 1591, whether innocently or by murder on Boris's instructions can never be known. It is a story as fabled as the murder of the Princes in the Tower, but more momentous. The suspected Boris ordered an enquiry after there had been violent local disorder; the death, it was announced, was accidental. For those who had instigated the rioting there was torture and mutilation; for the Nagoy family exile or imprisonment. Retired to a nunnery, the tsaritsa Maria, the mother of Dmitry, became the nun Marfa.

The sequel, preceded by a thickening crop of rumours, came twelve years later. In the interval, however, tsar Boris had exerted himself to meet fresh disaster. For three successive years, 1601–2–3, there had been a total failure of harvest over wide areas. In conditions of famine, such as only Russia among European countries has known, which were attended by cannibalism and by plague and pestilence, Boris organized the distribution of grain in Moscow and the provision of public works. These measures of relief, however, could not extend very far and across the length and breadth of Muscovy roamed hordes of the hungry in robber bands, plundering and murdering, their numbers continuously swollen by the drift of peasants left to fend for themselves by masters who no longer required their labour. All this was yeast in the revolutionary ferment.

The story that Dmitry was alive, that he had escaped the murderous intentions of Boris and that another child had been buried in his name in Uglich, spread eastwards from Poland. It found, like the legend of Perkin Warbeck, willing believers. In 1603 came the news that the Pretender had won recognition from the Polish king, Sigismund III, and was enlisting an army to regain the throne of his father which Boris had usurped. In Moscow the tsar denounced the imposture, the patriarch followed suit; the 'false Dmitry' was identified as Yury Otrepev, the son of a small landowner who had once served in the Romanov household, become a monk, filled a minor office in the patriarch's establishment and then fled to Lithuania. But this and all similar explanations were in vain; the Pretender's following grew irresistibly.

Who was he? Not Dmitry certainly. But almost as certainly not Otrepev either. It seems beyond doubt that he was an instrument of the tsar's boyar subjects—a dupe, though an innocent dupe, of the Romanovs, who had conveniently chosen Poland as his springboard. For the riddle of the whole astonishing story is that this Pretender genuinely believed he was the tsarevich; from beginning to end his behaviour makes it plain that he thought himself Dmitry. It was this conviction, this total absence of the precautions and evasions of the impostor, that so often convinced others. Unhandsome but intelligent and fearless, the Pretender merited a better cause than that of the great boyars who had contrived to use him.

Turned Catholic, with a mixed following of Poles, Cossacks, rebellious garrison troops and runaway serfs, he started out from Kiev for Moscow in the autumn of 1604. He met with little initial opposition, but, in failing to make junction with a body of Cossacks advancing from the Don, was routed by a Russian force and driven back. In the following spring he set out again, with messengers and proclamations preceding him. District after district declared for the Pretender; the capital awaited him. And there, in April 1605, tsar Boris died suddenly at the age of fifty-three.

It was now that Russia began to fall apart. The throne passed to Boris's son, Fedor, but Fedor's cause was lost at the outset. To the Pretender on his way to Moscow rallied the great boyars; now at least they could do so openly. Led by Prince Vasily Shuisky, who had once proffered sworn testimony that Dmitry was dead, they took the oath of loyalty to him and demanded that all do the same. A mob invaded the Kremlin and Fedor and his mother were done to death. A week later 'the true tsar Dmitry' entered his capital. There came to him from exile the nun Marfa, who promptly recognized in him her son.

The Pretender's brief reign marks an ominous interlude of quiet before the full storm of the Time of Troubles burst upon Russia. He took firm but restrained measures against Boris's chief henchmen; his recall of the Romanov and Nagoy families was graced by sympathetic gestures. A crowned tsar, he gave new vigour to the deliberations of the boyars' council. He made no anticipated cession of territory to Sigismund and did nothing to encourage the hopes of the Polish Jesuits in his train. Although he retained much of his popularity with the Russian people, what lost him favour in conservative Muscovite quarters was his all too evident preference for foreign (and more civilized) ways. Together with the greed of the Poles by whom he was surrounded after his marriage to the Polish Marina, a provincial governor's daughter, it contributed to his undoing. But the chief agency of his downfall was the boyars themselves, whose purpose he had already served.

It is necessary to distinguish the diverse threads in the intricate pattern of anarchy which was now unfolded. The great boyar families sought to restrict the power of the throne and to restore their position as an hereditary ruling caste. The military-service class of gentry were concerned to maintain their rights against the great boyars, the gentry of the provinces staking out a claim to share political responsibility with the gentry of the capital. The trading community of the towns sought relief from crippling legal disabilities. On the Polish side, Sigismund hoped to drain Russian strength by promoting civil war and the gentry looked for opportunity as soldiers of fortune; while the clergy, who in 1596 had established for the Russian population of Lithuania the Uniat confession, whose adherents acknowledged the supremacy of the Pope while retaining the outward ritual and the liturgical language of Orthodoxy, in a tide of Jesuit energy did not despair of winning Muscovy to the cause of Rome. As for the Cossacks, with freebooting habit went an untutored vision of the rebuilding of Muscovy on the principles of Cossack freedom and fraternity. Finally, for the peasantry as a whole, or for the slaves and fugitives who fought in their name, the goal was deliverance from boyar and *pomeshchik* alike, and as such signified a social revolution.

Of these conflicts of purpose the boyar notables who had set the stage for the Pretender's appearance were soon made aware. Their own special contribution was a bid to secure the dynasty for one of themselves. With the earliest signs of danger Shuisky had once more changed his mind and announced that the Pretender was an impostor. Astonishingly, without hesitation or anxiety, the latter summoned an assembly of the land to consider the charge. Found guilty of treasonable falsehood, Shuisky was pardoned on the gallows and then restored to his rank and titles. His next step was more successful. It was to incite the people of Moscow, always the heart of Russian xenophobia, against the Poles and foreigners in the Pretender's retinue. A mob stormed the Kremlin, massacred and plundered, and then ran amok for two days. Among their victims was the false Dmitry. His death was the signal for the acclamation by a picked crowd in the Red Square, not by voice of the *zemsky sobor*, of Prince Vasily Shuisky as tsar.

The reign of chaos opened now. Tsar Vasily had hoped to insure his position on the throne by conceding the claims of his accomplices among the great boyars to a constitutional right in government, but the scales were by this time heavily weighted against him and against them. The military-service gentry, from whom in the end salvation was to come, cast their lot against the tsar almost at the same moment as popular revolt flared up.

Revolt originated in the southern borderlands and spread swiftly. It was as though the accession of Shuisky was a signal awaited simultaneously by slaves, peasants, Cossacks and the poorer gentry, with each element of society unaware of the mood of pent-up violence of the rest. The inchoate waves of protest—against the whole scheme of things directed from Moscow, against boyar oppression and the exactions of the landowners—coalesced in a movement of destruction and revenge, led by a runaway slave, Ivan Bolotnikov.

Bolotnikov summoned slave and serf to a war of extermination against their masters, exhorting them to kill, to seize the masters' wives and daughters and their possessions. There followed the prototype of Russian peasant *jacqueries*, a campaign of burning and pillage, torture and death. In the autumn of 1606 Bolotnikov made for Moscow, heading a host of 'thieves' which spread terror on the way. But at the critical phase of the campaign the class savagery of the rising lost him the support of the military-service elements which had made common cause with him, and the rebels were thrown back by the tsar's forces and retired on Tula. There, joined by a Cossack detachment under a leader who claimed to be no other than a (wholly imaginary) son of the tsar Fedor, it was besieged and starved into surrender. Bolotnikov was either captured or else vanished at this point without trace. But he had laid down a memorable pattern of peasant revolt.

Even while the fires of Bolotnikov's war were still raging there appeared yet another true tsar Dmitry—the third; a second had briefly come and gone months earlier. For through all official assurances that the Pretender was dead it seemed likely enough, so incomprehensible was the whole succession of events, that he was in fact alive. The new pretender, who is known as the Thief of Tushino, was a crude tool of those elements which had originally supported the first pretender, to whom he bore not the slightest resemblance. A bold, coarse ruffian, he was openly mocked as an impostor by them. Yet with little effort on his own part his following grew from day to day. A swarm of Polish adventurers, strong Polish military units, Cossacks from the Dnieper and the Don flocked to his side along with remnants of Bolotnikov's army and a new and variegated army of 'thieves'.

With this motley backing the Thief moved on Moscow, which he three parts encircled in the summer of 1608. A grotesque situation now developed, with Shuisky virtually imprisoned in the capital and the Thief installed as rival sovereign in an armed camp at Tushino, on the outskirts, where he maintained the semblance of a court and government of his own. The unruly pleasures of the camp had their attraction for the population of Moscow, which moved to and fro between the two sides. The Poles, constantly strengthened in numbers, were the ruling force in Tushino, where the Polish Marina chose to recognize in the Thief the husband from whom she had been parted; while under Polish leadership a detachment from the camp, lured by the prospect of rich booty, besieged for some sixteen months the Trinity monastery of St Sergius, a fortress which the monks defended with great spirit. It was from the Trinity monastery that the call to resistance eventually came.

With almost the whole of central Muscovy converted to the Thief's cause, Shuisky had resort to desperate measures. At the price, among other concessions, of ceding Karelia to Sweden, he secured the military aid of a Swedish auxiliary force. The effect, of necessity, was to bring Poland openly into the struggle. Sigismund gave prompt effect to a declaration of war against Muscovy by laying siege in the autumn of 1609 to the fortress-city of Smolensk, which then as now guarded the direct road to Moscow. The Thief bestirred himself simultaneously against the capital. But in face of the Swedish auxiliaries, and of the desertion of his Polish troops to Sigismund's battle for Smolensk, he was forced to withdraw, abandoning Tushino and falling back on Kaluga.

Chaos seemed complete, though in fact the worst was still to follow. Hostile from the start to the 'boyar-tsar', the military-service class were at last successful in dethroning Shuisky, and a confused and faction-ridden boyars' council now looked to the election of a new tsar for the restoration of order. So precarious was Muscovy's situation that the choice of an active minority fell upon the youthful Wladyslaw, Sigismund's son.

Since the offer to Wladyslaw was based upon conditions which have been described as the earliest draft constitution for Russia, it is interesting to speculate on what the consequences might have been if Sigismund had not desired the throne of Moscow for himself. A leading personage in the Muscovite delegation to him was Philaret Romanov, whom the Pretender had made a bishop and the Thief had raised to the patriarchate. Sigismund detained him as a virtual prisoner while pressing his siege of Smolensk. The great fortress was captured and destroyed, and Sigismund returned to Warsaw and there waited upon events. Despair fell on Moscow; even the news in the last days of December 1610 that the Thief had been murdered by one of his followers brought little consolation to the boyars' council, which saw no alternative to recognizing Sigismund as tsar.

Yet a saving national pride was at work both in the capital and in the countryside. It went deeper than mere hatred of the Poles now in possession of Moscow. A restored confidence in the Russian land flowed from the exhortations of the aged patriarch Hermogen and from the bold messages which were sent out from the Trinity monastery to every part of the land. From that centre of Muscovite faith and strength, now heartened by the lifting of the siege, there came also supplies of money and of arms for the deliverance of the Orthodox realm. Only unity against the invader, ran the summons from the Church, could save Russia.

Effective unity was beyond the capacity of the mixed body of gentry, Cossacks and peasants who formed the first popular levy. Advancing from different directions towards Moscow in the early months of 1611, it gathered reinforcements on the way, was joined in the capital itself by a restless and expectant population and in Easter week besieged the Polish garrison in the Kremlin. The Poles were completely masters of the situation. They inflicted great slaughter on the ill-armed attackers, drove them back, burned down a large part of the city and immured themselves once more in the safety of the Kremlin. Defeat revived the bitter divergencies on the Russian side, in which the balance of strength lay with the undisciplined Cossacks.

By the autumn blackest night had fallen upon Muscovy. The Poles held in their hands Moscow, Smolensk and other cities in the south-west; the Swedes had seized Novgorod and adjacent lands in the north-west; another pretender claimed allegiance in Pskov; the voice of the patriarch Hermogen in the capital had been silenced by the Poles. There was neither government in Russia nor leadership of any kind, only a land laid waste and an abandoned people.

Tenacity of will, which is perhaps a Protestant and Puritan virtue, is no part of the Russian character. But endurance is, and at the extreme of endurance lies the capacity for recovery. When all seemed lost Muscovy recovered through the concerted efforts of the minor nobility of the capital and the gentry and trading population of the provinces. The lead in the formation of a second and more disciplined popular levy was given by Nizhny-Novgorod, whose *starosta* (mayor), Kuzma Minin, a prosperous butcher and cattle-dealer, raised a national fund for the purpose. A local boyar of soldierly reputation, Prince Dmitry Pozharsky, was appointed to the command. So confused was the situation, so envenomed by suspicion, that the whole movement was threatened at the outset by the apprehensions of the Cossacks in Moscow, still bent on realizing their dream of universal Cossackdom.

Pozharsky moved cautiously and in the spring of 1612 made

not for Moscow but for Yaroslavl, on the middle Volga, where he summoned a meeting of the *zemsky sobor*. The assembly assumed full civil and military powers, but, deliberating and delaying, prepared for the election of a new tsar before attempting to march on Moscow. In July, however, came the news that Sigismund was sending a relieving force to Moscow to assist the Polish garrison in the Kremlin, which was once more under siege by the Cossacks. For Pozharsky this was the signal to march. In the capital he barely escaped assassination at the hands of the Cossacks, of whom the greater number now deserted the fight while the rest sought to come to terms with him. The Polish reinforcements arrived in the thick of the argument and promptly attacked; the Cossacks were passive spectators of the battle almost until the end, when they could no longer sustain so difficult a part. The Russian force seized the fortified Kitaigorod, the ancient quarter nearest to the Kremlin, and four days later the exhausted and starving Polish garrison, which had been reduced to the grimmest horrors of siege, surrendered. Moscow was freed.

But even in the capital the Time of Troubles was not yet over, for the crown of liberation, the election of a new tsar, was still to be won. Invitations went out to all the principal cities of Muscovy to send delegates to a *zemsky sobor* which would choose a sovereign. The assembly of the land which met in January 1612 was the most widely representative in the history of that institution. It gave a voice to every class in the state, including the peasantry. From a prolonged and anxious debate emerged, first, the decision to exclude all foreign candidates for the throne in favour of a member of one of 'the great families' of Moscow; then the choice of the sixteen-year-old Michael Romanov, the son of Philaret. A link, however tenuous, with the old dynasty—a hint of continuity, however faint, with the line of Ivan Kalita—was thus preserved. In the middle of February Michael was acclaimed tsar in the Red Square in Moscow, and, though in fact he was not at the time in the capital but had taken refuge in a monastery near Kostroma, the people of Moscow swore allegiance to him.

What the Time of Troubles had meant in material devastation Russia was to discover under the early Romanov tsars. But the harvest of anarchy was ruinous in a deeper sense. In terms of retarded development, the Time of Troubles cost Russia scarcely less than the wars of religion soon afterwards cost Germany. Morally and spiritually, it arrested the clock for generations.

Only the serving class of the landowning gentry, the ruling caste of the future, and the merchant class of the towns, who between them had saved Moscow and brought the Romanovs to the throne, were the victors in the struggle. The entire population paid the

price of their victory. The boyars, like the English feudal nobility
in the Wars of the Roses, as a class had committed suicide; the
position of individual families was secured or even strengthened,
but the rest declined almost overnight and great names sank into
total obscurity. The Cossack hope was extinguished; continued
revolt had brought nothing but continued defeat. And for the
peasantry the only prospect in view was to be delivered more
completely into the hands of the gentry, the true arbiters of the
nation's destiny until 1861.

CHAPTER VII

THE EARLY ROMANOVS

IN SPITE OF their newly discovered sense of Russia as a national
state, it was a profoundly chastened people who recognized Michael
Romanov as tsar. At the end of the long night of chaos to which
all classes and factions in the land had made their disruptive contribution the light of a natural order of rule returned to a Russia
severely restricted in territory and crippled in strength. In 1613
the country was on the brink of economic collapse. The empty
treasury, the unsown and wasted fields, the burned and pillaged
estates, the desolation and decay of the capital and the fearful scars
of battle everywhere were eloquent of the renewed impoverishment which the country had suffered.

Brute impoverishment, indeed, with its accompanying load of
taxation, dulled and stifled the energies of the nation for the next
century. Western conceptions of progress have admittedly never
captured the Russian mind or imagination unreservedly, but it
remains true that the seventeenth century, an era of high adventure
and rising prosperity in the west, was characterized in Russia by a
pervading moral and material stagnation. The pace of western
influence perceptibly quickened in this century; to the extent that
the remedy for Russian backwardness had already been recognized
Peter the Great found the ground prepared for him. But innovation,
which the great majority mistrusted, lay lightly on a thin crust of
society. The horizons of seventeenth-century Russia were narrow,

No belated breath of the Renaissance had come to liberate the imagination, no reflected gleam of the Reformation (save in the disputed lands west of the Dnieper, where the counter-Reformation was in process) to quicken the spirit. It is a nice point of contrast, perhaps, that serf law was formally acknowledged in Russia within a few months of the execution of Charles I of England.

The immediate tasks of government at the accession of Michael, who proved a negative and characterless ruler, were to fill the treasury, to renovate the shattered machinery of administration, to restore civil order in face of Cossack threats and domestic disturbance and to counter the occupation by Sweden and Poland of Russian territory. For these purposes the sustained support of the *zemsky sobor* which had brought Michael to the throne was essential. Neither the tsar's family nor the surviving boyar notables were willing or indeed able to forgo this aid. Philaret, the tsar's father, who did not return from captivity in Poland until 1619, who was then consecrated patriarch and as effective ruler raised to an equal titular height with his son, had all the requisite qualities of a Russian autocrat, but at no time could he dispense with the support which the assembly of the land only could afford.

So began the brief phase, unique in Russian history until 1905, of a rudimentary scheme of representative government. A genuine if restricted inquest of the nation, the assemblies summoned by the first of the Romanov tsars were very different in composition from those convoked in the previous century. The boyars' council still stood at the centre of the assembly, but it was now dominated by the serving gentry, who, like the representatives of the trading community, were often present in an elective capacity. True, unless it was specially charged by the tsar to do so, the assembly initiated no new laws; in principle, its function was advisory only. But the part allotted to it nevertheless marked the transition in Russia from government by established custom to government by statutory decree.

Outwardly the assembly had all the potentialities of a permanent legislative body. Yet in fact it was never able to take root in the harsh and unfriendly soil of Moscow. It met no less than ten times during the thirty-two years of Michael's reign, almost continuously for the first three years, deliberating on issues of war or peace and on fiscal needs and expedients. But it was summoned five times only during the thirty-one years of the reign of Alexis, Michael's successor, and these occasions were all crowded into the first eight years of the reign. Thenceforth, having by this time shed a representative character, it met three times only, the last in 1698. Except at rare intervals in the long era of St Petersburg absolutism that followed, the representative idea was sunk in an enchanted sleep and only the noise of approaching revolution could wake it.

Parliamentary rule in any western sense of the term did not seriously intrude upon Russian minds until the earlier part of the nineteenth century, and seldom diverted the nation afterwards from very dissimilar currents of political thought. But the failure of the *zemsky sobor* undoubtedly cut short a hopeful prospect in the scheme of seventeenth-century government. Failure sprang from two causes. In the first place, it was never intended by the tsar, or by the remnant of the old aristocracy in alliance with the new, that the assembly should assume permanent powers; its representative character was no more than an expedient for transferring to the nation immediate responsibility for the maintenance of the new dynasty. That responsibility discharged, the assembly had outlived the occasion for which it was summoned.

More significantly, what deprived the assembly of continuing purpose was the increasing rigidity of the divisions between the several 'estates' or classes in the state. Amid the poverty and precariousness of the state's resources the principle of obligatory service took precedence of all others. Military and fiscal need dictated a strict segregation of classes, each with its appointed obligation. Between those on the one hand who rendered military service and those on the other who constituted the general body of taxpayers, between the landowning gentry, the clergy, the commercial guilds of the towns and the peasantry the state erected barriers of fixed and unalterable law. In this rigorous system of class segregation, which was consummated by the formal recognition of serfdom, there was no place for a corporate and popular instrument of legislation.

Serfdom, indeed, was the decisive factor in the eclipse of the assembly of the land and in so much else that helped to shape the course of events in the seventeenth and later centuries. It was a poison that drained away the energies of government under the early Romanovs. In Michael's reign foreign pressure and Cossack violence were countered with varying degrees of success. The Don Cossacks, though they would suffer no restriction of their right to order their own affairs, acknowledged the tsar in Moscow. Though the Swedes would not surrender the coastal strip they had won on the Gulf of Finland, the treaty of Stolbovo in 1617 restored Novgorod to Russia as the price of freeing Swedish arms on the eve of the Thirty Years' War. Though Poland, which had swallowed a great new slice of Russian territory, was still the deadly enemy and war was resumed in 1618, with the Poles once more reaching as far as Moscow, a truce was maintained for fourteen years by recognizing Polish possession of Smolensk and the border province of Seversk. The further resumption of war and the total failure of the Russian siege of Smolensk brought no additional losses and peace in 1634 even gained Polish renunciation of the claim to the throne of the tsars. All these assertions, however qualified, of reviving strength ministered to a growing confidence in Moscow. But there was no such sense of reassurance in face of the growth of serfdom.

The condition of hereditary peasant serfdom was formally recognized in the *Ulozhenie*, or code of laws, of 1649. This summed up the enactments of the previous century and was specially designed to consolidate the laws and sovereign decrees dating from the founding of the Romanov dynasty. What was primarily involved in the statement of serf law was the state revenue. For not the least injurious consequence of the legally undefined relationship of peasant and landlord was the opportunity it afforded for the wholesale evasion of taxation.

Peasant flight, which in Michael's reign had shown no sign of slackening, was a familiar problem for the tsar's keepers of the treasury. Together with continued flight, however, had gone a more subtle method of escaping financial and all other obligations to the state which was open to peasants and townspeople who were still technically free. By voluntarily forgoing their liberty and enrolling themselves among the household dependents of a serving landowner or monastery, they joined the ranks of the chattel population who were subject neither to taxation nor to conscript service. Both they and their master thus profited at the expense of the state. The bargain struck in respect of their liberty might be called off at any time, but in the meantime this temporary or simulated bondage suited both parties. The disguise of chattel status had its advantages not only for free peasants and the poorer townsmen but also for the humbler members of the serving gentry themselves.

In these circumstances one of the first and most pressing needs of government under Michael had been to undertake a census of lands and population for taxation purposes. The chief end in view was to restore to the peasant community all runaways and to reimpose tax-paying obligations upon all who had contrived to evade them. Begun in 1619, the work met with every kind of obstruction and delay, was half-abandoned, resumed again and completed in 1628. From this point the peasant-landlord relationship was frozen into immobility and the names inscribed in the village registers listed the serf population of Russia. The census marked, in effect, the real point of departure in law at which the peasant on both the private estate and state land forfeited the right of movement. The time limit for the recapture of fugitives was in 1642 extended to ten years, and four years later was completely abolished. Three years later still came the *Uloʒhenie* and the categorical statement of serf law, or the right of security as it was called (*krepostnoe pravo*), by which the landlord secured the labour of his peasants and the state secured the payment of peasant taxes by making the landlord responsible for their collection.

The promulgation of the code had been preceded a year earlier by riots throughout the tsar's dominions. For some days the situation in the capital, where the habitually restive *Streltsy* garrison were on the point of revolt because of accumulated arrears of payment, was critical; the tsar himself was rudely menaced by a mob and gained immunity only by discarding his chief counsellor. It was the fear of renewed disorder which had hastened the work of codification.

The code did nothing to moderate smouldering resentments. Rather the reverse happened. Peasant grievances had already been brought to the point of crisis by events elsewhere. Across the western frontier serf revolt in Little Russia had merged in the fearful war against the Polish gentry of the Zaporozhian Cossacks under their elected *hetman* Bogdan Khmelnitsky.* Serfdom in Poland was still more unbridled than in Russia, and in the Lithuanian lands, where the Polish population was still relatively small, the animosities of religion and nationality nourished the hatred of the Russian Orthodox peasants for their alien masters. The Zaporozhian Cossacks, among them a 'registered' minority in the military service of Warsaw, lived in a state of undeclared war against the serf-owning Polish squires. Khmelnitsky himself had suffered outrage at the hands of one of them and vainly sought redress. He had looked in turn to the khan of the Crimea and to Alexis for aid; Moscow he had tempted by an offer to recognize the tsar as ruler of the free Zaporozhian host. Though it was clear that Khmelnitsky's hopes were fixed on gaining the whole of Little Russia for Cossackdom and not for the tsar, Moscow hesitated. Unless support were given, the long deferred prize of Kiev and the Dnieper lands might for ever remain with Poland or even pass to the Turkish overlord of the Crimea.

While Alexis hesitated Khmelnitsky struck. In the spring of 1648 two Polish forces in succession were slaughtered by his Cossack-Tatar army advancing from the south and the signal was given for a historic *jacquerie*. The Khmelnitsky massacres in the Ukraine, crudely romanticized in Russian revolutionary folklore, still live in Polish—and Jewish—memory. The Polish serf competed with Cossack and Tatar in blind atrocity: the gentry were hanged, burnt, flayed, torn limb from limb; priests were shot or hanged at the altar; the Jews—then as afterwards the commercial

* Chmielnicki, in the accepted style of transliteration from the Polish.

middlemen and factors of the landed Polish gentry—suffered name-less horrors. Khmelnitsky's final triumph came in September with the annihilation of an army of the flower of the Polish nobility, characteristically dressed in ermine and gold. The Cossack leader was now undisputed lord of almost the whole of Little Russia. The entire Little Russian population professed itself Cossack.

From that position of strength he negotiated a treaty with Jan Casimir, the Polish king, by which Polish forces were banned from Little Russia and recognition given to the supremacy of the Orthodox Church there. For more than a year Khmelnitsky ruled in somewhat grandiose fashion as a conqueror. But Poland recovered, war was resumed, and again the Cossacks turned to Moscow. Still Alexis hesitated, and meanwhile Khmelnitsky, abandoned by his Tatar auxiliaries, rapidly lost ground. Decision could no longer be postponed in Moscow; the ambition of centuries of restoring the Russian borderlands to Russian rule was now at stake. In January 1654 the Zaporozhian *rada*, the popular assembly, proclaimed tsar Alexis suzerain of Little Russia and protector of the autonomous Cossack host. Three months later Alexis, 'tsar of all Great, Little and White Russia', declared war against Poland. A year later Poland's northern foe in the person of Charles X of Sweden followed suit.

Swift and sweeping success attended the tsar's armies. An ill-garrisoned Smolensk, for the possession of which so many bloody battles and sieges had been fought, fell that year, and by the end of the following year Moscow had captured a string of fortress-cities in White Russia. Only Moscow's alarm at the Swedish success in occupying Warsaw and Cracow and winning over to Sweden's side some of the Polish territorial magnates saved Poland from collapse. By the treaty of Vilna in 1656 she ceded to Moscow the whole of Little and White Russia and both countries made common cause against Sweden.

The ensuing tangle of events is not easily or briefly unravelled. Khmelnitsky died in 1657 and his successor, still pursuing the dream of an independent Cossack state, now looked to Poland for support. Poland herself, as so often in her mercurial history, passed from catastrophe to resurgent strength and again fell back into impotent disunity. By a whirlwind campaign in 1660 she had regained almost all that had been surrendered by the treaty of Vilna, but then fell victim once more to the dissensions of crown and nobility. In the struggle among the Zaporozhian host for the authority of *hetman*, in which one faction leaned on Moscow, another on Warsaw and a mutinous remnant finally took service under the sultan, the greater part of Little Russia was laid waste. Both sides were exhausted when in 1667 Russia and Poland agreed to divide between them the prize of these now desolate lands and signed the treaty of Andrusovo.

By the terms of the treaty Poland retained Lithuania and Russia acquired Smolensk and the left bank of the Dnieper. The right bank remained Polish, save for Kiev, which by agreement passed into Russian hands for two years only but which in fact Poland could never regain. For in relation to her eastern Slav neighbour Poland had passed the zenith of her power; from now onwards Russian strength grew in Europe and Poland's declined. For that very reason the treaty allowed Russia to orientate her policy towards alliance with Poland against the more formidable Swedish and Turkish barriers to Russian expansion. By the treaty of Moscow in 1686 Russia and Poland pledged themselves to eternal friendship and peace.

Throughout the war with Poland the material for a peasant conflagration had accumulated in Muscovy and periodically blazed up. The growth of serfdom sharpened peasant anarchy. The tsar's judicial servants and tax-gatherers, notoriously venal, shared with the serf-owners in the spoils of government. Corruption thrived on the irresponsible powers of local officials and unrestricted rights of punishment; the extremes of peasant servitude bred extremes of peasant cruelty and violence; over large stretches of the country-side banditry was endemic, and in the towns as in the rural wilds the darkest crimes were everyday occurrences.

The twenty odd years between the promulgation of serf law and the rebellion of Stenka Razin were filled with a succession of local risings. The cost of Muscovy's wars was paid for in scarcity and high prices, in harsher and more arbitrary taxation. In 1650 there was a savage rebellion in Pskov, which was more briefly echoed in Novgorod. During an outbreak of plague in 1655, which took a great toll of lives and brought the country's affairs almost to a standstill, violence raged unchecked in the central regions. In the summer of 1662 revolt stirred in Moscow through well-founded suspicion of the fortunes made in high places after the introduction some years earlier of a copper coinage in place of silver. For a time the capital was in the hands of an enraged mob, and once more the tsar was threatened in person. On this occasion the *Streltsy* were called out and there followed a punitive campaign of extreme ferocity. Some seven thousand people were executed and twice as many suffered torture, mutilation, exile or confiscation of their possessions.

The worst hatreds were kindled on the private estates. In spite of the penalties of capture, peasant flight continued on an increasing scale. The greatest lure was still the adventurous freedom of the Cossack country, from which the state-organized hunts for fugitives were jealously excluded. These periodic armed expeditions, which began in 1664 and continued for a century, reflected the constantly worsening conditions of serfdom. It was not to the land only that the peasant was attached but to the landlord, whose authority over the person of his serfs grew steadily more absolute. The law required him not to inflict death on any of his peasants by way of punishment, but in point of fact he was in no way legally responsible if death followed. Punishment apart, the sale of peasants without their land was a normal practice to which the law soon extended its protection, and to this there was added in time the custom, often involving the separation of families, of offering peasants as a personal gift or in payment of debt.

The rebellion led by Stenka Razin, a rebellion of peasant serf, exploited townsman, poorer Cossack and subject tribesman of the Volga lands against the self-owning gentry and all officialdom, is historic and legendary. It is a fount of popular ballad and epic, a spring of revolutionary folklore. Bloodthirsty and barbarian, Stenka Razin lit a candle that was never put out. He enters upon the scene of history as the leader of a predatory band of Cossacks of the Don. Peasant flight to the Don country, where cultivation of the soil was forbidden in order to avert the menace of serfdom, had divided the older Cossack settlements from the horde of hungry newcomers. Since the first retained in their own hands the best fishing and hunting grounds, the newcomers—the 'naked', as they were called—cast about for adventure. But the traditional Cossack sport of plundering Turk and Tatar on the shores of the Black Sea was now obstructed by the Tatar forts guarding Azov at the mouth of the Don. In a famous episode of Cossack arms in 1637 the fortress of Azov had been captured in a surprise raid, victoriously held against a prolonged siege and twice vainly offered to the tsar. Since the lower Don was closed to adventure the 'naked' Cossacks turned towards the Volga.

The prelude to revolt in the spring of 1670 was a series of audacious exploits that stirred the popular imagination. Piracy on the busy lower reaches of the Volga was crowned by a campaign of massacre and pillage of Persian settlements on the Caspian shore. A victory-flushed host defied all the tsar's officials on the return to the Don. These accomplishments set the Volga and Don lands echoing with Stenka Razin's name and fame. The spectacle of the treasure he had brought back with him and the conquering hero's largesse drew to his side an army of the destitute and the loot-hungry.

Now his thoughts turned from the riches of Persia to the fraternity of the Russian land. What had begun as normal Cossack adventure turned to a dubious war of liberation against the masters,

F

the oppressors of free Cossacks and serf peasants alike; brigandage blazed into a vast social conflagration. Stenka Razin led his army against the tsar's governors on the middle and lower Volga. The peasantry and the rabble of the towns were with him as soon as he had moved; the *Streltsy* garrisons promptly came over to his side. Death, torture and rapine followed the horsetail standard of revolt in the manor houses, administrative offices and merchant dwellings of the Volga provinces. Tsaritsyn, Astrakhan, Saratov, Samara in turn opened their gates to the Cossack hero. For Stenka Razin, while protesting allegiance to the tsar in Moscow, proclaimed the rule of Cossack freedom throughout Russia. His emissaries went before him, rousing the whole countryside, stirring the displaced Finnish tribes of Mordvin, Chuvash and Cheremis settlers to revolt, organizing massacre and plunder in the Oka lands, reaching as far as Moscow itself and beyond to the Solovetsky monastery in the White Sea. A vast stretch of the tsar's dominions was lit by the glare of peasant insurrection.

The flames were spreading towards Moscow itself when the battle turned against Stenka Razin. A foreign-trained body of troops, which had saved Nizhny-Novgorod from the rebels, turned south and routed him at Simbirsk.* The legend of his magic dissolved, the patriarch formally anathematized him, the Don Cossack settlements refused him shelter. He was betrayed, taken to Moscow, suffered with great fortitude hideous tortures and was quartered alive. The revolt was not over, however; the avenging fires continued to burn on the private estates long afterwards. The tsar's punitive columns levelled unnumbered villages to the ground and left standing gallows everywhere, but it was years before peasant resistance in the Volga regions was entirely quelled.

The rebellion of Stenka Razin, cruel beyond all measure, brought to the surface a kind of barbarian idealism in seventeenth-century Russia. The great schism in the Russian Church which was almost contemporary with it illustrated an almost unteachable fear of reform. There had long been a movement in the higher ranks of the clergy to draw Russian Orthodoxy into closer unity with the Eastern Church as a whole, and in particular to restore the liturgies in use, which had been corrupted in the past by copyists' errors, to complete conformity with Greek usage. The movement came to a head with the consecration as Russian patriarch in 1652 of Nikon, the only figure in Russian ecclesiastical history in the mould of a great prelate of the west. With the help of Greek and Russian scholars in Kiev Nikon set in hand the revision of the service books. In so doing he created consternation and horror among the Russian Orthodox faithful.

* Now Ulianov.

The changes he introduced might elsewhere have appeared insignificant; the most substantial of all required that the sign of the cross be made with three fingers and not with two and involved a slightly different spelling of the name of Jesus. But change in any form flouted the invincible conviction that Russian Orthodoxy alone was the true Orthodoxy. The strict letter of established ritual was the heart and soul of faith; the faithful had nothing to learn from Greek scholars, subjects of the infidel Turk. In this climate of bigotry the mass of the lower clergy were joined by a section of the hierarchy in opposition to Nikon's reforms. Schism was widened by the overbearing pretensions of Nikon himself.

Religious revolt spread to all classes of the population. It split the Church wide open. The movement for a return to the old belief (*staraya vera*) gathered momentum, and not all the repressive measures launched by the leaders of the Church could arrest it. The schismatics (*raskolniki*), or Old Believers (*starovertsi*), were armed against every denunciation for heresy, every form of persecution. They suffered exile and death, and in exile and death made converts. They prophesied the coming of anti-Christ and hastened their own departure from the world by self-immolation, locking themselves in barns and dwellings which they then set alight. For eight years the monks of the Solovetsky monastery withstood a siege by regular troops in defence of the old belief. There were large numbers of schismatics among Stenka Razin's following. The greatest figure of all among the Old Believers was the archpriest Avvakum, fanatical, eloquent and heroic, whose superb autobiography, the earliest work of Russian literature composed in the spoken language of the people, is the indubitable masterpiece of the century. The martyr's crown which Avvakum won in 1681, long before Nikon had fallen from power, inspired among his followers a renewed passion of self-destruction before the coming of anti-Christ.

Nikon's triumph, in the normal order of things, was his undoing. Appointed 'grand sovereign', like Philaret, by the pious and suggestible Alexis, he had gone on to strain the limits of ecclesiastical ambition. In presuming to claim supreme authority, in his own terms, for the sun of the Church over the moon of the state he had raised every secular power in the land against him. Deposed, while still protesting his authority as head of the Church, from the patriarchal throne and exiled to a distant monastery, he had nevertheless completed his work. He had, in the first place, precipitated the decline of the Church during the next two and a half centuries. And he had created in holy Russia a vast body of religious dissent, which was perhaps the real source of the spiritual energies of the Russian people from now onwards and which was almost always to be identified with popular movements against authority. On the dissenters before all others fell the rigours of persecution in the name of Orthodoxy throughout the years to come.

The prevailing conservatism of sentiment and custom in the Russia of the early Romanovs affected the entire nation. It was perhaps the one thing that bridged the immense chasm dividing the privileged landowning class as a whole from the peasant majority. As always, backwardness itself bred resistance to change. Yet through all conservative prejudice the lesson of foreign example was slowly being learned. Side by side with the cult of national exclusiveness grew the reluctant habit of learning from Europe. Guided by Ordyn-Nashchokin, the earliest of the true 'westerners', Russia's ruling class began to sit at the feet of the foreigner. For the people as a whole, as for Nashchokin himself, such things as foreign dress were an abomination, a profanation of the Russian idea. But foreign mercenaries helped to train a regular Russian army, foreign prospectors searched for mineral wealth, foreign doctors, engineers, craftsmen and even scholars were made welcome. Germans were conspicuous in Moscow. From the foreign suburb (*nemetskaya sloboda**) of the capital came, among other things, European furniture, carriages, musical instruments and clocks. But these were for the enterprising few among the great nobility; for the nation at large life remained fixed in the immemorial pattern of the village community, a cluster of chimneyless earthen or wooden huts, filth and raggedness, the 'darkness' of poverty, ignorance, superstition and drunkenness. Nobility and people alike awaited the prodigal energies and the draconian methods of Peter the Great.

CHAPTER VIII

THE LEGACY
OF PETER THE GREAT

THE REIGN of Peter the Great is the watershed of modern Russian history, the great divide between Muscovy and imperial Russia, the iron bridge between the harsh paternalism of Moscow and the

---

* *Nemets*, from *nemoy* (dumb), was the name by which a German had always been known in Russia, and was stretched to include all European foreigners.

harsher regimentation of St Petersburg. It brought a semi-Asiatic and medieval state into fruitful but shallow contact with the civilization of the west and established Russia among the great powers of Europe. As the architect of the empire of the tsars and an example for the age of Stalin Peter is the most significant ruler in Russian history.

Insecurity attended his accession to the throne. Tsar Alexis died suddenly in 1676 at the age of forty-seven. By his first wife, Maria Miloslavsky, he left two sons, Fedor and Ivan, aged fourteen and ten; by his second wife, Natalia Naryshkin, the four-year-old Peter. Both Fedor and Ivan were sickly, the one half-paralysed and the other almost blind and witless; the boy Peter enjoyed abounding health. Even while Alexis lived the Miloslavsky and Naryshkin factions had been at bitter odds in rivalry for the succession. With the due acclamation as tsar of Fedor the Naryshkins were driven unceremoniously from court and Peter and his mother relegated to a safe distance. Fedor died six years later. In the midst of continued sordid faction the signal event of his brief reign was the formal abolition of the obstructive system of *mestnichestvo*.

By all the unformulated rules of succession the throne was now Ivan's. But the Miloslavskys had made lively enemies at court and in the Church, and these, attempting to dispense with the formality of an assembly of the land, hastened to proclaim Peter. At this point there appeared on the scene the formidable Sophia, Ivan's sister, a shrewd, ambitious, plain-featured woman with a cultivated prince charming, Prince Vasily Golitsyn, for lover. Sophia had recourse to the *Streltsy* garrison of the capital, who once more had accumulated a load of grievances. The tale that Ivan had been done away with sent armed detachments to the Kremlin. Before Peter's eyes several members of his family and their supporters were hacked to death as the prelude to three days of bloodthirsty rioting in the capital. There followed the proclamation of Ivan and Peter as joint tsars under the regency of Sophia. Both tsars appeared together on state occasions, when Peter's vigour and high spirits habitually caught the eye of foreign envoys. But while Sophia and Ivan dwelt in the pomp of the Kremlin Peter and his mother lived in secluded and simple fashion in the village of Preobrazhenskoe (Transfiguration), on the outskirts of Moscow, not far from the German suburb.

There Peter's ordinary schooling ceased. He had learned to read and write—the missionary educator of Russia could never spell correctly—and had acquired a smattering of Greek and Latin. But his studies henceforth were entirely of a practical kind. The absorbing passion of his boyhood, not an uncommon one either then or afterwards, was playing at soldiers. But with Peter the game was played in all earnestness and with a studious interest in the science of fortress-building and of mechanical engines of war. His playmates were drawn from the children of those in attendance upon his mother and from the neighbouring villages; nobleman's child and peasant's child were equally welcome in his toy army. They formed the nucleus of the famous regiments in later years of the Preobrazhensky and Semenovsky Guards and the most favoured constituted a small corps of boon and trusted companions.

From Dutch, Germans, Scots and Swiss in the German suburb Peter acquired a knowledge of mathematics for artillery practice and instruction in sailing, and from his games of Mars and Neptune, as he called them, sprang the army and navy which he created. Of restless and gross appetite, he acquired from the foreign colony a great deal more besides, including a German mistress. In 1689, at the age of seventeen, he was unwillingly married to Evdokia Lopukhin, of a noble Russian family, whom he cast off even before she bore him a son in the following year. By that time he was firmly seated on the throne.

For Sophia had overplayed her hand. She had given hostages to fortune in invoking the aid of the *Streltsy*, had converted allies into enemies by assuming the title of autocrat and incurred loud unpopularity through the failure of the campaign, led by her prince charming, against the Crimean Tatars. Her period of rule bristled with disappointments, or was made to appear so by the supporters of Peter's cause. In the Far East, where Russian colonization had already reached Kamchatka and the Pacific, progress was checked by Chinese arms in the Amur river valley, from which Russia agreed to withdraw by the terms of the Treaty of Nerchinsk in 1689. This, too, was turned to her disadvantage. In an atmosphere of thickening court intrigue crisis was not long delayed.

It came towards the end of August 1689, when the news reached Preobrazhenskoe at night that a *Streltsy* band were on the way to murder Peter. The news was false and may well have been deliberately concocted, but there was wild alarm and he was hurried on horseback through the forest to the Trinity monastery. The experience left its mark on him for the rest of his life in a nervous twitch on one side of his face which sometimes spread in ugly contortions to the rest of his body. With the report of his flight came a prompt alignment of forces; he was joined by his toy regiments, then by several *Streltsy* companies and bodies of regular troops and finally by many notables among the Moscow nobility. There was never the least doubt that popular sentiment was with him. Sophia was confined to a convent, Golitsyn was exiled and a few hangings took place. At seventeen Peter was effective tsar.

But he did not at once assume the reins of power, preferring instead to direct the manoeuvres of a play army which for some time had ceased to be a play army. Only in 1694, after the death of his mother, did he begin to take over the functions of government. Two years later Ivan died, and the chapter of nominal joint rule was ended.

Peter, who became Peter the Great and emperor, attempted to refashion Russia with the western instruments of progress. He desired nothing more of Europe than the skills and the knowledge which she possessed; with these he sought to throw off the inheritance of Russian backwardness and to build upon new foundations a greater Russia. What he set out to achieve he did not and could not achieve, for all the inertia, ignorance and incapacity of the Russian people stood between him and his goal. A semi-Asiatic and medieval land before he set to work upon it, Russia remained largely semi-Asiatic and medieval after he had done. In attempting, in Kliuchevsky's phrase, to evoke initiative in an enslaved society Peter was courting failure. Yet the change he accomplished, superficial in so many respects, fragmentary, chaotic and prodigal in wasted lives and wealth, constituted a real enough revolution. And Peter's example, perfunctory though his immediate successors were in following it, continued in some degree to shape the polity of the empire until the end, and shapes the polity of the Soviet Union to-day.

The lead he gave, which at the time clashed with every national prejudice, became in the nineteenth century a theme of passionate contention between slavophils and westerners, provoking a great flow of soul on the true destiny of Russia. Yet the whole historical and philosophical argument was in a sense unreal. For imperial Russia could neither have been created nor have survived save by imitation, however crude and at whatever cost, of the methods of the west. Those methods had already been tried out by Peter's forerunners. His originality lay in recognizing their logic. Since all that was conservative and stagnant in Muscovite habit sprang from the cultural tradition of Byzantium, the secular forms of europeanization were a necessity of state.

The case against Peter the Great is formidable. It is not answered by the liberal argument for progress or by the apology for revolution from above. But neither is it advanced by the charge that he destroyed an indigenous culture and disrupted an organic unity of the nation. With the beards and caftans which Peter abolished went a debased religious formality; with a common mode of thought in Russian society went the division of Russian society into two nations. The cleavage between rulers and ruled was not projected by the contrasting symbols of Moscow and the new city of St

Petersburg; it was inherent in the historic order of the Russian state. The real count against Peter the Great—and perhaps, after all, it overshadows all the rest—is that in attempting the impossible he set a killing pace. He drove his country forward along strange paths with pitiless unconcern, without thought of the sacrifices he demanded or the costliness of his errors. It is that taskmaster's obduracy which wears so familiar a look to-day.

Peter's reforms were undertaken in the first place through military necessity. War and expansion were the dominant themes of his reign. The schooling for Russia which he sought from the west was technical and utilitarian; Europe could fit Russia for war and expansion by teaching her not only gunnery, shipbuilding and navigation but also administration, manufacture and trade. In thus planning to educate his subjects Peter had no single and inclusive scheme of reform in mind. He attacked his problems piecemeal, often creating new and greater disorder by hasty improvisation; only in the last six or seven years of his reign, indeed, did he set himself the task of repairing the confusion he had made. At no time did he threaten to disturb the existing twin pillars of the state. Autocracy and serfdom were both profoundly strengthened by his innovations.

In varying degrees, Catherine the Great, Alexander I, Nicholas I and Alexander III all had both ability and character enough to sustain in their own person the comprehensive role of autocrat. To the requisite ability and character Peter joined a demoniac freakishness of nature. Quick and lively in mind, he made up for a certain want of depth by devouring curiosity and inexhaustible nervous energy. A giant in stature, he delighted in feats of physical strength, was never ashamed to stoop to the humblest manual tasks and was always willing to learn. It was a favourite boast of his that he had mastered fifteen trades, including dentistry. In a gross age his manners were exceptionally gross and ran to a passion for revolting horseplay. And there was in him a dark streak of the pathological. Not even Ivan the Terrible exceeded Peter the Great in the savagery of his punishments. Though not always faithful to his friends, he was capable of deep attachment to them: to the Swiss Lefort, the great favourite of the early years of his reign, and most of all to 'my dearest friend', 'my brother', 'my heart', Alexander Menshikov, reputedly a pastrycook's boy, who rose to be the tsar's right hand in war and in peace and who proved the greediest and most unscrupulous of a robber band of imperial administrators. With men like these Peter to the end of his days indulged in gargantuan drinking debauches and extravagances of lust and blasphemy under the auspices of a companionship which he styled the Drunken Assembly of Fools.

The first test of his mock battles and sieges came in 1695 with the assault on the Tatar fortress of Azov. The prize of the southern steppelands still eluded the farthest reach of Moscow; some hundreds of miles of perilous no man's land divided the southern limits of Russian agricultural settlement from the shores of the Black Sea. The capture of Azov was designed to free the whole of the Don valley steppe. But ordinary methods of siege in 1695 were in vain, since supplies and reinforcements reached the enemy by sea. The next move therefore was to build a fleet of river galleys in order to blockade Azov. In a combined operation in the following summer the attempt was renewed and the fortress duly fell. Peter had demonstrated the new arts of war in Russia.

From this initial victory sprang the project, at its focal point the recurring Russian dream of the possession of Constantinople, of a coalition of European states to dismember the Turkish empire. The project was pursued in the course of Peter's celebrated grand embassy in Europe, where it met with scant sympathy and was laid aside. But the embassy itself was historic. Included in the company of two hundred which left Moscow for foreign parts in the spring of 1697 were various youthful members of the Russian nobility sent to study shipbuilding, 'navigation science' and similar mysteries, and also the giant Corporal Peter Mikhailov of the Preobrazhensky regiment of Guards. It was the first time a Russian sovereign had travelled abroad.

The party journeyed by way of Riga, Courland and East Prussia to Holland. For a week the 'tsar-carpenter' worked in the shipyards of the small town of Zaandam, then moved on to Amsterdam, and, at the invitation of William III, came to England, whose shipwrights he cherished ever afterwards. He stayed in England for four months, visiting docks, arsenals, museums, the Tower of London, the House of Commons (the sitting he attended left him cold); talked with Fellows of the Royal Society; sat for his portrait —now in Hampton Court—to Kneller; and left behind a trail of profuse and wanton damage in John Evelyn's house in Deptford which had been rented for him. Throughout the whole tour it was the coarse and disgusting habits of the Russian party that made perhaps the strongest impression.

Peter and his Russian barbarians, however, had not failed in their more practical purpose. The tsar returned home wiser in knowledge and stronger in resources, having negotiated the purchase of naval and military supplies and commissioned the services of foreign technicians and skilled workers. It was in Vienna, on the way back, that news reached him of a revolt of the *Streltsy* in his absence and its successful suppression. Peter hastened his return. Suppression of the revolt had not erred in clemency, but his darkest suspicions were aroused and he ordered a new enquiry. Torture and confession were the prelude to as dreadful a feat of punitive ferocity as any in the history of the tsars. The block, the gallows, the wheel, the rack, slow fire and the knout were pressed into service in a holocaust of public executions. The tsar presided over the labours of a series of torture chambers in Preobrazhenskoe and possibly dispatched some of the victims himself. Mutilated bodies were put on show in the Red Square in Moscow through all the months of the winter. The *Streltsy* companies, their ranks thinned by close on two thousand executions and unnumbered sentences of exile to Siberia, were disbanded, and the dubiously implicated Sophia was shorn as a nun.

The horror which this vengeance excited in the population of the capital, versed as they were in the spectacle of death and torture, capped the effect of the tsar's decree on the compulsory wearing of European dress and the shaving of beards. On the day after his return to Preobrazhenskoe occurred the famous incident in which Peter himself cut off the beards of some of his foremost nobles. The logic of this essay in enforced westernization was impeccable; since in foreign eyes the long beards and the long-skirted robes of Muscovite custom were eastern and barbarian, the claim to equality with Europe necessitated the adoption of short dress and shaven chins. Yet the beard was, in Russian eyes, the very badge of Orthodoxy. 'Where will you be', the patriarch had demanded years earlier, 'on Judgment Day? With the saints whose faces are decked with beards or with the shaven heretics?' The tsar's decree illuminated all that was impious to the majority in his westernizing reforms. From their sense of outrage, strongest among the Old Believer element of the merchant and trading community, grew the image of Peter as anti-Christ. The law finally permitted the wearing of a beard on payment of a beard licence, but otherwise only peasants and priests might go unshaven.

The dismemberment of Turkey postponed, Peter's eyes turned to the Baltic seaboard. During the three years in which he prepared for war with Sweden he launched out on an impetuous first instalment of measures of reorganization. The state revenues were taken in hand; beard licences were joined to a succession of other novel fiscal devices; the whole apparatus of local government was overturned, though this was as yet only a beginning; and a similar beginning was made with the reform of central government. A new standing army was created, and the development of the iron foundries of the Urals was hurried on with the aid of 'possessional' serf labour—that is, the labour of peasants on state land who were enserfed to private or state industry. Amidst all his preparations for war Peter found time for the reform of the Russian calendar, which until then had been reckoned from the beginning of the world. January 1 was now adopted in place of September 1 as the beginning of the Christian year 1700.

The most dangerous military adventures are those undertaken in the expectation of a short war. The command of the Baltic that Peter eventually wrested from Sweden cost Russia dear. The Great Northern War, as it is called, lasted twenty-one years, brought the mass of the Russian people to threadbare poverty and fastened upon them a completer and still more degrading servitude.

The war began in August 1700, on the unsubstantial basis of an alliance with Poland and Denmark and the formal conclusion of peace with Turkey. All his energies notwithstanding, Peter's preparations had not gone very far. But Russian troops at once marched towards the Gulf of Finland and besieged the Swedish fortress of Narva. Charles XII of Sweden was barely eighteen years old and of unknown military quality. At Narva the new Russian army was driven headlong in flight, abandoning virtually the whole of its artillery and baggage to an enemy greatly inferior in numbers. Peter's complete loss of nerve on the occasion is notorious. But Charles's fatal error was to postpone the invasion of Russia until he had settled scores with Poland, Sweden's hereditary enemy. The six years during which his armies campaigned to and fro in Poland, ever victorious but ever more deeply embroiled in the luckless fate of the Polish kingdom, gave Peter the opportunity to learn his lesson.

He did, in truth, learn it. The system he now adopted of maintaining the strength of the army by constant levies on peasant households was remorseless, but it met his insatiable need and long survived his death. Conscription was for twenty-five years. Discipline was to match, though not so ferocious then as it became afterwards.

The fruits of this military reorganization ripened quickly. One army helped to keep Charles at full stretch in Poland; another, with Menshikov leading a reformed cavalry, recovered the coastal strip of the Gulf of Finland which long ago had been lost to Sweden and moved nearer to the mouth of the Neva. In the autumn of 1702 Peter himself assisted in the capture of the fortress of Noteburg, which he re-named Schlüsselburg. It was indeed the 'key city' to the sea. A little distance away, in May 1703, rose the newly built Russian fortress of St Peter and St Paul. And just beyond the fortress walls, on a desolate stretch of wind-blown marsh, Peter laid the foundations of his city, his future 'paradise', St Petersburg, Russia's window on the west.

This first stage of the Great Northern War was rounded off by

the preliminary labours of construction of a Baltic fleet—already
the naval base of Kronstadt was rising from the sea—and by the
triumphant assault on Narva in 1704. Tied down by politics and
diplomacy at this time more than by war, the grim and silent
Charles bided his time. He himself had known nothing but victory.
And while he waited domestic confusion gathered around Peter.
His policies had dislocated the whole mechanism of state and
strained the endurance of almost every class of the population. No
tsar had so consistently courted the hostility of his subjects. There
was chaos in the state finances; local administration had collapsed
on the lower Volga and elsewhere; the Bashkirs of the Urals had
risen in revolt; the clergy were incensed against the tsar and the
schismatics were in open rebellion. Most threatening of all, peasant
unrest in the autumn of 1707 burst into flame with the insurrection
of the Don Cossacks, still a refuge for runaway serfs, under their
ataman Bulavin. The ghost of Stenka Razin once more walked
abroad.

All Cossackdom was stirred, fired by the old dream of republican
independence. The Cossacks of the Ukraine under their *hetman*
Mazeppa were on the brink of joining hands with the Cossacks of
the Don; Mazeppa, indeed, uncertain of the outcome of the war,
had for some time been in secret correspondence with the Swedes.
At a time when he could ill afford to spare the troops Peter sent a
large detachment to the Don, where during the following months
revolt was put down mercilessly.

By that time Charles had moved. Early in 1708 he advanced
through Poland at the head of a strong and seasoned army. At
Grodno Peter fell back on the classic Russian strategy of retreat,
the implacable Russian tactics of scorched earth. With reinforcements on the way from Livonia, Charles took the direct road to
Moscow, then broke off and headed south to join forces with
Mazeppa. A double disaster overtook him: the Livonian reinforcements were scattered by Peter, with the loss of the artillery and
stores on which Charles had been counting, while Menshikov,
suspecting treachery, moved swiftly against 'Judas' Mazeppa's
stronghold after the *hetman* had made his way almost alone to
Charles's camp.

Throughout the winter of 1708–9 the Russian army kept guard
on the eastern bank of the Dnieper. In the spring Charles struck
out once more and, following the line of the Vorskla river, besieged
the Russian southern frontier post of Poltava. There, on June
27/July 8, with the Swedes at a hopeless disadvantage, was fought
the critical battle of the war. It was short but decisive. Poltava
marked the emergence of Russia as a leading military power in
Europe. The significance of the victory was apparent at the time,

and amid their rejoicing the subjects of the tsar were all but reconciled to Peter and his ruinous and heretical reforms.

Poltava freed Peter's hands; dangerously so, as it happened. Much that remained to be accomplished in the north was put in hand; the Baltic provinces of Livonia and Estonia were subdued, Karelia and a large part of southern Finland were wrested from the Swedes. But these victories only excited larger dreams of conquest, a deeper intoxication of glory. The tsar's eyes now turned southwards, where originally his gaze had been fixed, to the Crimea.

Once more, as at the impetuous start of the struggle with Sweden, Peter met humiliating failure. It was the sultan, with Charles at his side, who made the first move and declared war. It was now that Peter fastened upon Russia the role, sustained for another two centuries in war and diplomacy, of protector of the Orthodox subjects of the Ottoman power in the Balkans. Scantily prepared for the arduous campaign, his army marched south, and, exhausted by the enemy's harrying tactics, was confronted by a vast and well-ordered Turkish army on the river Pruth. Negotiation, even on the most abject terms, was the sole alternative to surrender. The loss of Azov, and of all that had been won by the treaty of 1700, signified the complete collapse of Peter's southern ambitions.

Years of tireless war and of tireless Russian diplomacy followed in an attempt to bring the struggle in the north to a conclusion. Peter was absent from Russia for long intervals, restlessly hurrying from place to place and project to project. A resounding naval victory in the Baltic in 1714—the first in Russian history—even though it endangered Stockholm itself, brought peace no nearer, since it aroused alarm in England and drew English sea power closer to Sweden. Still Peter persisted in a grand design of reshaping the system of European power. It was no longer a barbarian tsar who on a second visit to the west in 1717 courted the favours of the court of Louis XV; but, though his courtesies were more polished, Peter's bid to replace Sweden as the ally of France was received with negligent curiosity only. Direct peace overtures next year were halted by the death of Charles, indomitable to the last, in a siege in Norway. A brief resurgence of Swedish strength faded amidst the havoc of the Russian invasion by sea in 1719, and, after further diplomatic delays, peace negotiations were set in train which ended in the signature of the treaty of Nystadt, to which England was a party, on September 10, 1721. Russia had achieved the principal ambition she had pursued during the twenty-one years of the Great Northern War.

From Viborg to Riga the Baltic coast was Russian. Though almost the whole of Finland was given up, part of Karelia was acquired together with the Baltic provinces*. Russia now faced both ways, west as well as east. In recognition of victory the Senate which Peter had established as the supreme instrument of central government conferred upon him the title of *Peter Patriae, Imperator, Maximus*.

Even this was not sufficient to satisfy the emperor's thirst for glory. Hard on the heels of peace with Sweden came war with Persia, from which he temporarily won the long western coastal fringe of the Caspian. Almost on his death-bed he was planning military expeditions to the extremities of the Eurasian plain, towards the frontiers of China and India.

The Senate, which in a revised form survived until the revolution of 1917, represented one of Peter's major institutional reforms. It came to birth in 1711 as a corrective to an earlier and sweeping scheme of decentralization, under which the country was split up into eight vast administrative units, known as *guberniy*, or 'governments', each with its own system of territorial division. The plan was meant to replace the entire apparatus of the old boyars' council and the *prikaẓi*. It left a gaping void at the centre and at the same time created chaos in local government. The Senate, appointed as an inner council of nine at the time of the war with Turkey to conduct affairs in the tsar's name and to serve as a supreme court of justice, thus found itself charged with the supervision of the 'governments'.

Even so, the whole system was unworkable and complete confusion prevailed in the collection of state revenues. Reconstruction of the central administration came in 1718, the year which marks the opening of Peter's final and considered phase of reform. In that year the ministerial 'colleges' which he had devised on the Swedish model in place of the old system of *prikaẓi* took over the separate administration of the army, the navy, foreign affairs, commerce, finance, justice, industry and mining. Over each college presided not a single minister but a board of twelve with collective responsibility. Effective co-ordination of the work of the colleges was still lacking, but some advance towards it was made in 1720, by which time there were twelve 'governments' responsible to the Senate. Although this was now the chief organ of executive power, in 1722 Peter set above it the new office of procurator-general. It was a curious and distinctively Russian institution, serving as 'the eye of the sovereign' in every sphere of government, that of the Senate included, and designed through its representation in every college and every administrative division to provide the tsar with a domestic system of espionage.

---

* The Baltic provinces retained a distinctive place in the scheme of Russian empire and contributed in the German nobility of 'Baltic barons' a notable corps of bureaucrats in civil and military administration.

Inevitably, the new structure of civil government was extended to the affairs of the Church. In 1721 the office of patriarch was abolished and in its place was set up the Holy Synod, a ministerial college of ecclesiastical members subject to the secular arm. It was the logical conclusion of Peter's policy of secularization. Anti-clerical conviction, the desire to counter the obscurantism of the Church and its continued opposition to his westernizing reforms, and the need to possess himself of the Church's wealth all ran together. Already the monastic lands had come under a large measure of civil control, and part of their revenue was being diverted to the state. This share in the spoils of ecclesiastical power was steadily enlarged. The shock to the faithful of the abolition of the patriarchate had been softened by Peter's tactics in leaving the patriarchal throne formally unoccupied since 1700, but the subordination of the authority of the Church to the Senate was no less drastic for that. It finally ensured the identification of Orthodoxy with the autocrat's will and made it certain that the Church would share the fate of the monarchy.

One further measure which Peter introduced, and which in all essential respects was retained until 1917, similarly exercised a pervading psychological influence upon the regime. This was the Table of Ranks, which established for all classes who owed service to the state a hierarchy of fourteen grades* of individual merit. The claims which Peter made upon the servants of the state exceeded in stringency all that had gone before. Service, whether in the army or navy or in the civil administration, was for life. All entered at the lowest grade and all were given the opportunity to rise to the top; service, in this sense, was a career open to talent. Promotion to the eighth grade carried with it the nobleman's privilege, among others, of owning serfs. The fruits of this system of official ranking, which established through a Prussian style of honorifics in the mode of address a new order of precedence at court and in society, were unexpected. From it developed the petrifaction of the bureaucratic order of imperial Russia. The system bred only fear and inertia in the lower ranks of the bureaucracy and gave to the upper ranks their peculiar odour of bleak and sterile formality.

The serving classes were driven relentlessly. The obligations laid upon the gentry were defined in precise forms of registration and training from which none were exempt while Peter lived. They were sent to school to study mathematics, engineering, foreign languages; they were to be educated, if need be, by force. He went so far at one time as to forbid them to marry unless they had undergone the system of schooling between the age of ten and fifteen which he

* From the word *chin*, meaning grade or rank, came the term *chinovnik*, used of any official in the vast apparatus of bureaucracy.

had prescribed for them. Only after his death were the chief energies of the gentry spent in releasing themselves from the bonds of service he had forged for them.

But the full weight of Peter the Great's exactions fell upon the peasantry. On them was laid the burden of financing the tsar's wars and conquests, of paying for his army, his navy, his investment in industry, his foreign specialists, his schemes of reconstruction. In the unending search for revenue peasant fortunes were affected in three ways. The fetters of serfdom were viciously tightened; the peasants on state land were all but completely assimilated to the condition of serfs; and serf law was extended to new classes of free peasants. All three processes were consummated in the decision to substitute for the direct tax on the peasant household a poll-tax to be levied on all males of the household. This turn of the screw was decreed in 1718 after a census of households had once more revealed widespread financial evasion on the part of the landed proprietors. In the further census which was put in hand army units were employed as in a punitive campaign to enforce the registration of the technically free or half-free elements among the peasantry. It was now that the great body of monastic dependents on the land were caught in the net of serfdom. The poll-tax, or soul tax, was levied for the first time in 1724. It obliterated all distinction between the different categories of bondsmen on the private estates. Save for those who were permitted to escape serfdom by joining the army—a concession withdrawn after Peter's reign—all were impressed into the body of tax-paying serfs and all were delivered more completely into the hands of the proprietors, who acquired powers of police supervision over their lives through the introduction of an interior passport system. What was in some ways the hardest fate of all fell upon the serf labourers in mine or factory.

Next to the conscript military levies and the burden of taxation it was the building of Peter's city which made the cruellest demands upon his subjects. Peter could not wait to see his dream of paradise realized. From every part of Russia he recruited droves of workers who, herded like cattle, laboured almost with bare hands to clear the island stretches of swamp on which the city was raised. In conditions that bred recurring epidemics, tens of thousands of lives were sacrificed to his prodigal haste. To St Petersburg he transferred at the earliest opportunity the court and the seat of government. Never during his lifetime did it bear much resemblance to the city of Elizabeth or Catherine, the city of artificial beauty of Rastrelli and Quarenghi and Cameron, of parks and fountains and rose-pink palaces. But while he lived it stood for the tutelary light of the west against the Byzantine dark of Moscow.

Peter's schemes of europeanization drew their chief support at home from a small minority with a smattering of western education. He created special academies of technical training; he commissioned translations of foreign books, which were printed in a simplified alphabet and a type devised by himself; he emancipated women from the oriental seclusion of the *terem* and arranged for 'assemblies' of men and women which were designed to teach good manners and the arts of polite conversation; he founded, in 1703, the first Russian newspaper, the *Moskovskia Vedomosti* (*Moscow News*). It was Peter who brought to birth the Russian Academy of Sciences, though it was not formally opened until a year after his death. If during his lifetime the Russian landowning gentry as a class remained rude and ignorant, it was through no lack of effort on the part of Peter the Great himself.

He ruled Russia with a rod of iron. He ruled his family in similarly despotic fashion, and with strange effects long after his death. He had cast off his wife, taken their son Alexis from her and prescribed for him a strict course of study. Mutinous and unwilling to learn, the boy grew up to hate his father. Peter married him off to a German princess, Sophia Charlotte of Wolfenbüttel, who in 1715 bore a son named Peter and died soon after. By that time Peter the Great had publicly married the Baltic servant girl named Catherine who had been Menshikov's mistress before she became his own. She, too, had a son named Peter among her eleven children (of whom two only, Anna and Elizabeth, survived early childhood) by the tsar. Until the clouded phase at the end it was a strangely successful marriage, comradely and tender, as Peter's extraordinary letters to her show. Only Catherine could soothe an explosiveness of temper in the tsar in his later years which frequently bordered on hysteria.

On Alexis were focused all the hopes of the conservative elements in Russian society outraged by Peter's reforms. The injured tsar offered him the choice between mending his Muscovite ways and renouncing the succession. Alexis chose the latter course and fled to the Emperor Charles VI in Vienna. The climax came in 1718, when he was induced to return, was charged by his father with treasonable plotting against the state, was imprisoned, tortured, interrogated and sentenced to death. The sentence was never executed, but two days after it was pronounced Alexis was found dead by his gaolers in the fortress of St Peter and St Paul. The cause of death, it was announced, was apoplexy. Three years later came the reckless decree, its consequences then unforeseen, by which the succession to the throne was put at the disposal of the reigning sovereign.

It is unlikely in the extreme that there will ever be lasting

G

agreement in Russia or outside Russia on the merits of Peter the Great's achievement. The simple verdict of Soloviev was that 'a great man is always and everywhere the representative of his nation'. To this comforting doctrine the severely critical judgment of Peter proffered by Miliukov is perhaps a healthy corrective. For the rest, though the curious shifts of Soviet interpretation during the past quarter of a century belong to politics rather than to historiography, they illustrate the wide margin of choice. The bare facts may be recapitulated. Peter made of Russia a great European power and an empire. He lifted from her a fraction of the Byzantine and Asiatic past. He directed Russian energies towards the laborious imitation of western technique, though at the unavoidable cost of widening a cultural schism in society and breeding a perpetual nostalgic regret. He instituted the age of bureaucracy. He broadened the foundations of industry but left agriculture as backward as it was before. He bled the peasantry white by his reforms and degraded still further the condition of serfdom. He bequeathed to Russia a system of dynastic marriages, chiefly German, which profoundly affected Russian foreign policy after him. And he inaugurated the historic debate on Russia's path of destiny.

He bequeathed also, in the Guards who had sprung from his toy soldiers and whom towards the end he employed increasingly on special missions to execute his will, the power to make or unmake the sovereign ruler of Russia for a century after his death.

CHAPTER IX

THE
SUPREMACY OF THE GUARDS

PETER THE GREAT died on January 28/February 8, 1725, after a chill incurred in attempting to save from drowning some soldiers whose boat had capsized in the estuary of the Neva. On his death-bed he had tried with his last breath—unavailingly—to name a successor. In a symbolical sense, perhaps, it was a confession of failure: he had laid on Russia a burden of government which no one after him could bear.

The ten-year-old son of the unfortunate Alexis, Peter, was the only surviving male of the Romanov line and the demonstrable heir. But instantaneous action was taken by Menshikov and the group of new dignitaries of the state around him to proclaim the accession of Catherine, Peter the Great's widow. Though she had been crowned empress in the previous year, Catherine was without any lawful claim to the throne. That she should nevertheless have succeeded Peter was by choice of the Guards, the arbiters of the imperial destiny.

With Peter the Great's aristocracy at their head and the army behind them, the regiments of the Guards made or unmade the emperors or empresses of Russia from Catherine I until Alexander I. It was they who inaugurated the era of palace revolutions. Throughout the melodramatic changes and chances of court intrigue in the Russia of Peter's successors the threads of conspiracy around the throne always led back to the Guards' barracks in St Petersburg. Between 1725 and 1762 the throne passed, in a capricious and bewildering sequence, from Peter the Great's widow to his grandson, who as Peter II reigned for three years and died of smallpox at the age of fifteen; from Peter II to Anna, the widowed Duchess of Courland, who was the daughter of Peter the Great's half-brother Ivan, the joint tsar of their youth; from Anna to the newly born son of her German niece, who as Ivan VI reigned in his cradle for a year and was then deposed; from Ivan VI to Elizabeth, the daughter of Peter the Great by Catherine; from Elizabeth to the Germanic Peter III, the son of her sister Anna; and from Peter III, without a shadow of right in the succession, to his wholly German wife, who as Catherine the Great was in some ways the most Russian sovereign of them all and the only one in any respect fit to assume the mantle of Peter the Great. Throughout this fantastic sequence it was the nobility of the Guards who in the last resort gave their sanction to every choice of a new occupant of the throne.

The whole period, a peculiarly corrupt and inglorious period of Russian history, has one salient domestic aspect. This is the conversion of the numerically swollen *dvorianstvo*, the class of non-taxpaying gentry in military or administrative service, to a hereditary nobility freed from all obligations of service. By the time Catherine the Great usurped the throne in 1762 this class had succeeded in emancipating itself from the very condition of its original status of privilege. There was thus created an order of aristocracy which contradicted every principle of the state established by Peter the Great. The serf-owner's complete immunity from service brought with it, moreover, more absolute forms of ownership. Indifferent to the purposes of westernization but often wedded to the costly graces of western culture that set the fashion in St Petersburg, the landed proprietors established a despotic and extortionate rule over their peasantry in which serfdom was indeed indistinguishable from slavery.

The two years of the reign of Catherine I, whose robust health declined amidst the pleasures of a recklessly extravagant court, were marked by an attempt on the part of Menshikov, now at the summit of power, and of his closest rivals to subdue the principle of autocracy to their own oligarchic interest. They set up a body of six persons, superior in authority to the Senate, with the title of Supreme Privy Council and vested with the right of inspection of all proposals on domestic and foreign affairs submitted to the throne. Only the personal jealousies in the council hindered its complete exercise of a sovereign power.

These jealousies, in which once more, and almost for the last time, the old nobility were arrayed against the new, were very much in evidence from the moment the throne passed by general consent to the twelve-year-old Peter II. Menshikov sought to marry the tsar to his own daughter. The Dolgorukis, scions of the ancient aristocracy, had their own candidate for an imperial marriage. In this clash of supreme ambition Menshikov fell. He was disgraced and sent into exile, leaving the Dolgorukis to prove themselves a match even for him in greed and unscrupulousness. But Peter died early in 1730, on the very day he was to have married into the Dolgoruki family, and the latter's attempt to forge a death-bed testament naming the bride as successor to the throne deceived nobody.

Once more the Supreme Privy Council, now dominated by a Golitsyn, took temporary control. It offered the throne to Anna, whose claim was of the slenderest kind, on strictly formulated conditions. Without the council's consent she was not to declare war or peace, not to impose new taxes, not to confer new patents of nobility, not to exercise authority over the Guards, not to marry and not to name a successor. In circumstances of penury and neglect in Courland Anna submitted; the conditions were assailed by anxious factions; and in the end the Guards came to Anna's rescue even before her accession. She came to the throne with the principle of autocracy unimpaired and the Supreme Privy Council shattered. None of its members escaped her patient and malevolent revenge.

The Guards learned to regret their error. The ten years of Anna's reign form as ugly and forbidding a chapter of Russian history as any. The empress brought with her a Teuton horde from her petty court in Courland whose exactions exceeded even normal Russian bounds. At their head was her favourite Biren, trivial, empty and infinitely rapacious, a lasting object of Russian hate and anti-foreign sentiment. It was now that the German Baltic bureaucracy took firm root in St Petersburg; their principal representatives in Anna's reign, both formerly in the service of Peter the Great, were Ostermann and Münnich, the one directing civil affairs and the other military. Both were able men, but both were the servants of a peculiarly rancorous despotism. Though she may once have been intelligent, Anna had been soured by experience. Evil-tempered, senseless in her love of luxury, devoured by *ennui*, she found distraction in the grossest cruelty and in a passion for debased forms of entertainment. She filled the court with dwarfs and misshapen creatures and her parks and gardens with every manner of beast on which she could fire from palace windows. She delighted in methodical outrage. The 'era of Biren' was yet another reign of terror, during which thousands were executed and many thousands more were tortured and exiled. Yet the empress was in no position to resist the continued demands of the new nobility. During her reign one restriction after another was lifted from them. Within a year of her accession, for instance, she instituted the Corps of Pages, in which the sons of those of highest rank completed their training as army officers instead of in the ranks as formerly. In 1736 the *dvorianin's* term of service, which had originally been lifelong, was commuted to twenty-five years, and from then onwards special exemptions were granted from year to year.

Anna had named as heir an infant grand-nephew of three months, who became Ivan VI, and had appointed Biren regent. The Guards' opportunity came soon after her death; Biren was arrested and deported to Siberia. He was replaced by Ivan's mother, whose entourage was even more purely German. The Guards turned their eyes upon the thirty-two-year-old Elizabeth, the youngest daughter of Peter the Great. Though she had at no time shown a desire for the throne, she had been under strict observation during Anna's reign and even now was obliged to move with circumspection. Prompted by the French envoy in the capital, stage-managed by the Guards, hastened by a Swedish declaration of war which signalized that country's readiness to intervene, the *coup d'état* of December 6, 1741 was neatly contrived. Elizabeth rode with a small escort of the regiment to the Preobrazhensky barracks, where oaths of loyalty were exchanged, and proceeded to the imperial palace, where Ivan and his mother were put under guard and Elizabeth announced her accession. The rest followed in due order: the Senate swore allegiance to her, Ostermann and Münnich were summarily banished, and Ivan VI was confined for the rest of his life in a secret cell in Schlüsselburg. It was a model palace revolution.

Yet the joyous acclamation was premature: this was not quite a feat of national deliverance. Elizabeth, who reigned from 1741 to 1761, was her father's daughter in Russian sentiment, though this did not prevent her from exchanging German influence at court for the still more pervasive influence of France. Her reign confirmed the sway of French fashion at the higher levels of society and the adoption by the Russian nobility of the language of France in place of their own. But she was also her mother's daughter, a full-blown flower of peasant greed and sensuality. A fine figure of a woman, vain, gluttonous, enamoured of clothes (she left at her death a wardrobe of fifteen thousand dresses), a creature of light and easy loves (her most celebrated favourite was a Ukrainian Cossack, a former choirboy, Alexis Razumovsky), Elizabeth had all too little time for affairs of state. Her prodigal extravagance was swollen by the cost of the new constructions, among them the Winter Palace, with which she helped to create the illusion of another Versailles in St Petersburg. Personally amiable except where her feminine vanity was involved, when she was often inordinately cruel, as a ruler she was merely irresponsible. It was her own appetite which stimulated the appetite of the landed proprietors. During her reign serfdom was extended to further categories of monastic labour; the ownership of populated land was confirmed as an exclusive right of the nobility; and peasant risings throughout the whole period were accompanied by mass flight to Siberia, to the Caucasus and even to Poland. The nobility were permitted to shorten their term of service by having their names inscribed at birth in regimental registers.

The course of foreign relations in Elizabeth's reign demonstrated the growing strength of the Russian army and the increasing weight thus brought by Russian diplomacy into the European balance of power. At the outbreak of the Seven Years' War the greater threat to Russian interests appeared to come from Frederick the Great. In 1757 a Russian army invaded and devastated east Prussia and pressed on into Brandenburg. The slaughter on both sides at Zorndorf, near the Oder, in the following year, and the joint Russian-Austrian victory the year after at Kunersdorf brought disaster close to Frederick. It came closer still with the raid on Berlin by Cossack and Kalmuck troops in 1760 and a brief occupation of the Prussian capital which long afterwards woke shuddering memories. What saved Frederick and Prussia was the death of Elizabeth on January 2, 1762 and the reversal of Russian policy which followed.

The Russian type of autocracy breeds monsters. The common

view is that none was quite so destitute of character or intelligence as Elizabeth's successor, Peter III. But there is almost certainly a wide margin of exaggeration in Catherine the Great's too plausible memoirs, which have shaped the conventional verdict upon him. Revolting and ludicrous, Peter III is yet a pitiful monster, with a strange gleam of reason about him. The son of Elizabeth's sister Anna, who had become Duchess of Holstein, as a youth of fourteen he had been sent for by Elizabeth soon after her accession. Wholly German and Lutheran in upbringing, he had reluctantly accepted conversion to the Orthodox Church. In 1745, at the age of seventeen, he was married to a petty German princess, a second cousin, brought to St Petersburg for the purpose. She was Sophia Augusta of Anhalt-Zerbst, who was received into the Orthodox Church as Catherine and who in the process shed her German skin with ardent calculation. The marriage was a grotesque affair. Peter was coarse, exceedingly ugly and freakish in habit; his hero and model of military genius was Frederick the Great. Catherine was of lively charm and intelligence, adroit and ambitious; from the precocious childhood dream of a crown she passed quickly to the conviction that she was destined for the throne of the tsars. In 1754 she bore a son named Paul, whose paternity is one of the classic unresolved doubts of the history books. There is, up to a point, every reason for believing, as was believed at the time, that Paul's father was Saltykov, the first of the long line of Catherine's lovers (and hence that there was not a drop of Romanov blood in the last seven occupants of the Russian throne); beyond that point is Paul's resemblance in appearance and character to Peter III.

His patent unfitness for the throne notwithstanding, Peter was heir apparent. The junior court he kept in St Petersburg, in which Catherine's graces of mind and bearing shone with studied effect, was a centre of diplomatic intrigue and a source of jealous anxiety to Elizabeth. Catherine stumbled in her secret dealings with the English ambassador in the capital, Sir Charles Hanbury-Williams —she was in English pay for a time—and again in secret correspondence afterwards with her supporters, but in both instances she recovered. The empress kept watch over her, not very successfully so far as Catherine's amours were concerned, and, having taken Paul under her own charge, was all but ready to prefer him to Peter as her successor. Her death, apparently hastened by the melancholy of an aging voluptuary, left Peter in possession.

The six months of his reign were crowded with portentous incident. For the nobility humiliation and triumph were mixed in equal parts; for the nation at large injury was at moments relieved by the prospect of a less corrupt order of rule. The start was lamentable: hostilities with Prussia were concluded on terms that outraged every instinct of Russian pride in victory. Russia, it is true, stood to gain little from continuing the war; Peter had not brought peace too soon. But all that the vanquished Frederick had lost was restored to him and the treaty of peace was translated into an alliance.

A momentous domestic gesture broke into this Russian desert of peace-making. On March 1, Peter issued the famous manifesto proclaiming the emancipation of the nobility, who were now statutorily freed from every form of military or other service. Except in the emergency of war, all obligation to the state was lifted from their shoulders. The manifesto was acclaimed with delight by its beneficiaries. That in the logic of things—the logic of the whole historic order of the state—the emancipation of the serfs should have followed did not disturb them; this was an issue between themselves and the crown. Not that Peter gained any popularity as a result. He could indeed do nothing but offend. He ridiculed the court, affronted the Church—the measure for the complete secularization of its properties was originally his—and even tried to break up the regiments of the Guards. The gleam of reason was not lacking here. But at the same time he put his Holstein troops into tight Prussian uniform, drilled them enthusiastically and would have made war on Denmark in the duchy's interest. During all these months Catherine played her cards with unvarying composure, allowing others to weave the separate threads of conspiracy. Two of the five Orlov brothers, among them the lover whose son she had borne a couple of months earlier, could already answer for the Guards when Peter finally proposed to divorce his consort and marry his mistress.

The rest rounds off a celebrated palace revolution, which was consummated in a sordid epilogue. On the morning of July 10, 1762 Catherine left Peterhof and appeared before the Izmailovsky and Semenovsky regiments of the Guards, who took the oath of allegiance to her as empress and autocrat. A vast body of troops gathered in front of the Winter Palace. At Oranienbaum the unhappy Peter hesitated, delayed and was lost. Confined in the charge of one of the Orlovs to an estate a few miles from the capital, he died there a few days later in a scuffle with his captors, apparently strangled by Orlov himself. Catherine spoke of a fatal haemorrhage in announcing the empire's loss.

Little occurred in the whole of this sordid period of nearly forty years to encourage confidence in the future. The energies released by Peter the Great were halted; reform was all but totally obscured by the greed and extravagance of the ruling forces in society. Yet there were hopeful features in an otherwise comfortless scene. Education slowly expanded through the endowment of new schools, not all of them restricted to the children of the nobility. The first Russian university, feebly though it shone for a half-century, was founded in Moscow in 1755. The polymath Lomonosov, who was of free peasant stock, gave a quickening impulse to Russian scientific studies and at the same time fostered the beginnings of modern Russian literature. And in the empress Elizabeth's reluctance to impose the death penalty it may not be fanciful to recognize the compulsion, amidst so vast and barbarous a cruelty, of that broad humanity which is the central myth of Russian idealism.

CHAPTER X

THE AGE OF CATHERINE

No PERIOD OF Russian history is comparable in outward splendour with the age of Catherine the Great. This is the spectacular age of St Petersburg, the golden age of the nobility, the legendary age of Russian opulence and glitter. For the privileged enclave in society who had experienced its *douceur de vivre* the memories of the reign awoke ever afterwards a passion of regret. In extravagance and ostentation the life of the court, duplicated on a smaller scale in the palaces of the aristocracy, was a match for Versailles. It was almost a match also in intellectual polish and pretension. The great figures in society, who drew upon the seemingly inexhaustible wealth of their estates for the luxury they imported from Europe, took their cue from the imperial votary of European enlightenment and followed Catherine in her addiction to the liberal thought of the *philosophes*.

To this cultivation of aristocratic splendour and intellectual freedom was joined an enveloping pride of empire. Russian territorial aggrandizement in Catherine's reign was greater than in any reign since Ivan the Terrible. By war and diplomacy Russia advanced her frontiers in the south and west to what were almost the ultimate limits of expansion in Europe, absorbing in the one direction the Crimea, the Black Sea steppe and its northern shore, in the other the predominantly Russian provinces of Poland together with Courland. Simultaneously Russian settlement spread more widely through the vast spaces of Siberia. The age had its greatness, indeed, whatever Catherine's personal title to greatness may have lacked.

Yet the brilliant surface of achievement, as so often in Russian history, barely disguised the accumulation of decay. All the glitter of the age was paid for in an aggravation of existing evils. Whatever the sentiments she derived from Voltaire, in the dubious circumstances in which she came to the throne Catherine had no choice but to court the favour of the emancipated nobility. The alliance she struck with them left intact all the prerogatives of autocracy, but for their part it enabled the nobility to stretch authority over their peasants to the point at which they themselves were enthroned as local autocrats. Serfdom was never more inhuman in Russia than in the reign of Catherine the Great. It was extended throughout her dominions, and more particularly to the whole of the Ukraine, the Don country and large areas of the Caucasus, by the enormous grants of state land, with its free or semi-free peasants, which she made to her favourites and followers. Catherine's liberalism, in brief, stopped short at affairs of state. Even as a speculative exercise it could not easily survive the Pugachev rebellion in 1773–4 and was finally extinguished by the French Revolution.

Like other enlightened despots among her contemporaries, the empress of Russia enjoyed play-acting. Enlightenment in Catherine was, indeed, not much deeper than her vanity; despotism, on the other hand, was implicit in her ambition. Frederick the Great, notoriously shrewd in these matters, described her as very ambitious and very vain. Vanity was only too evident in her profession of advanced opinions, in her tireless correspondence with the great intellectual figures of the day, in her purchase of Diderot's library for the Hermitage palace, in her own versatile but unoriginal authorship. For all her liveliness of mind and astute grasp of affairs Voltaire's 'Semiramis of the North' is above all else an egotist who wishes to be flattered. Even her commanding gifts in administration and diplomacy were furbished with theatrical little tricks of self-advertisement. And vanity entered largely into her appetites. Though she could apparently suffer hurt, no woman was more completely mistress of herself in sensuality. Except in the closing passion of her life, when as a woman in her sixties she chose as lover a handsome but exceptionally stupid and greedy young cavalry officer of twenty-two, her amours in no way interfered with her personal conduct of state affairs. Her lovers were all, in her own phrase, her 'pupils'. It was their personal homage that she demanded, paying for it in munificent gifts of hard cash, estates and jewels, and frequently retaining it by regular payments after she had cast them off. They numbered in all at least twenty; Saltykov,

Poniatowski, Grigory Orlov, Vasilchikov, Potemkin and the rest —they were of all kinds and temperaments, but all ministered to her inordinate love of flattery. In diplomacy and love alike Catherine was resolved to cut a great figure.

The anxieties confronting her at the outset of the reign prompted a quick bid for popularity wherever it might be won. The manifesto proclaiming the emancipation of the nobility had been the signal for widespread peasant riots, which became more violent as the belief spread that Peter III's successor, the usurper Catherine, had chosen to suppress a supplementary decree emancipating the peasantry from their masters. The distribution of grants of land in the right quarters helped to quell these disturbances, though it could not prevent the recurrence of peasant risings and the appearance of false pretenders to the throne throughout the thirty-four years of the reign. Catherine similarly appeased the Church by affecting a willingness to revoke Peter III's decree secularizing all Church property. In point of fact, after a preliminary show of hesitation she pronounced in the early part of 1764 for the complete confiscation of all episcopal and monastic lands. Later in the year one of her chief personal anxieties was removed by the murder by his gaolers, after an attempt to rescue him from his secret cell in Schlüsselburg, of the luckless Ivan VI, who in the eyes of many had been the rightful sovereign.

The most ambitious undertaking in the early years of the reign by which Catherine sought to counter the impression made by her *coup d'état* was the Legislative Commission which she summoned in Moscow in 1766 in preparation for a new codification of the laws. She had the writer's itch—hence her plays, satires, historical treatises and the rest—and for more than a year she addressed herself in a fine rapture of enlightenment to the task of drawing up an Instruction (*Nakaz*) for the commission. It was an impressive document, very advanced and humane in its statement of abstract principle, even though its highest flights of liberalism were struck out from the imperial draft at the anxious suggestion of those nearest the throne. Almost the greater part of the document derived from Montesequieu's *Esprit des Lois*, though Catherine brought no little ingenuity to the labour of adapting Montesquieu to the exigencies of autocracy in Russia. It is conceivable that there was a flicker of sincerity in this display, since she was herself not inhumane, but it is unlikely that she looked for practical results from her work. There is no shred of evidence that she ever seriously considered the abolition of serfdom.

The Legislative Commission consisted of a body of between five and six hundred delegates representing the chief agencies of government and all the peoples of the empire and comprising all the various classes in society, the serf peasantry alone excluded. It met in a blaze of publicity. Together with the imperial Instruction the delegates were equipped with the recommendations of their particular social group or local community. In a series of more than two hundred sessions, which occupied a year and a half, they voiced their grievances and their specific dissatisfactions with the existing scheme of local administration, of taxation, of justice, of law. No subject was excluded from the interminable debate; there was argument of a sort even on the condition of serfdom. But what the whole protracted review of affairs revealed more clearly than anything else was the irreconcilable conflict of interest of the different elements in the assembly. Society was still too rigidly stratified to permit of a measure of agreement on the ends of legislation, the nobility too strongly entrenched to consent to any social policy in their disfavour. The commission brought to light local abuses and corruption which Catherine in later years was willing to remedy in her reform of provincial self-government; but, like her own *Nakaz*, in all else it accomplished precisely nothing. She availed herself gladly of the occasion of war as a pretext for ending its labours.

The war in question was the first round of the war with Turkey, of which the almost unforeseen consequence was the first partition of Poland. In a Europe thickly strewn not with enlightened despots only but also with dynastic ambitions it was to be expected that Catherine would conduct Russian foreign policy in person. But the empress could with some justice claim that diplomacy was her special province. She saw herself, indeed, as most of her successors on the throne of Russia were to see themselves, as the sovereign manipulator of the system of European power. Poland's misfortune was that Catherine's designs met a not wholly dissimilar Prussian aspiration.

It was the territory of the Ottoman empire in the Balkans that originally tempted Catherine, not Poland. Beyond the as yet unconquered last stretch of the southern steppe lay Constantinople, the crown of Russian ambition, but in the meantime the Orthodox faithful in the sultan's Danubian lands provided opportunity for an encircling policy. Poland, whose southern marches met the Ottoman empire, presented a small obstacle to be surmounted first. She had become progressively more dependent upon Russia. A king without authority, reduced to desperate shifts at home and diplomatic subterfuges abroad to maintain himself, a diet of faction-ridden gentry dominated by a score of great territorial magnates and sustained in irresponsibility by the *liberum veto*, an oppressed majority without civil rights of any kind—for Poland this signified, in truth, anarchy tempered by civil war. It was to Russia's interest to perpetuate the anarchy and thus keep Poland in subjection. As an instrument of Russian domination there was always the power to intervene in defence of the Orthodox minority in an implacably Catholic country.

Yet even in Poland constitutional reform was in the air. For to the humiliation of dependence on Russia was joined danger from Frederick the Great's Prussia. In September 1764 Russian persuasions, backed by a show of force, had lifted to the throne in Poland Stanislas Poniatowski, who had been Catherine's lover and who was to be the last of Poland's elected kings. But earlier, in the spring of that year, Frederick had at last succeeded in winning Russia from her alliance with Austria to alliance with himself. Two different maps of Europe were unrolled before Russian and Prussian eyes. While Catherine's gaze was upon the Turkish Balkans Frederick's was fixed upon the Polish provinces which divided Brandenburg from Prussia.

The unabashed power politics of the eighteenth century are notoriously in evidence in the partition of Poland. Admittedly there were degrees of initial guilt: Catherine was not quite so clever as she thought and the prime mover, and the principal beneficiary, of the partitions was Prussia. But Catherine was not seriously behind in the diplomatic play of greed and chicanery.

In spite of Russian concern, Poland had gone ahead with a far-reaching revision of the constitution. But in 1766, after the diet had rejected the demand on behalf of the non-Catholic elements for full religious rights, Catherine resorted to military measures. The diet yielded in the following year and a treaty signed early in 1768 conceded to Russia all but formal sovereignty in Poland by requiring Russian assent to any change in the Polish constitution. The irregular 'confederate' war against the occupying Russian army continued, however; the Polish patriots were driven back almost into Turkish territory; and an apprehensive sultan made common cause with them and declared war on Russia.

The imbroglio of the European powers in the course of the war is history of an unedifying kind. The separate policies which sprang from Russian greed, Frederick's fear through all his scheming of being involved once more in war, and Austrian jealousy all converged upon the fate of Poland. Turkey alone could not contain Russian arms. In the early autumn of 1769 a victorious Russian army on the Dniester blazed a trail for the occupation of the Turkish provinces north of the Danube. In the summer of the following year the destruction of the Turkish fleet in the straits of Chios by the Russian Baltic fleet, half-crippled though it had been by the voyage from the North Sea into the Mediterranean, was followed by more Russian victories on land. The whole of the

Crimea was occupied. But with every fresh Russian success the prospect of a general European war drew nearer. The exorbitance of Catherine's conditions of peace after the sultan had requested the mediation of Austria and Prussia finally yielded to Frederick's insidious argument: Russian military strength was too fully extended and safety and the harmony of the powers lay, he contended, in his original plan of common participation in the partition of Poland. Throughout 1771, while Russia continued to wage war against Turkey, the diplomatic bluff and bargaining went on at a rattling pace. On July 25/August 5, 1772, the treaties of partition were at last signed in St Petersburg.

It was a momentous event in European history. Prussia gained what she had coveted, Austria acquired Galicia and to Russia fell a large stretch of White Russia. For Poland the fatal annexations were those by Prussia and Austria. She could have survived the loss to Russia of what was for the most part ethnically Russian territory, but a glance at the map will show why she could not survive the menace of those other and essentially strategic losses.

Russian hostilities against Turkey, disappointing in their later stages, were interrupted more than once by abortive peace negotiations, but peace came in July 1774 with the signing of the treaty of Kuchuk-Kainardji. This was, for both Russia and Europe, a scarcely less momentous event. The immediate rewards to Russia, large enough in themselves, held ominous significance for the future. First, the treaty proclaimed the complete independence of the Crimea. Since this was independence without the substance of power, eventual Russian annexation of the Crimea was assured. Next, a Turkish indemnity apart, Russia was finally confirmed in the possession of Azov and gained the Kerch straits and the mouths of the Dnieper and the Bug. Here, in the extension of the cultivable steppe to the Black Sea littoral and access to ports from which to export surplus grain, were factors of great consequence to Russia in the nineteenth century. But the treaty also registered other and subtler gains. Together with the freedom of the Black Sea for her commerce and the right of access through the Straits to the Aegean, it recognized Russia's interest in the religious rights of the Orthodox subjects of the sultan. Not a little of the politics of nineteenth-century Europe sprang from the seemingly minor concessions which Russia wrested from the Porte in 1774.

The treaty of Kuchuk-Kainardji was concluded at the height o the great domestic crisis of Catherine's reign. A vaster eruption than the rebellion of Stenka Razin a century earlier, the Pugachev rebellion came near to overturning the whole order of state. In the Bolshevik calendar it marks the birth of social revolution in Russia because of its enormous extent, its destructive passion and the part played in it by the industrial serfs. It erupted at a time when risings against the usurper Catherine had not yet died down and after the epidemic which in 1771 spread from the Turkish front to Moscow, and thence to the central provinces, had created widespread disorder. Among the Cossacks of the Yaik,* where the rebellion started, and the Cossacks of the Don resentment at the encroachments of the civil power upon their liberty had flared up in revolt.

A former Don Cossack with an adventurous and roving past, Emelian Pugachev appeared in the Yaik country in the summer of 1773 in the guise of Peter III. Others had assumed that identity before him, but within a brief space Pugachev had gathered a large following, consisting of Cossacks, fugitive peasant serfs, serfs in the mines and industrial enterprises of the Urals, religious dissenters, Bashkirs, Kalmucks, Kirghiz and other Tatar and Finnish elements. The capture of the fortified posts along the Yaik swelled his army. It advanced to the siege of Orenburg,† the administrative centre of the region, amid a great stir caused by Pugachev's proclamations. Himself illiterate, he found means to issue edicts which promised an end to serfdom, vengeance upon the nobility and the dethronement and strict seclusion of Catherine. In obligatory fashion he established a court in a ragged encampment flying the flag of Holstein in which his principal henchmen bore the names of her favourites. Though in these circumstances the siege of Orenburg hung fire, the call to insurrection was answered over a vast area of the Volga countryside. Landowners and their families were tortured and murdered; manor houses were burned down; garrisons and regular detachments sent to quell disorder rose and slaughtered their officers; officials, merchants and priests were shot or hanged; arson and pillage swept nearer to Moscow. Action against the rebels, long delayed, drove them back for a time towards the Urals, but the fires broke out again and raged more fiercely, enveloping Kazan, reaching to Nizhny-Novgorod and threatening Moscow itself. Only then, when many in the old capital visibly awaited Pugachev's arrival, did Catherine show anxiety. Large bodies of picked troops moved against the rebels in the summer of 1774, inflicting hideous reprisals, and Pugachev himself, harried and hunted down, was surrendered by Cossack loyalists. He was taken to Moscow in an iron cage and executed in the following January.

The hatreds of the rebellion bred a different and enduring hate. Directed in the first place against the serf-owners, the Pugachev *jacquerie* left behind a passion of revenge which no conciliatory gesture or measure of reform in later years could eradicate. Peasant

---

* After the Pugachev rebellion the name of the river Yaik was changed to the Ural.
† Now Chkalov.

memories were kept alive by the ferocity of punitive expeditions which levelled villages to the ground and left gallows standing throughout the countryside. The landowners returned from their refuge in the towns or emerged from hiding and regained confidence in a more exacting despotism. Catherine for her part bent her mind to logical necessities of local administration. She was at the height of her passion for Potemkin, the most celebrated of her favourites, whom she had secretly married the year before. Their affair lasted for two years only, after which Potemkin himself, bold, brilliant and of very Russian temperament, superintended the order of succession of her favourites while remaining by her side until his death in 1791. It was with Potemkin's aid that the empress, after extinguishing what remained of Cossack autonomy, instituted a comprehensive reform of the structure of local government.

The largest possible measure of decentralization, it was clear, was essential for the maintenance of law and order throughout the empire. In place of Peter the Great's vast 'governments' Catherine established less unwieldy units of local government in the shape of provinces with a population of between 300,000 and 400,000 and subdivided into districts of between 20,000 and 30,000. By the end of her reign there were fifty such provinces. Headed by a governor, each was staffed by collegiate bodies of officials separately charged with legal and administrative functions—the whole scheme was based upon the strict separation of powers. The governors were equipped with far-reaching authority; governors-general, placed at the head of two or three contiguous provinces, represented the crown and were directly responsible to the Senate. In each district (*uezd*) the principal administrative offices were filled largely by government officials who had risen to the ranks of the nobility. The whole bureaucratic system, top-heavy and rigid, fitted the basic requirements of autocracy and the alliance of crown and nobility. Notwithstanding the reforms which came a century later, after the emancipation of the serfs, in its main outlines it endured until 1917.

The all but exclusive rights of the landowning nobility in local administration were reinforced by Catherine's charter of the nobility in 1785. This confirmed and codified the privileges they had won since the death of Peter the Great and formally invested them with a corporate organization. Exemption from compulsory service, exemption from taxation, exemption from loss of rank or estates, exemption from corporal punishment—these, and a hereditary status of nobility, were rounded off by statutory recognition of the existing provincial and district assemblies of nobility, over which an elected marshal presided. Through the marshal of the nobility the assemblies conferred with the governor or governor-general or made direct representation to the Senate or to the crown. They also appointed the principal law officers at the district level. Although titular authority in local affairs was thus almost exclusively reserved for them, the higher ranks of nobility seldom played an active part in local administration. They had reason to be content, after all, with their status in law.

Simultaneously with the charter of the nobility Catherine issued a charter of the towns, providing for a similar form of corporate organization. But city government, stifled at the outset by the rigid demarcation of classes, had little local substance while industry and manufacture remained undeveloped.

Amidst all preoccupations with domestic policy Catherine pursued a tenacious course of her own in foreign affairs. Dreams of empire-building increasingly possessed her. Only now, indeed, after much of the Black Sea steppe had been secured, did the goal of a Russian Constantinople assume the form of practical politics. The smooth transition, after the death of Maria Theresa, from alliance with Prussia to friendship with Austria had enabled her in 1783 to ignore with impunity the terms of the treaty of Kuchuk-Kainardji and proclaim the annexation of the Crimea. With Potemkin's support she now developed the grandiose 'Greek project'. Already foreshadowed by her choice in 1779 of the name Constantine for a grandson, the younger son of the tsarevich Paul, this was a scheme to revive the Byzantine empire in the Turkish Balkans under Russian tutelage. Since Austria's eyes were cast in the same direction, a deal with Joseph II was obligatory. In 1787, in company with the Austrian emperor, Catherine undertook her spectacular and myth-making tour of triumph to the new southern territories. They had been rapidly populated through lavish grants of land to new and old favourites, and Potemkin, who stage-managed the fairyland illusion of prosperous and smiling 'Potemkin villages' on the route down the Dnieper to the Crimea, had been appointed viceroy there. The tour was designed as deliberate provocation.

It achieved its intended effect: in September of that year Turkey declared war. In an access of restored energy the Turkish armies more than held their own for a time against the Russian and Austrian forces. But the conduct of the principal episodes in the war passed to Suvorov, eccentric almost to the point of dementia but nevertheless the greatest of all Russian generals. In Suvorov's absence, after a siege that was lavish in the expenditure of human lives, Potemkin pressed the assault in the last days of 1788 on the Turkish fortress of Ochakov on the Black Sea and captured it at even greater cost. The scale of Russian losses sustained in 1790 in Suvorov's triumphant assault on the great fortress of Izmail on

H

the Danube was eclipsed only by the magnitude of the carnage wreaked in return on the defenders. Victory at this price was beyond Austria's capacity, however, and a year later she concluded a separate peace with Turkey. Russian persistence brought its reward, though at fearful sacrifice and in shrunken form. By the terms of the treaty of Jassy, concluded in January, 1792, Russia retained the Crimea and gained Ochakov and the Black Sea littoral between the Bug and the Dniester.

The Greek project was lost. Once more, this time largely through the ascendancy over Catherine of the last of her lovers, the youthful Platon Zubov, it was Poland who was required to restore the Russian sense of advantage. Partition had stirred heady and reckless passions in Poland together with a genuine conviction of the need for reform. When in May 1791 a new and liberal Polish constitution was proclaimed Catherine was too fully occupied with the war against Turkey to do more than protest. But a dissident section of the Polish aristocracy, more alarmed than Catherine at this time by the contagion of the French Revolution, came to her aid, and in the following May a strong Russian army crossed the frontier under pretext of defending Poland's rescinded liberties. The unhappy Stanislas yielded; the Polish secessionist movement formed in St Petersburg spread in Poland under the protection of Russian bayonets; the Polish patriots went into exile; and Catherine and Frederick William II of Prussia struck their bargain. The prompt Prussian occupation of western Poland may be thought to cap the likeness, or a likeness in reverse, to the technique of joint conquest adopted in 1939.

The second partition of Poland, the master-stroke of fraud and force in the diplomacy of the century of enlightenment, was conducted, it might be noted, in the name of peace-loving ideals. Poland had succumbed to Jacobin conspiracy and was a menace to her neighbours; the Polish frontiers must therefore be pushed back in order that her neighbours might sleep safely in their beds. The bargain gave to Russia further great slices of territory in White Russia and the Ukraine which had for the most part been acquired by Poland from union with Lithuania. To Prussia, however, it gave the parent lands of the Polish state, the lands between the Vistula and the Oder, including the city of Danzig. The Poles temporized in vain; Catherine's troops and envoys refused delay. A purged Polish diet ratified the separate Prussian treaty of partition only by maintaining unbroken silence at the famous 'dumb session' of September 25, 1793.

Poland had been reduced to a narrow strip of territory running from Courland in the north through Warsaw to Cracow, with a total population of some four million. This was a kingdom doomed

The Expansion of the Russian Empire in the eighteenth century

at the outset. The insurrection led by Tadeusz Kosciuszko, the greatest of Polish patriots—and Poland, it need scarcely be said, has always been famed for her patriots—was an affair of high and heroic romanticism. The hopes built upon the rising of the entire population of Warsaw and then of Vilna were shattered when joint Russian and Prussian forces took the field and were followed by an invading Austrian army. The end came, after Kosciuszko's defeat on the line of the Vistula, with the siege of Warsaw, the storming of the suburb of Praga and the dreadful slaughter of the civil population by Suvorov's army. In the third and final partition of 1795 Prussia acquired the land between the Niemen and the Vistula, which included Warsaw; Austria took Cracow and Lublin; and Russia possessed herself formally of Courland and gained the remaining stretch of Lithuanian territory. Hers was much the largest acquisition.

The brief era of Polish liberalism was over. Jacobinism had been extirpated by the guardians of peace and Poland as a state ceased to exist. Catherine had now time and opportunity to recognize the infamy of the revolution in France. Though not yet sated with military glory, for the time being she had no intention of combating the 'French plague' by force; that would come in the last year of her reign, when she was on the point of dispatching Suvorov to engage the French armies in northern Italy. At the moment, however, Russian forces were required for a mission nearer her heart. Bewitched by Zubov, she endorsed, and in her last months prepared to put in hand, his 'Eastern project', a lunatic variant of the Greek project, by which Russia would conquer Persia, stretch out towards the Indian sub-continent, take the Asiatic territories of the Ottoman empire in the rear and possess herself simultaneously by way of the Balkans of Constantinople and the Straits.

Zubov was a source of reckless mischief all through the closing years of the reign. Insolent and interfering at court, he lent an extra virulence to the punitive repression at home to which Catherine was driven by horror at the course of events in France. His, too, was an exacerbating influence upon the mutual suspicion which had long characterized the relations of the empress and the heir apparent, whose right she had originally usurped. Like so many earlier Russian sovereigns, Catherine was not reconciled to the obvious succession. After having rigorously shut him out from affairs of state she would have excluded Paul from the throne if she could. She did indeed plan to name Alexander, Paul's son, as her successor, and Alexander himself was informed to this effect and pledged to silence. But her death on November 17, 1796 found Catherine, ironically enough, unprepared.

In the perspective of history, not diplomacy or empire or the brilliance of the age gives the reign of Catherine decisive significance. The future to which it points is shaped rather by the irremediable worsening of the condition of the peasantry. From now onwards no agreed and practicable solution of the fundamental problems of serfdom is in sight. Proposals for reform will multiply, reform itself will extinguish serfdom; but the evils have gone too deep, the difficulties have grown too intractable, to give the liberal forces in society a fair opportunity.

At the end of the reign Russia had a population of 36 million, the largest of any state in Europe. It had increased threefold in the seventy years since the death of Peter the Great, partly through territorial acquisition but in the main by natural increase. Of these 36 million it is estimated that 34 million were peasants, of whom nearly 20 million were serfs on private estates; the remainder, state or crown land peasants, were not far removed from the strict condition of serfdom. As yet the growth of population pressed heavily upon the means of subsistence only in the central regions. Agriculture almost everywhere was still primitive, regulated for the most part by the three-field system, with open fields divided among the peasant households in the village in the traditional pattern of long, narrow strips, and the use of a light wooden plough (*sokha*) that only scratched the surface of the soil. Estates, especially those of larger size, were often mere *latifundia*; the rich owner lived in St Petersburg, the poorer in the provincial capital, both as rack-rent landlords. On the majority of estates the serfs might number anything from a hundred to a thousand. But the age was noted for its fabulously rich serf-owners, many of them the special recipients of Catherine's bounty, and there were scores who were only a degree less blessed than the Count Sheremetev who possessed 300,000 serfs. Serf dues in rent (*obrok*) commonly consisting of both cash and kind, were the rule in the north, in the less fertile areas which had once been the property of the state; labour dues (*barshchina*) were the normal payment in the black-earth areas and were most often fixed at three days in the week. But it was here, under the stimulus of the expanding trade in grain, that the owners had grown most exacting, the labour dues on many estates having been extended to as much as six days in the week.

Into these varying degrees of economic slavery, to which the payment of state taxes added a growing burden, there entered a deepening moral degradation. The everyday conditions of existence for the peasantry steadily became more brutalized in the golden age of the nobility. The discipline of serfdom was maintained more than all else by corporal punishment; never was the practice of flogging in Russia so extensive, never was the knout considered so sovereign a remedy for peasant failings. Against the injustice or the barbarity of punishment inflicted by his master the peasant had, in effect, no redress. In 1767, almost at the very moment when Catherine had presented her enlightened Instruction for the guidance of the Legislative Assembly, an imperial decree prohibited all complaints by a serf against his master under threat of the severest penalties. Already, indeed, the serf-owner was equipped with the legal right to punish a peasant if he so desired by deporting him to convict labour in Siberia. And through all the years of the reign the trade in 'souls' continued, both in private sales and the public auction of serfs. Patrons of art among the seigneurs of the countryside maintained serf companies of actors or musicians, and a serf sent abroad to study stage design returned to Russia still a serf.

There could be no orderly transition from this state of affairs to a better and more humane scheme of society. The iniquity was plain, the moral revulsion already apparent. In 1790 Alexander Radishchev, a member of the nobility who had been educated abroad, pictured peasant poverty and the evils of serfdom in an eloquent little book bearing the innocent title of *A Journey from St Petersburg to Moscow*. 'Worse than Pugachev!' exclaimed Catherine in horror, and the sentence of death passed upon Radishchev, the proto-martyr of Russian literary radicalism, was commuted only to penal servitude for life in Siberia. A little later Nicholas Novikov, who once had found in the empress a contributor to his satirical journals and who had rendered no little educational service to the country as a book publisher, was sent to solitary confinement in Schlüsselburg for entertaining dangerous thoughts in his advocacy of the ideals of Freemasonry. The foundations of the literary censorship in Russia were firmly laid in these closing years of the reign; even Catherine's own Instruction now came under an official ban. Yet at the same time—and the paradox governs the whole of the next century—literature shone with an inextinguishable light. It had not yet entered a golden age, but in the continued labours of Lomonosov, in the plays of Fonvizin and Sumarokov, even in the foreign classicism of the poetry of Derzhavin, the age of Catherine gave promise of greatness to come.

CHAPTER XI

THE SON OF CATHERINE

OVER THE BRIEF reign of the emperor Paul move grotesque shadows. Great events were astir in Europe at the turn of the eighteenth century, in Russia as elsewhere new ideas were abroad among the educated classes and new economic pressures were at work in society, but the whole course of Russian affairs during those four years was exposed in the first instance to the incoherent play of Paul's caprice and aberration of mind.

Consistently irrational in behaviour though he was, Paul cannot be dismissed as merely insane. Except in his most unbalanced phase during the closing months of his life, he did not lack something of strange intelligence or even purpose. He had been sane enough in earlier years, though always uncertain of temper and a prey to vertiginous excitement. Very ugly, though capable of dignity and sometimes of charm, of demonstratively serious tastes, even in youth his interest in affairs of state had been strongly marked. There, in part, the trouble lay; in the eyes of both himself and his mother Paul had always been a rival claimant to the throne. For his own part the claim had been implicit in his early requests to be admitted to the responsibilities of government, in his criticism of state policies under Catherine and in proposals of his own of a more or less liberal character. They had been coldly received; by turns Catherine ignored and slighted him. Even his children, or at least the two eldest—there were eventually ten in all—were taken from him to be brought up under the empress's own supervision. In 1783, when he was aged twenty-eight, she had confined him to a somewhat secluded mode of existence at Gatchina, just outside the capital. There his energies were spent in a furious pedantry of military parades and exercises. Like Peter III, who had idolized Frederick the Great, Paul took the Prussian army for inspiration and made of Gatchina a smaller Potsdam. In his frantic interest in niceties of military uniform he had much in common with his English contemporary, the Prince Regent. Professedly liberal, still thwarted in his desire for political responsibility, as heir apparent he found sympathy in unexpected quarters. Hating his mother, hating the favourites who similarly slighted him, distrustful with some cause both before and after his accession of Alexander, his eldest son, his mind was increasingly clouded by rancour and obsessions of revenge. In the end, no doubt, the vestiges of reason in him were eclipsed by the corruption of despotic power.

The conventional nineteenth-century view of Paul as a madman pure and simple is largely derived from the evidence in which the memoirs of a later period abound of his behaviour at court and on the parade-ground. That view has been modified by closer study of his application to problems of state. But the case which has been made out for him as a reformer or potential reformer rests upon slender argument. The reforming pretensions were admittedly there, since like every Russian autocrat Paul looked now and then for popularity. But his liberalism as emperor was as erratic, as regardless of consequences, as his contrary impulse of repression. It sprang above all else from the desire to undo Catherine's work and to assert his will by changing everything, by reforming everything that she had established during her rule.

He came to the throne at the age of forty-two with the fixed resolve to turn his back upon Catherine's policies and to reverse the direction of her rewards and punishments. Mental instability apart, it is the pressure upon this personal resolve of unchanging reasons of state which gives his own policies their curious ambiguity. He began by staging a grim spectacle: his father's body was exhumed from the monastery of St Alexander Nevsky, borne in procession in a coffin behind which walked the murderer Alexis Orlov bearing the imperial crown, and laid by the side of Catherine in the cathedral of St Peter and St Paul, the traditional resting place of the emperors of Russia. Potemkin's corpse was likewise disinterred and buried in a common pit. These feats of retribution achieved, Paul's symbolic gestures became more uncertain. He would have had no difficulty in ridding himself, as he had often threatened to do, of those who had lived in the sunshine of Catherine's favour, but in the event he disturbed surprisingly few of them. Fitfully he released from prison or exile many who had earned her displeasure, Radishchev and Novikov among them. But it was another and very different matter to attack the entire privileged class who had made common cause with her. The nobility were still a necessary aid and support of autocracy.

The craving to mar what Catherine had made, however, was stronger than mere prudence; more than all else, it would seem, the power he had so long been denied must be made visible. A decree—long premeditated- -issued at his coronation established for the future the principle of succession to the throne from father to son; there was to be no more uncertainty, no further occasion for palace revolutions. It was from this point of departure that Paul went on to amend the terms of Catherine's charter of the nobility. He could not as yet wholly withdraw it, but by dissolving their assemblies he could, and did, deprive the nobility of the privilege of collectively petitioning the crown. By what was largely a verbal subterfuge he could, and did, make them once more subject in law to corporal punishment. That he was thus the first sovereign to reduce the privileges which the nobility had accumulated since the death of Peter the Great is strictly true. It is perhaps equally true that he showed a complementary desire to mitigate the evils of serfdom, though the evidence here is more confusing.

It is sometimes claimed for Paul, who at his accession restored to the serf peasantry the right of taking the oath of allegiance which had been in abeyance since the time of the empress Elizabeth, that he restricted serf labour dues to three days in the week. This is to mistake a characteristic gesture of his for something more. The manifesto on the subject which was issued simultaneously with the decree on the principle of succession merely urged that Sundays and days of high Church festivals should be left free, and recommended that the serf's working week should otherwise be equally divided between the cultivation of his master's land and the care of his own plot. Vaguely formulated, the announcement ignored the great diversity of local peasant custom and conditions and in any case was not meant to be of binding force. Admittedly it went a little way towards conceding the necessity of delimiting serf obligations, but Paul never went beyond it. Whatever relief, in point of fact, he may have won for the peasantry was only an incidental product of the desire to injure the great landowning nobility. Perhaps the natural bent of his mind appears in his frequent assertion that the peasants owed their masters absolute obedience and in his no less frequent recommendation of flogging as a punishment. The truth is, no doubt, that in this as in all else consistency is not to be looked for in Paul. But no sovereign, not even Catherine, made as many new serfs by prodigal grants of state land to new beneficiaries.

Every Russian emperor after him was, like Paul himself, a hierophant of the drill, discipline, uniform and military regulations of the Russian army. But none approached the heights of his tyrannical pedantry. The remarkable thing is that he left behind a residue of serious reform; Paul's army reforms are, indeed, his least equivocal achievement. Though he was chiefly moved by hatred of Potemkin's memory and by the desire to blot out all traces of Potemkin's work, he effected a healthy purge of army administration and restored a lost efficiency to the regiments of the Guards. But all this was accompanied by disciplinary extravagances almost beyond belief. Tightly encased in resplendent Prussian uniform so that they could scarcely breathe, adorned with pigtail, powdered hair and shako, rigid as automatons, his troops paraded before him in an extreme of apprehension. Insults, blows, savage punishments and unpredictable favours were all part of the routine of inspection; for those of highest rank every review was an ordeal. A similarly insensate punctilio prevailed at court, although here, together with every sort of humiliation for breaches of etiquette, went sudden showers of awards and decorations. Dismissal followed on the heels of promotion, for with imperial delusions of magnanimity went sudden suspicion. Even Alexis Arakcheyev, whose notoriety was still to come but who in the meantime had served Paul faithfully at Gatchina, fell from favour; while opposition to some of the emperor's military reforms at one time earned for Suvorov and almost the entire military hierarchy dismissal from the army.

Paul had not long to wait, however, to recognize his need of Suvorov. At his accession he had firmly chosen to remain at peace with revolutionary France. He resembled his mother only in the contempt he expressed for Napoleon and the republican idea, but his course was set by the need to reverse Catherine's decision to send an army under Suvorov to fight in Italy. With the collapse of Austrian resistance to Napoleon, however, Russian anxieties mounted and English persuasions were redoubled. In 1799 Russia had no interest in a war against Napoleon, and the balance of official opinion in the capital was for neutrality. But Paul, too, saw himself as the arbiter of Europe's destinies. What eventually brought him into the second coalition against France was nothing more momentous than Napoleon's seizure of Malta, whose Knights of St John Paul had by freakish circumstances taken under his wing.

The brilliance of Suvorov's campaign of 1799 in northern Italy is legendary. The swift succession of Russian-Austrian victories under his command—Cassano, which opened the way to the occupation of Milan, victory on the Trebbia, the bloody triumph of Novi—drew Suvorov's eyes toward the road to Paris. There followed the normal Austrian hesitations dictated by greed, the substitute plan of operations in Switzerland and Paul's wanton meddling in strategy. The end came, after Suvorov's forced march to the St Gotthard pass and the storming of the Devil's Bridge, with his escape from catastrophe by the famous retreat over the Alps into Germany.

The brief second coalition faded in glory and confusion for Russia, with Austria proved faithless and England found wanting in the combined Anglo-Russian offensive against the French in Holland. But the abrupt Russian transition to a policy of virulent hostility towards England owed less, perhaps, to disillusionment in war than to the soaring fever of Paul's mind. Napoleon, now first consul, wooed him plausibly; Rostopchin, a new and magniloquent adviser, returned to the vast perspectives of Catherine's Eastern project and directed his gaze to the Turkish Balkans and the Straits and to more distant horizons. In a whirl of secret or half-secret Russian-French negotiations Paul came to terms with Napoleon, with whom he agreed to divide the mastery of Europe. It was England and England alone, he was now convinced, which in the eastern Mediterranean as elsewhere menaced both legitimate Russian ambitions and the restoration of order in Europe. With a strict return to the principles of armed neutrality in the Baltic as a pledge of goodwill, in the last months of his reign Paul outlined to Napoleon his scheme of conquering India. In February 1801 a force of some 20,000 Don Cossacks, fantastically unprepared and lacking even maps, marched eastward towards the dim distances of Khiva and Bokhara and thence to the possession of the Indian subcontinent. A month later a much depleted force had reached Orenburg. But by that time Paul was dead.

He had in every conceivable way alienated the essential support of autocracy in Russia. The mass of his subjects had suffered little from the shocks and penalties of his errant absolutism, but the nobility had endured outrage. Arrests, punishments, dismissals and a spate of punitive and arbitrary regulations had kindled dangerous passions. Fuel had been added to the flame by the losses sustained through the cessation of trade with England, the chief export market for the products of their estates. Now came the prospect of war with England. Among the nobility at court a palace revolution was once more in the air. For their separate part, too, a small liberal section of the nobility had been brought to despair by the stringency of the emperor's anti-revolutionary precautions. Those printing establishments which had not already been shut down by Catherine were beset by the severest restrictions; the import of foreign books was virtually prohibited; and it was all but impossible in the first year of the nineteenth century for students to leave Russia or for a foreigner to enter it. The hopes of many rested on the heir to the throne, Alexander, whose addiction to humane philosophical principles was widely known.

The plot to dethrone Paul was probably hatched towards the end of 1799. Among the court officials, military officers and foreign envoys in some degree privy to it was the English ambassador, Sir Charles (afterwards Lord) Whitworth. There can be no doubt that Alexander himself was fully aware from the start of what was in train. It was only the insensate despotism of the emperor's whims, however, that drove the conspirators to the plan of assassination. The plan ripened at a time when Paul, gripped by fear, had installed himself in the barely completed Michael Palace which he had built in the style of a fortress in the capital. He scented plots and conspiracies everywhere, imposed a curfew in the capital at nine o'clock in the evening and leaned upon the protection of Count Pahlen, the military governor of St Petersburg and the commandant of the palace guards. It was Pahlen who guided the conspiracy. He was aided by the men who, having been sentenced to exile from the capital through Paul's suspicions, at this moment were recalled by him. And it was Alexander who chose for the attempt the night of March 23, 1801, when his own regiment of the Semenovsky Guards were on duty at the palace. Could he have failed to know, in spite of all the assurances he had requested, that what was being prepared for his father was not merely abdication? Having gained entry to the palace, the conspirators, nerved for the task by heavy drinking, proceeded to the emperor's bedroom, demanded his abdication and then strangled him with an officer's scarf.

CHAPTER XII

ST PETERSBURG
AND REVOLUTIONARY EUROPE

IF, DURING THE TWO centuries which divide the Russia of Peter the Great from the Bolshevik revolution, there was any period in which the spell of the authoritarian past might have been overcome, the forms of the state liberalized in a constitution and the course of Russian development merged with the historic currents of the west, it is the earlier part of the reign of Alexander I. Or so, for a moment, one is tempted to think. For the oppressive closing years of Catherine's reign, the ruinous caprice of her successor and the French Revolution itself had not been without effect upon thoughtful minds in Russia. In the years before 1812 it was above all the emperor who appeared convinced, perhaps more convinced than any of his subjects, that Russia's needs could be met only by a scheme of constitutional government and the abolition of serfdom.

And it might be supposed that Alexander's will would be sufficient to secure his ends.

Yet a legacy of misfortune and political error on the scale of the Russian past is not easily cast off. Where in the vast, undeveloped and venally administered empire were the resources of legality and consent which would be required to transform from top to bottom a system of government and society basically unchanged since Peter the Great? And how, precisely, was so radical a transformation to be made? The example of the west bore no relevance to Russian conditions, and in any case the points of contact between the bureaucratic absolutism of St Petersburg and revolutionary Europe were still few. Whatever, in fact, the force of Alexander's conviction, the opportunity he offered or appeared to offer was beyond the grasp of Russian society. There was only the narrowest foundation of the rule of law on which to raise a structure of constitutional government, only a flickering idealism to light the way towards the ending of serfdom. And Alexander, for all his strangely compounded liberal impulse and despotic self-will, was not the ruler to try to impose either on Russia. For the truth is, of course, that the only form of constitution he was prepared to concede was one which left intact the sovereign principle of autocracy, while no one had better cause than he to know that the nobility would give their assent to the liberation of the serfs only on the impossible condition that it did not injure them.

Unfailingly courteous and gentle, the show of weakness in him constantly belied by an intransigent temper, Alexander is the most complex and most elusive figure among the emperors of Russia. Napoleon called him 'the sphinx', 'the Talma of the north', 'the cunning Byzantine', and the descriptions match Napoleon's experience at his hands. But they are valid in a more general context. Dissimulation came almost by the light of nature to Alexander. Originally a need he had cultivated in youth in professing dangerously divergent loyalties as the pupil of Catherine and his father's son, it became an overmastering habit. No tsar, perhaps, was more of an actor, not even the false charmer of a brother who became Nicholas I. Yet at the same time none was more visibly driven by dominant but mysterious impulses. He remains always 'the enigmatic tsar', a riddle of a man who, in Pushkin's words, carried his secret with him to the grave.

One element in the riddle is his extraordinary personal fascination. Debonair and graceful (he was slightly lame through a fall from his horse), captivating in the warmth of his address, he is the earliest and most striking representative of the famous Romanov charm. Like all people who learn to rely upon charm, he became progressively more insubstantial in character, the outlines of his personality blurred by the succession of flattering parts he chose to play; in the end, perhaps, he could not distinguish between what was real in him and what was assumed. He had been brought up by Catherine in the invigorated air of the enlightenment and had been given as principal tutor the Swiss La Harpe, who with republican views and a somewhat pedantic cultivation affected a veneer of Jacobinism. Alexander's education was of a fitful kind even before his marriage in 1793, when he was not yet sixteen, to a princess of Baden, but he acquired excellent English as well as French, both of which he continued to speak better than Russian, and he preserved through all the irrationalism of his concluding phase of rule something of the rarefied doctrine of reason instilled into him in early years. Certainly when he came to the throne at the age of twenty-three an aura of ardent liberalism clung to him.

Psychological analysis will not conjure the demon that drove him in later years to restless travels and tours of inspection in Russia and journeys abroad, but from the beginning certain elements of mental conflict in him are plain. The events of the night of March 23 in the Michael Palace lay always on Alexander's conscience; the guilt of parricide and a lurking fear for himself were joined in an ineradicable obsession. He could give his trust to nobody. And then, perhaps as a means of release, there was the pursuit of glory. Alexander from the first was in competition with Napoleon. He had taken very kindly to his father's fearsome military style at Gatchina—not for nothing did Pushkin call Alexander a crowned drill-sergeant—and his faith in the rigours of military discipline and blind obedience stretched to a stubborn confidence in his powers of leadership in war. He saw himself constantly as military saviour of his country and indeed of Europe.

There is, in a sense, no real break between the period of liberalism up to 1812 and the years of reaction that followed. The cloudy projects of a form of representative government for Russia and the mystical principles of the Holy Alliance had a common source, it would appear, in a sense of personal insecurity. The early dreams were never completely abandoned. Together with the harshest repression in the later period went continued pledges of reform and instructions to his ministers to draft a scheme of peasant emancipation. But in the years before 1812 Alexander kept idealistic hopes alive by small instalments of liberal legislation. Once again, at the opening of a new reign, the sovereign had made a bid for popularity. Alexander restored civil rights to some thousands of persons who had been deprived of them by Paul; he recalled to the capital many whom Paul had summarily banished; he closed down the department of political police known as the secret chancery; he gave permission for students to travel abroad,

lifted the ban on the import of foreign books and allowed the
penalized publishing houses to operate again; and he restored in
full the privileges conferred by the charter of the nobility. As for
the Cossacks who had been dispatched on their mission of conquering India, they had promptly been recalled. And while all
this made an encouraging start to the reign there seemed every
prospect of greater things to come. The liberal promise in the air
of the capital was concentrated in the deliberations of the small
group of young men around the throne, 'the young friends' as
they were styled, whom the emperor had constituted into an
unofficial committee.

The group consisted of three aristocratic intimates of his youth,
Adam Czartoryski, Paul Stroganov and Nicholas Novosiltsev,
and a fourth in Victor Kochubey, all of them sharing his outlook,
all familiar with western Europe and all early types of the Russian
anglomaniac. For a year and a half they sat in committee, with
Alexander sometimes presiding in person, discussing and drafting
schemes of reform and exciting some apprehension in conservative
official quarters. There need have been little anxiety. The committee
were young and generous in mind but prudent.

The practical fruits of their labours were indeed small. At the
end of 1801 the right to own inhabited land, hitherto restricted
to members of the nobility, was extended to all free classes in
society and even to state peasants. More than a year later effect was
given to a law which prescribed the conditions in which individual
serfs might purchase a holding of land by agreement with their
masters and thus acquire a status of all but unqualified freedom.
Few landowners, however, availed themselves of the law, which,
together with a ban on the sale of serfs in the open market, represented the farthest practical advance towards peasant emancipation
made during the reign in the strictly Russian parts of the empire.
One other achievement of these early years, though it had little
enough to do with the grant of a constitution, was the creation,
in place of Peter the Great's unwieldy colleges, of ministries*, of
which the individual heads were given the right of direct communication with the emperor. This system, which was more fully
developed in 1811 and which enabled ministers to function as a
committee, still left all the executive threads of policy in the
autocrat's hands, but it nevertheless established the pattern of
central administration for another century. The simultaneous
renovation in 1802 of the Senate as the supreme judicial organ in

* There were originally eight ministries, dealing with foreign affairs, war, the navy,
the interior, finance, commerce, justice and education, the last representing an
entirely new field of state activity. Three more were instituted in 1811, among them a
ministry of state security.

the empire was a much less substantial change, since the Senate's right to examine imperial decrees in the light of existing law was more nominal than real.

Alexander had made peace with England soon after his accession, but from 1805 to 1808 Russia was again at war and his interest in reform lapsed. It sprang to life once more under the guidance of an adviser of remarkable capacity, one of the ablest political minds in nineteenth-century Russia. Michael Speransky, born in 1772, the son of a village priest, had filled a succession of government posts with unexampled brilliance. He had been brought to the attention of the emperor, who in 1809 laid upon him the task of devising a comprehensive system of constitutional government. Almost the sole advice proffered by the emperor took the form of a request to make haste slowly in effecting the transition to a new order.

Speransky's draft constitution is a monument of political wisdom adapted to historical Russian circumstances. It belongs, alas, as has been remarked, only to the history of ideas, but even more than Alexander's personal sentiments it illustrates the wasted opportunity of the reign. Though practicable reform ruled out any open challenge to the existing order, it was plain enough that a constitutional regime could not be reconciled with the unqualified principle of autocracy. On the basis therefore of a scheme of limited representation, Speransky proceeded to devise a new legislative structure; through the strict separation of powers he planned a complete remodelling of the administrative and the judicial apparatus. Between them these measures of reconstruction, it seemed to him, might pave the way for a constitutional monarchy.

The representative idea was projected in an ascending order of election to a *duma*, a council or parliament, for each canton, each district and each province. At the canton level the body of electors was confined to the propertied classes, which included various categories of state peasants; one seat was reserved for every landowner and there was one for every five hundred state peasants. The canton duma would elect a representative to the district duma, which in turn would send a representative to the provincial duma. This hierarchy of local institutions was to be crowned, on the same indirect principle, by an elective duma for the entire empire. At the apex of the legislative structure would stand the State Council, whose functions were advisory and whose members were appointed directly by the throne. This was to serve as the link between the autocratic prerogative and administrative authority as re-shaped by a more closely co-ordinated system of ministries. A separate hierarchy of judicial institutions was similarly to be crowned by a remodelled Senate. Though the extension of civil rights to the entire population was an integral part of the project and therefore called for the abolition of serfdom, Speransky hesitated to approach the subject at this stage. But there is a telling irony in the fact that the Bolsheviks adopted precisely this hierarchical structure for the system of representation by soviets.

The State Council was set up in 1810, with Speransky himself as state secretary, and for a hundred years afterwards it continued to invest its rigid conservative bias with a semi-constitutional character. The improved ordering of the ministries apart, however, this was the sum total of Speransky's project to be realized. Inevitably, he had alarmed the bureaucracy and the place-holders at court. The further charge of financial reorganization laid upon him gave them their opportunity. On patently false grounds he was accused of treasonable relations with France. Like Nicholas II a century later, Alexander was never more himself than in his manner of dismissing an apparently trusted adviser. The crisis of 1812 was approaching, and the emperor looked for support among the traditional great servants of the crown. After an affectionate farewell Speransky was banished to Nizhny-Novgorod, and thence to Perm, from which he was permitted to return only at the close of the reign, on the eve of another and very different career under Alexander's successor.

The drama of 1812 was in the making for seven years. Although Alexander had originally chosen neutrality, the progress of Napoleon's military ascendancy in Europe had left Russia with no choice but to enter the third coalition in 1805. After the catastrophe of Austerlitz the Russian army had withdrawn behind its own frontiers; but, with both Vienna and Berlin occupied by the French, with French armies marching into Poland while Turkey struck across the Balkans, Alexander stubbornly resumed the fighting. Defeat at Friedland in June 1807 had its sequel in the calculated risk of the bargain struck with Napoleon at Tilsit, in the celebrated and unrecorded talk on the raft in the Niemen, in the following month.

Precisely how calculated was the risk on Alexander's side has always been matter for conjecture, and the analogy with the Soviet-Nazi pact of 1939 does nothing to remove uncertainty. Though still capable of prosecuting the war, Russia was admittedly wearied, Napoleon seemed invincible and the significance of England's war at sea, then as afterwards, was not apparent to Russian eyes. But why did the tsar, in proffering a full-blown alliance, draw upon himself the palpable threat of invasion by restricting the Russian room for manoeuvre in a duchy of Warsaw carved out of Poland's gains in the partition of Poland? Was it, after all, not so much Byzantine dissimulation that guided Alexander as the greed written into the secret clause of the treaty which pledged Napoleon's support for Russian claims to the Turkish Danubian provinces (though not to Constantinople, which for Napoleon was *l'empire du monde*)? Yet this was not a pledge to be taken seriously. Tilsit, in brief, which left in Alexander a rankling sense of humiliation, continues to raise as many doubts as the later pact.

It did, however, as did the pact of 1939, provoke a sustained duel of wits. The meeting of the emperors at Erfurt in the following year changed nothing; but, while military preparations in Russia took count of France as a potential enemy, as an ally Alexander had nothing to fear from Napoleon in pursuing designs against Sweden. In 1808 Finland, which for six centuries had been part of Sweden, was overrun and in the following September was formally incorporated as an autonomous grand duchy into the Russian empire. The war with Turkey was now resumed more vigorously, though the full fruits of Kutuzov's victories on the Danube were sacrificed to the need for meeting the threatened invasion of the Grand Army. In the treaty of Bucharest, signed in May 1812, Russia was content to acquire only Bessarabia.

Long before then all doubt had vanished that the alliance with France could not hold. Suspicion on both sides was exacerbated by the exchange of personal discourtesies over Napoleon's proposal of marriage with Alexander's sister Anna and by the evasion of economic agreements. Increasingly Russia ignored the provisions of the continental blockade against England. The preparations for battle were unconcealed on either side of the Niemen for more than a year before the event, with both Alexander and Napoleon bidding for Polish support.

There are several Russian aspects of the war of 1812 that may still be distinguished with advantage. The scattered disposition of the Russian armies over so extended a front was an initial folly which Napoleon was quick to detect. It seems certain that (as in 1941) Russia entered upon the war with no coherent strategy; Alexander had certainly contemplated the necessity of retreat in the light of Rostopchin's famous *dictum*—'The emperor of Russia will always be formidable in Moscow, terrible in Kazan, invincible in Tobolsk'—but counsels were hopelessly confused at the start of the campaign and the high command's plan of disengagement and withdrawal adopted by the Scottish-Russian General Barclay de Tolly was, in fact, countermanded by Alexander himself. It is more than doubtful whether there was any great stir of national feeling during the initial phase of the Russian retreat. High patriotism among the nobility, yes, but it is hard to discover elsewhere. If, like a later conqueror, Napoleon had seriously attempted to placate the civil population and had disciplined his army, he might well have assumed the role of liberator for the peasantry, who made little attempt to execute the scorched earth policy which they were instructed to follow. Almost up to Borodino patriotic feeling in the countryside was still for the most part quiescent. It was only the occupation of a deserted and burning Moscow which finally transformed the war into 'the war of the fatherland'. The burning of Moscow was, of course, largely accidental. But national sentiment flamed more brightly with the enemy's withdrawal, and it was the harrying by irregular Cossack and peasant bands of the defeated Grand Army in their long retreat which above all else gave the war of the fatherland its exalted and sacrificial character.

Napoleon and his armies were driven from Russian soil and the goal of Russian policy was achieved. Or so it seemed to Alexander's soldiers, including their commander Kutuzov, whom the emperor out of dislike and jealousy had with great reluctance appointed to succeed Barclay de Tolly. It did not seem so to Alexander himself. Invasion and its sequel had worked strangely upon him; the fires of Moscow, in his own words, had illumined his soul. Still racked for a time by despair, he found resolution in the end in what appeared to be religion. A brooding mystical impulse, nourished on constant reading of the Bible, gradually possessed him. His mission was plain: Providence had laid upon him a task of retribution and the power to command peace in Europe. In January 1813 the emperor of Russia, the leader of a new European coalition, advanced with his troops westwards across the Niemen. There followed the battle of the nations at Leipzig, the march to the Rhine, the triumphant entry into Paris and Napoleon's abdication. It was the hour of Alexander's greatest glory.

The horizons of the Congress of Vienna were largely bounded by the traditional objectives of Russian diplomacy in the Balkans and the Baltic and by the crucial issue of Poland. There is little trace of mystical sentiment in Alexander's peace-making, as little as in Russian peace-making in 1945, to which it bears so close a resemblance. From the first it threatened to dissolve in a new conflagration the grand alliance which had forged victory. But fears of Russia's western expansion were mitigated by the exclusion from 'Congress' Poland of Danzig and Posen, which formed the Prussian share of the duchy, and of Galicia as the Austrian share, and by Alexander's pledge to rule in Poland as a constitutional monarch. Harmony was not fully restored, however, even during the Hundred Days. Byron's autocrat of waltzes and of war came to London, renting Mrs Piozzi's house in Streatham as Peter the Great had rented John Evelyn's house in Deptford (and, in a studied intervention in English party politics, behaving with galling disdain towards the Prince Regent). So to Waterloo, which somewhat dimmed Alexander's glory since Russian forces could not have arrived upon the scene in time, though they duly made their appearance once more in Paris.

From the alliance of Russia with Austria, Prussia and England for the maintenance of the peace settlement and the subjection of France Alexander passed to the conception of the Holy Alliance. It was in June 1815 that he had his first and famous midnight interview with Julie de Krüdener, the penurious widow of one of his Baltic barons, whose dubious piety and gifts of flattery had gained for her a fashionable following as a mystic seer. Her personal influence upon Alexander, in spite of their continued correspondence, was short-lived, but it was under her sway that he formulated those Christian principles of faith and justice to which the sovereign rulers of Europe in the Holy Alliance were required to subscribe. What precisely he meant by these principles, or with what sincerity he advanced them, it is impossible to say. Neither Metternich nor Talleyrand was capable of thinking of politics in terms of personal sentiment; but up to a point Castlereagh was, and for him, though he alone of the statesmen of the period believed Alexander was sincere, the Holy Alliance was a thing of 'sublime mysticism and nonsense'.

Yet something of genuine idealism may well have lurked there, some flickering illumination of spirit may have touched the vanity of the imperial guardian of law and order in Europe. The era of unbridled repression in the name of faith and justice, of the defence of legitimism against revolution, the support of the *status quo* in Europe through military intervention, was still to come. Not until the signature by Russia, Austria and Prussia in 1820 of the Troppau protocol, which cemented the common interest of all three countries in the final dismemberment of Poland and in which the master hand was not Alexander but Metternich, were the last vestiges of Alexander's profession of enlightenment extinguished. Only then did he begin to repent of the liberal delusions of his youth. From 1815 to 1820, however, his reactionary policies were confined to the Russian territories of the empire. He kept his pledge to confer upon Poland a liberal constitution, in which a large measure of autonomy rested upon the principle of an elected diet and legal guarantees of civil liberty. In the Baltic provinces the peasants were emancipated, though without land. But not a gleam of constitutionalism fell upon the strictly Russian parts of the empire. And from 1820 onwards the maintenance of stability abroad was joined to a comprehensive programme of reaction at home. The great test of Alexander's adherence to the cause of the Holy Alliance came with the liberal-nationalist revolt in Greece against Turkish domination. Could the *status quo* take precedence over Russian interest in the Orthodox subjects of the sultan? It could and did, though British diplomatic pressure undoubtedly helped to resolve Alexander's doubt.

At home bigotry and obscurantism held the field. In the bureaucratic climate of St Petersburg the ghost of revolution was never laid after 1789. Projects of reform of every kind were still submitted to the emperor, who in private still acknowledged the evil of serfdom, but he now relied upon servants or advisers of a different type. Foremost among them was Arakcheyev, the all too faithful instrument of Alexander's will.

It was on Arakcheyev—the 'hyena', as the ambassador Joseph de Maistre called him—that Alexander laid responsibility for the 'military colonies', the most hated feature of the entire reign. Instituted in earnest in 1816, they had been devised by the emperor himself as a means of lightening the financial burden imposed by an enormous standing army. In the areas designed as military colonies the local state peasants were charged, in return for exemption from taxes, with the maintenance of a unit of the regular army and were themselves trained for military service. Simultaneously peasant cultivators and soldiers, they were subject to the most brutalizing military discipline, their manner of life prescribed and regimented for every moment of the day. Service in the military colonies was hereditary. The colonists' children were put into uniform at an early age, the womenfolk of the household were registered, camp conditions of life prevailed in the fields and in peasant dwellings. The whole routine of slavery for these impressed peasants—they may have totalled a half million by the end of the reign—was enforced by a system of punishments in which a murderous form of 'running the gauntlet' figured prominently. Arakcheyev, a creature of notorious brutality, made his contribution to the inhumanity of this regime, but largely as Pharaoh's taskmaster. In spite of constant riots in the colonies and of the palpable failure to effect economies or to promote military efficiency, Alexander persisted obstinately in the execution of the scheme.

Equally characteristic of Alexander's guidance in domestic affairs after 1815 was a gross illiberalism in education. Here, too, the action of his ministers masked the strange workings upon the emperor of his esoteric pietism. The early promise of a Ministry of Education and of a large measure of university autonomy vanished in 1817, when a newly designated Ministry of Education and Spiritual Affairs was put in the charge of the procurator of the Holy Synod, Prince A. N. Golitsyn, who was followed by the equally conservative Admiral Shishkov. Zealots of their own stamp were given their head in missions to institutions of higher

134 SHORT HISTORY OF RUSSIA

education. In the name of Orthodoxy dangerous thoughts were proscribed, university faculties were purged, the teaching of history and philosophy emasculated and theological aids devised for the advancement of learning in the natural sciences. And the censorship was more widely established on a new administrative basis.

Yet this was the period of the rise of a high order of periodical journalism in Russia and, more significantly, of the beginnings of the golden age of Russian literature. The greatest of Russian poets, Alexander Pushkin, born in 1799, a poet of divine ease, grace and proportion but one whose lightness and lyrical verve are untranslatable, had by the end of the reign already exorcized the pseudo-classicism of style which an earlier generation had derived from France. Here now was a native style of poetry, a living mode of literary language unfettered by Old Slavonic, a new imaginative awareness of things specifically Russian. The linguistic ground had been prepared and the new prosody introduced by Vasily Zhukovsky, who revealed in his translations from the poetry of western Europe the rich and flexible literary resources of educated Russian speech. Zhukovsky himself owed much to the innovations of Karamzin, grammarian and scholar, founder of the *Vestnik Evropy* (*Messenger of Europe*), which survived as the most weighty of Russian periodicals until 1917, and author of a new mode of sentiment in fiction and of a monumental *History of the Russian State*. And then there was Krylov, the most authentically Russian of fabulists; the elegiac poet Batiushkov; the dramatist Alexander Griboyedov, author of an incomparable classic of Russian comedy, *Woe from Wit*, and many more.

From this unfolding of the imagination in the reign of Alexander I sprang the tragedy and romantic pathos of the Decembrist revolt. Like the flowering of literature, the revolt stemmed from the privileged nobility—or, rather, from a handful of the younger and better educated among the nobility. Poets and amateurs of literature held pride of place among the Decembrist conspirators.

They took their name from the insurrection in St Petersburg on December 14,* 1825. For the most part junior officers of the Guards, the majority were members of the minor nobility, though some, including all the original members of the first of the secret societies, bore great aristocratic names. Reared in the fashionable liberalism of the early part of the reign, in Germany and France they had been witness, in the words of one of them, to events which had changed the destiny of mankind. The chill winds of the Russia to which they returned from the wars in 1815 struck

---

* December 14—'the fateful day'—is the Old Style date (N.S., December 26). It echoes throughout nineteenth-century Russian historiography and political literature.

harshly upon their spirit. Victory in the war of liberation had turned to the defeat at home of every generous impulse, every prospect of liberty they had entertained for their own country.

On the eve of revolt there were in all probably fewer than three hundred persons directly involved in the conspiracy, though the number in sympathy with them was more considerable. The secret societies in which the conspiracy originated took their original character from Freemasonry, to which not a few of their members had been introduced in Europe and from which they borrowed both a vague moral philanthropy and the ritual of secret organization. In 1816 a group of six young officers, headed by Prince Trubetskoy, colonel of the Preobrazhensky Guards, formed the Union of Salvation, or the Society of True and Faithful Sons of the Fatherland. They met to discuss literature and the hope of reform in Russia. In this latter interest they were encouraged by the belief that the emperor himself was still on their side. Later they were joined by the most remarkable figure among them all, Paul Pestel, a staff officer, who had especially distinguished himself at Borodino. Born in 1793, the son of a governor-general of Siberia, Pestel was a man of brilliant parts, widely read, forcible in argument and of strong personality. In mind and character he bears an obvious degree of likeness to Lenin. Into the vague talk of constitutional government, the prospects of liberating the serfs and the means of educating public opinion Pestel introduced a sharper note of controversy.

Amidst growing dissension the Union of Salvation was dissolved in the following year and revived in the Union of Welfare, which seemed willing to exclude all political discussion. But Pestel's views had hardened. He had come to the conviction that the end to be sought was not reform but revolution, not a constitutional monarchy but a republic. This could be achieved only by armed insurrection and the murder of the emperor and the imperial family, after which it would be essential to establish a temporary dictatorship, equipped with the necessary apparatus of repression, in order to undertake the reconstruction of society. In the uncompleted *Russkaya Pravda* (*Russian Justice* or *Truth*—a title which goes back to the code of laws of the Kievan era), composed during the three or four years before the insurrection, Pestel projected in some detail a half-prophetic scheme of Russian revolution.

Though the extremism of his views had the effect of reinforcing more moderate attitudes in the society, it also gained converts. In 1820 came a fresh jolt towards conspiracy. While at Troppau the report reached Alexander of what was described as a mutiny in the Semenovsky Guards, his own regiment, whose soldiers had in fact been goaded into protest by the excesses of cruelty of a new commander. Shocked and suspicious, the emperor proceeded to post the officers of the regiment to other duties, and Pestel was moved to staff headquarters of the southern army at Tulchin, in the Ukraine. A year later, after an imperial decree aimed in the first place at the masonic lodges had prohibited all forms of secret society, the Union of Welfare, ostensibly wound up by consent, went underground.

From now onwards the conspirators were grouped in two separate bodies: a Northern Society in St Petersburg, where as time went on the leading place was filled by the poet Kondraty Ryleyev, and the Southern Society, much more radical in character, centred in Tulchin. There, in the last phase, contact was established with a Polish secret society and then with the United Slavs, a small body of pan-slav visionaries. But communication between south and north was always difficult. In March 1824 Pestel paid a visit to St Petersburg in a vain attempt to reconcile differences and to overcome misgivings. Nothing could as yet be settled, nor was firm agreement in sight. And Alexander was by now aware of the fact of conspiracy, for its threads stretched to the society of the court. Yet he seemed lost in apathy, indifferent to exhortation or warning. He had spoken increasingly of late of abdicating, of the charms of existence as a private citizen in Switzerland or as a botanist on the Rhine. He had long been separated from the childless empress—other loves apart, he had had several children by a Polish mistress who was the wife of a court official—but in September 1825 he went to join her in Taganrog, on the Sea of Azov, where she was convalescing after illness. There he was himself taken ill and died on November 19/December 1 at the age of forty-eight.*

The interregnum that followed combines a farcical comedy of errors with a tragedy of indecision. It took time for the news of Alexander's death to reach St Petersburg and still more time was required for the progress of negotiations between St Petersburg and Warsaw. For in Warsaw as Russian commander-in-chief was Constantine, the dead sovereign's brother and the presumed heir to the throne, and in St Petersburg was Nicholas, a younger brother. But was Constantine indeed heir? Or had he formally waived his right to the succession, as Nicholas had cause to suspect, after contracting a morganatic second marriage? Nicholas remained in doubt until the sealed manifesto drawn up years earlier by Alexander was opened and confirmed his right to the throne. Even then he

* It is desirable, perhaps, to record the legend that Alexander did not die in Taganrog but only vanished from sight in order to re-appear in western Siberia in 1836 as a *starets*, or religious hermit, who had adopted the name of Fedor Kuzmich. The latter died in Tomsk in 1864. Alexander's coffin in the fortress of St Peter and St Paul was opened in the 1920s and found empty; but there are other and simpler explanations for this than the fantastically incredible one which would support the legend.

hesitated to proclaim his accession, since no member of the imperial family was more unpopular with the regiments of the Guards, until after Constantine had formally and in person announced his renunciation. And this Constantine declined to do. In the event Nicholas swore allegiance to Constantine in Warsaw and Constantine swore allegiance to Nicholas in St Petersburg. Only the betrayal of the projected military rising in the south finally compelled Nicholas to act. December 14 was appointed as the day on which the State Council, the Senate and the army would take the oath of allegiance to him.

For three weeks before the event the members of the Northern Society met daily in tense but irresolute discussion. Pestel had won some sort of tentative agreement to military action in the spring of 1826, but there was now no strategy of insurrection on which to build. Yet plainly there could be no further delay. In putting their faith in the proclamation as emperor of Constantine (who, in fact, was as forbidding a military martinet as Nicholas) the conspirators entertained hopes of drawing the troops in the capital to their side. But as junior officers they were in no position to bring their units over with them. There was, in truth, no plan, no initiative, no confident purpose to support a call to arms. Eloquent and heroic, gripped by a premonition of doom, Ryleyev reached the point of no return in a passion of self-sacrifice. On the morning of December 14—an hour after the members of the Senate had already taken the oath—some 3,000 soldiers, consisting of the Moscow regiment and a handful or two from other units, assembled in the Senate Square, in the shadow of Falconet's great equestrian statue of Peter the Great. The leaders came and went, some returning to brood in desperate inertia on the scene, while others, including Trubetskoy, who had been chosen as dictator, stayed at home. Nothing passed during the bitterly cold hours of the morning and afternoon that bore the least resemblance to an insurrection. Formed into a square, their muskets loaded, the uncomprehending insurgent troops stamped their feet to keep warm and cheered for Constantine, divided by a short distance only from the loyal regiments, perhaps three times their number, drawn up in parade on the neighbouring Admiralty Boulevard. Thousands of onlookers stood by. The murder by one of the conspirators of the military governor of the capital, General Miloradovich, and the refusal of a hearing to Nicholas's intermediaries precipitated the end. Nicholas was slow to use force, but as the light fell the danger grew that the government troops might be seduced from their duty. Cannon were brought up and the order was given to fire. The first volley scattered the insurgents, and in an hour it was all over. The number of victims is unknown, but they included a crowd of innocents, for the ice of the Neva had been broken by grapeshot and there were many drownings. The rounding up of the conspirators followed swiftly that evening.

The rest was braver but even more forlorn. By the time the summons to revolt from St Petersburg had reached the south the plot had been betrayed. Pestel was arrested a day before the insurrection in the capital, and the desperate attempt by Sergey Muraviev-Apostol at the head of a southern regiment to occupy Kiev was easily overcome.

Half-hearted, romantic and jejune, in the nature of things the Decembrist rising was condemned to failure. And yet the margin of defeat may have been narrow. Perhaps, after all, only a fraction more realism and determination was needed to bring the government troops over; perhaps a successful military insurrection in the capital would have touched off popular revolt. The bare fact remains that on December 14 the conspirators almost willed their own defeat, and that the cost of defeat was the eclipse of liberal hopes for a generation afterwards. That, however, was not the only consequence of failure. Alexander Herzen, with whom the tradition of Russian revolutionary agitation begins, pointed the moral of this first attempted revolution in the empire of the tsars with a political programme. Theories, he said, inspire convictions, example shapes conduct. The fate of the Decembrists in challenging autocracy created a popular martyrology and a summons to action for the revolutionary movements which came after them.

CHAPTER XIII

THE GENDARME OF EUROPE

TSARIST RUSSIA endured more than one iron age, but that description was specially earned by the thirty years of the despotism of Nicholas I. In the articulate minority who represented 'unofficial' Russia the peculiar tyranny of Nicholas's rule bred a hatred which echoes in Russian literature right up to the Bolshevik revolution. Of no emperor of Russia have more damning or more contemptuous things been said. The reign marks the formal inauguration of the police state in Russia, the growth of a conscious revolutionary purpose in Russian society and the hardening of western suspicion of Russian policies to the point of russophobia.

The events of these thirty years threw into ominous relief the lost opportunities for reform in the previous reign and demonstrated the fundamental instability of the regime which Alexander had passed on to his successor. For within an enveloping political absolutism the system of bureaucratic tyranny, barrack-room discipline and police supervision which Nicholas imposed on Russian society bore only a delusive appearance of strength. Behind a façade of civil order and military power lay corruption and incompetence, a massive inertia and decay. The imposing system broke down in humiliating failure, as the dying emperor himself recognized, in the early disasters, diplomatic and military, of the Crimean War.

The springs of policy, domestic and foreign, under Nicholas were in no way new. With the maintenance of the rights of autocracy as a sovereign principle the emperor confronted familiar problems: administrative and judicial chaos, Poland, the Ottoman power in decline and—above all else—serfdom on the one hand and revolution in Europe on the other. In serfdom he saw, in his own words to the State Council, 'the unmistakable evil of Russian life'. But at the same time he was appalled by the danger of touching it: that, he was convinced, would tear the state apart. In the revolutionary spirit abroad Nicholas detected the source of universal corruption. Faithful to the legitimist ideals of the Holy Alliance, he accepted the obligation of defending crowned rights and existing frontiers, casting Russia for the role of gendarme of Europe. All this was in a recently established tradition of Russian imperial rule. What was new in Nicholas's conduct of affairs was the prodigious edifice of administrative authority which he erected for perfecting order in the state and regulating the lives of his subjects. The limitless proportions, the ubiquity, the automatism, the pedantry and punctilio of the apparatus of bureaucracy set in motion by Nicholas I are faithfully illustrated in the pages of Gogol. The apparatus was the emperor's own instrument for discharging in detail his duty and thus ensuring the safety of the realm. As conscientious in every way as he was unimaginative, Nicholas, if he could, would have retained in his own hands every administrative function in the land, and indeed drove himself to death in the attempt.

He brought to his appointed obligations an indefatigable energy and the habit of a ruthless military disciplinarian. The vision he entertained of Russia was always of an endless parade ground and barracks. Not personal cruelty so much as the brutal authoritarianism of his military style won for him the notorious title of Nicholas Palkin, Nicholas the Flogger. Discipline, and the symbols and ceremony of discipline, possessed him almost to the exclusion of all else. He gave unwearied attention to the details of military uniform and himself devised the uniforms which at various times were made obligatory for different classes of the population, from the bureaucrats themselves to the students. Like Alexander, though perhaps with better reason, he trusted nobody; unlike Alexander, he was of cold and narrow intelligence. The histrionic streak in him, which enabled him to cultivate a fine presence and to assume with no little success an air of candour and sympathy, was powerfully reinforced by vanity; even at his most autocratic Nicholas was always the actor. There is, in spite of everything, an ineradicable hint of imposture in the spectacle of his devotion to duty. It blunts the edge of the stern sense of vocation which Nicholas brought to all the follies and misfortunes he visited upon Russia.

The falseness of his sympathetic charm of manner was displayed at the outset of the reign in Nicholas's close personal investigation of the Decembrist conspiracy. From the Winter Palace where they were brought after arrest, or from solitary confinement afterwards in the fortress of St Peter and St Paul, the conspirators were conducted into the presence of the emperor. No professional *agent-provocateur* could have been more successful in winning the confidence, often the penitent devotion, of his victims and in extracting from them full and indeed over-full confessions. After months of patient inquisition of some six hundred persons in all, one hundred and twenty were brought to trial by a special court. Among the members of the court was Speransky, seemingly unperturbed by the ghost of his liberal past. Sentence of death by quartering was pronounced on five, including Pestel, Ryleyev and Sergey Muraviev-Apostol, and death by decapitation on thirty-one others. In the event only the five suffered the capital penalty, which was commuted to hanging. The death sentence had been virtually in abeyance since the reign of Elizabeth, and their execution excited a stir of horror. It swelled the romantic pity and pride which for so long afterwards attached itself to their name and to the memory of the lesser martyrs in penal exile in Siberia.

The Decembrist revolt was the crystallizing influence in Nicholas's domestic policy, and perhaps in his foreign policy also. He believed ever afterwards, or pretended to believe, that he had delivered Russia from irretrievable ruin. To his younger brother Michael, on the very day after the insurrection, he declared: 'Revolution stands on the threshold of Russia, but I swear it will never enter Russia while my breath lasts.' Until the very end he remained implacable in revenge, hardened against forgiveness or trust. It was unallayed suspicion on his part that multiplied the agencies of inspection in every sphere of administration. The tasks of government were for himself alone, not for the State Council or the Senate, still less for the committee of ministers, all of which he was generally content to ignore, but as a comprehensive instrument of his will he had recourse to a special apparatus of his own. This was the imperial private chancellery, hitherto concerned for the most part with matters of a personal or formal character, but now reorganized and expanded until it became in effect the omnicompetent organ of the central power. That this vast new mechanism of bureaucracy, fed by an unceasing flow of paper, soon acquired all the portentous incapacity of the old only sharpened the emperor's resolve to widen its operations.

What was to prove the showpiece of the private chancellery was its Third Section, an institution of evil fame. Originally charged with the supervision of foreigners, the detection of forgery, surveillance of religious sectarians and places of political detention, it was rapidly transformed into an immense organization of secret police. As such it was an agency of government wholly independent of the normal processes of law. Served by a newly created gendarmerie and a network of informers on a vastly more extensive scale than had previously existed in Russia, it fortified the peculiar Russian tradition of the state within a state. Throughout its existence (it was formally merged in the Ministry of the Interior in 1880, a year before the assassination of Alexander II) it was headed largely by the industrious breed of German Baltic barons. The extra-legality of the Third Section derives a pointed incongruity from the achievement of the Second Section, under Speransky, who was put to work on the long-delayed codification of the laws since the *Ulozhenie* of 1649 and who in 1832 completed a massive labour of compilation which stands almost alone on the credit side of official activity during the reign.

Though from the beginning he had set his face against dangerous innovations, Nicholas continued to profess a desire for reform. From the written depositions of the Decembrists he had learned far more of the country's discontents than any of his advisers could tell him. But reform, he made it plain, would be instituted from the throne; the last thing he desired was the pressure or persuasion of his subjects. Hence the secret committee appointed towards the end of 1826 which sat for six years discussing the reorganization of the State Council, the reform of the Senate, the amelioration of peasant conditions, and so on, and the profusion of secret committees afterwards, all of which left matters essentially where they were before. For the events of 1830 and of 1848 and of all that came between bore witness to the perils of change. If serfdom was the great evil of Russian life, its maintenance was yet a safeguard against the greater evil of universal revolution.

Nicholas had not recovered from the shock of 'the infamous July revolution' of 1830 in France when rebellion in Poland burst upon him in the following November. The rising exposed the nerve centres of the alliance with Prussia (the empress of Russia was the daughter of Frederick William III) and with Austria on which rested their common defence of legitimism. Nicholas had not forgotten the Polish part in the Decembrist plot. Formally crowned king of Poland in 1828, he had done nothing to repair the widening breaches in the liberal Polish constitution conferred by Alexander which Alexander himself had made. For the autocrat of imperial Russia, as in a different fashion for his educated Russian subjects, a Polish constitution was indeed the strangest of anomalies.

The Polish revolt, originally prepared by secret societies, was touched off by Nicholas's decision to include Polish units in the army which after the July revolution he had been on the point of dispatching to the Rhine. It had all the intemperance of Polish nationalist fervour. The diet in Warsaw not only proclaimed an independent republic but demanded the restoration of the Lithuanian provinces. The appeal to the west was met by sympathy in Britain and in France, but neither country stirred. And the Poles themselves, as always, were disunited, the radical elements at odds with the conservative magnates, while the body of the peasantry remained for the most part unmoved. The Polish army slowly gave way under the pressure of a Russian army of 150,000 in the spring of 1831, and in the late summer Warsaw surrendered.

What Nicholas still needed to learn of the faithlessness of the Poles he discovered in the punitive rage of his restoration of order. While Polish columns were on their way to Siberia Alexander's liberal constitution was effectively replaced by an organic statute and Congress Poland formally absorbed as an integral part of the Russian empire. A campaign of stern though as yet incomplete russification followed: the continued use of the Polish language in the schools was conceded only under strict conditions, Russian officials were installed in all the principal organs of local administration, and both the Polish Catholic Church and the equally suspect Uniats in the former Polish-Lithuanian territories came under severe penalties. In 1839 the Uniat Church was virtually dissolved.

Poland was disposed of for the rest of the reign: it now contributed merely a single note to the swelling harmony of domestic order which Nicholas had prescribed. But in spite of the Holy Alliance a European harmony eluded him as yet. The critical foreign preoccupation during the reign, and indeed for the rest of the

century and afterwards, was with what was still called the eastern
question. Turkey no longer represented the extreme limit of
western diplomatic intercourse with the east, but for the western
powers as for Russia the eastern question still did euphemistic duty
for the real issue posed in 1774 by the treaty of Kuchuk-Kainardji—
the control of the Straits. It was Nicholas who coined the term 'the
sick man' of Europe to point his argument for the dismemberment
of the Turkish empire. For Nicholas's Russia what was at stake
in the first place was not the Danubian principalities of Moldavia
and Wallachia, not the Slav and Orthodox subjects of the Porte,
but the command of the Bosphorus and the Dardanelles.

At the beginning of the reign the whole issue had been projected
in the Greek revolution. Here Nicholas had been guilty of back-
sliding. Against all his legitimist principles he had been brought
round by Russian interest to reverse Alexander's policy and support
the Greeks against the sultan. Russian squadrons had joined the
British and French in the resounding action in 1827 against the
Turkish fleet in Navarino Bay. A single-handed war with Turkey
had followed next year. By the treaty of Adrianople in 1829 the
Porte conceded effective autonomy to Greece and an informal
Russian protectorate over the Danubian principalities. The Russian
hold on western Transcaucasia was simultaneously tightened.
The eastern Caucasus had already been drawn more securely into
the Russian sphere by renewed war with Persia, though the
mountain tribes under the warrior-priest Shamil waged a heroic
guerrilla war of independence for another thirty years.

It was now that the conflict of St Petersburg and London in
the Near East became envenomed. What with the pretensions of
Russian military power to support her eastern diplomacy on the
one hand and the fantasy of British alarms for India on the other,
rivalry verged on extreme bellicosity. In the jockeying for diplomatic advantage, in which all the great powers took a hand, Russia's
policy towards the Porte underwent a significant tactical change.
Her gains in the Balkans had antagonized Austria and threatened
the Holy Alliance. Now, in competition with Britain and with a
reviving France, dismemberment could wait; what Russia desired
at all costs was to retain a solid pretext for intervention in the
Balkans. Her opportunity came in 1833, when the sultan, threatened
by a powerful rival in the person of Mehemet Ali, his pasha in
Egypt, reluctantly accepted the assistance of a Russian expeditionary
force at the Bosphorus for the defence of Constantinople. The bill
was promptly presented and took the form of the treaty of Unkiar-
Skelessi.

The letter if not the spirit of the treaty has sometimes been mis-
understood. It did not confer upon Russia, as was widely supposed

then and afterwards, the right to demand that the Straits should be closed to all foreign warships other than her own. Nicholas would have desired nothing better, but correctly judged that as yet that goal was beyond his reach. The diplomatic significance of the treaty lay in the all but exclusive influence which Russia temporarily acquired in Constantinople through an 'alliance for peace'. But in the west the alarming vision unfolded of the transformation of the Black Sea into a Russian lake. Thus while Nicholas, after the endangered Holy Alliance had been re-affirmed by the three autocratic powers, counted on Austrian support in pursuing further designs on Turkey, Palmerston kept up a steady anti-Russian pressure. Six years later the conflict between the sultan and Mehemet Ali was resumed and, in the face of reactions in the west which brought Russia and Britain to the brink of war, Nicholas saw the necessity for retreat. By the Straits Convention of 1841 Russia tacitly abandoned her status of privilege in Constantinople by acknowledging with the other great powers that the Straits should remain closed to all foreign warships while Turkey was at peace. That convention survived until the eve of the first world war. But for Russia, and in a different degree for Britain and France also, the catastrophic sequel of the whole affair came at the close of Nicholas's reign.

The long diplomatic prelude to the Crimean War apart, the course of Russian foreign policy during the later years was governed by the force of Nicholas's anti-revolutionary sentiments. For all his obtrusive vanity there was something perversely messianic in his dream of policing Europe. He was, for all practical purposes, his own foreign minister, though it is certain that Nesselrode, who held the titular office for the entire thirty years of the reign, was a good deal more than the clerkly instrument he is sometimes said to have been. 1848, the year of revolutions, roused his master to fury. After the revolution in France in February of that year Nicholas was only reluctantly dissuaded from ordering an army of 400,000 to march westwards. His offer of assistance to Prussia was declined. But the revolution in Galician Poland and in Hungary was another matter, and the youthful new emperor of Austria, Francis Joseph, did not ask in vain for help against the Magyar and Polish-assisted rising under Kossuth. It was a Russian army under Paskevich which kept the Habsburg dynasty alive.

This inflamed reaction to events abroad was matched by a new extreme of repression at home. After 1848 the obscurantism of official Russia turned to stifling darkness. All pretence of seeking ways and means of reform was abandoned. Police rule grew more arbitrary: every hint of intellectual dissent was suppressed, the most venial political offences earned a sentence of deportation to Siberia, and the numbers condemned to *katorga**—confinement in a Siberian penal settlement—rose sharply. Even the most reliable executants of Nicholas's domestic policies were dismissed on suspicion of liberal sentiments. Among them was Count Sergey Uvarov, for sixteen years the emperor's Minister of Education, who in protecting Russia from the contagion of the corrupt west had constituted himself the chief apologist of the regime.

From the start of the reign the disciplined conformity which Nicholas demanded of his subjects had necessitated a further hardening of social divisions. This was plainly reflected in educational policy. In 1828 the opportunities for secondary and higher education which, at least in theory, had been made available in the previous reign without distinction of class, were restricted by administrative regulation to the children of the nobility and officialdom. Peasant illiteracy was all but universal, but the law was designed to confine such prospects of education as might nevertheless be open to a peasant child to the negligibly small number of parish schools. The pace in educational reaction was now set by Uvarov, a scholar turned sour and ambitious, who on his appointment in 1833 applied himself to the task of combating subversion in all its forms. His purpose, in his own words, was to retard the development of Russia by fifty years. What was necessary was to build dams against the revolutionary flood from Europe. The strongest dam would be formed by the triple alliance of Orthodoxy, autocracy, nationality: the first signifying the unqualified doctrinal authority of the Church, the second devotion to the person and to the police rule of the emperor, and the third (*narodnost*) standing rather ambiguously for a prescribed mode of patriotism or nationalism.

This official design for living and thinking was backed by all the resources of coercion. In 1835 the universities were brought into line. Such autonomy as they had retained was taken from them, together with their advisory powers in local secondary education, control of which passed to a hand-picked ministry inspectorate. New professorial appointments required ministerial sanction; instruction in theology and Church history was made obligatory for all students; and the whole emphasis of university training was diverted from learning to the requirements of an expanding bureaucracy. Once more permission to study abroad was severely curtailed, though not before a crop of Russian intellectuals of a new type had been raised in the universities of Germany. After 1848 entry to the Russian universities was hedged by fresh precautions, curriculums were re-drawn and the teaching of such subjects as foreign constitutional law suspended, and

* The literal meaning of the word is the gallows.

K

finally, since sedition was still rife among the young, the number of students in the universities was reduced in all faculties except theology and medicine.

A key part in the control of dangerous thoughts was played by the censorship. This was exercised in the first place by the indefatigable Third Section, whose researches often reached ludicrous heights of suspicion, but also by a host of other agencies, including almost every ministry. Nicholas—for whom public opinion and dangerous thoughts were one and the same thing—himself assumed the role of censor in chief, extending his vigilance to errors of style and conferring a special form of patronage upon Pushkin. In expiation of his offence as the friend and suspected accomplice of many of the Decembrists the poet was required to submit his work before publication to the emperor's critical scrutiny.

From Nicholas's point of view, censorship was a prime necessity of state. For whatever else was stifled by the tyranny and petty persecution of the bureaucratic machine he had brought into being, it was not thought or imagination. In as oppressive an intellectual climate as Russia had known literature flowered as never before. Censorship was often circumvented by clandestine circulation in manuscript form, still more by the adoption of an 'aesopian' language of allusion in controversial matters, but poetry and prose alike flourished brilliantly even without these aids. Among Pushkin's poetic contemporaries were Baratynsky and Yazykov; after him came Lermontov and Tiutchev: in all, a period of some thirty years of poetic achievement of astonishing originality and splendour. And it was the age of Nicholas that nurtured the distinctive realism of the Russian novel, which took firm root in Gogol and the early Dostoevsky, and with which above all else Russia repaid her literary indebtedness in the past to Europe. There was little to comfort the political police in the rebellious passion of Lermontov's later poetry or in the satirical rage of *Dead Souls*, but more dangerous than these were the new currents of critical and speculative thought. They flowed from diverse layers of society: from the nobility, from the merchant class, from the children of priests and minor officials. It was the contribution to what looked suspiciously like public opinion of a newly emergent power in Russian society—a body of persons of various classes (*raznochintsy*) engaged in literature and journalism—that required the closest attention. The Russian intelligentsia had, in fact, arrived on the scene in the 1830s.

Their principal intellectual stimulus still came from abroad. Russian realities exercised their conscience, the legacy of the Decembrists lay nearest to their heart, but what originally shaped the thought of the younger generation whose leaders were Belinsky,

Herzen and Bakunin was German idealist philosophy. From the
abstractions of Schelling, of Fichte and Kant, above all of Hegel,
the 'circles' and student groups in Moscow and elsewhere drew
the stuff of vivid and impassioned Russian debate. They fed on
the honey-dew of metaphysical speculation, casting back to first
principles in reviewing the Russian past and attempting to read
the future. Since they meditated in a political void and enjoyed
liberty only in speculation, their thought ran easily, as the thought
of the Russian intelligentsia ran ever afterwards, to extremes. They
represented a mere handful among a total Russian population at
this time of perhaps forty-five million, but theirs was a truly decisive
influence upon the thought and destinies of their country.

From their argument sprang first a dichotomy, then a peculiar
amalgam, of socialist and Russian nationalist ideas. It was
represented in the middle years of the reign by two contending
intellectual currents, westernism and slavophilism. Both had a
common source in the sense of the Russian past, during which the
course of national development had visibly alternated between the
imitation of the west and the assertion of a specifically native
inheritance. Where, in these dark and forbidding years, was the
path of Russia's true destiny? The question had originally been
posed by Peter Chaadayev in a philosophical essay which had
eluded the vigilance of the censor in 1836 and which burst upon the
reading public like a thunderbolt. Chaadayev, a bold spirit, discovered
no meaning in the Russian past, condemned the fatal influence of
Byzantium and maintained that Russia, which had failed to acquire
the traditions of either the west or the east, had also failed to evolve
a distinctive culture of her own. For this heretical reasoning he was
formally declared insane. But his example was not wasted. The
argument was taken up with furious energy by Belinsky in the guise
of literary criticism. It should always be borne in mind that throughout the whole period from the reign of Nicholas I to the Bolshevik
revolution literary criticism was a medium, and for much of the
time the sole medium, of discussion of public and political affairs.
An epochal figure in the intellectual history of Russia, Belinsky
firmly established the tradition of 'social' or 'civic' criticism which
has both enriched and sterilized the critical values of literature in
Russia ever since. In his own time it provided powerful support
for the westerners in their controversy with the slavophils.

The entire quasi-philosophical argument revolved to a large
extent round the legacy of Peter the Great. The westerners took
their stand on a doctrine of progress, of historic necessity. It was
true, they conceded, that her past had endowed Russia with distinctive traditions of her own. But common laws governed her
future. All that divided her in substance from the civilization of

the west was the backwardness originating in centuries of resistance to Asia, and all hope for the future lay in following where Europe had led. There could be no other path of progress, no material and intellectual advance by other means. The westerners were, without exception, ardent radicals, but in the circumstances of censorship in the thirties and forties it was only in the most guarded and theoretical terms that they could proclaim the necessity for abolishing serfdom and autocracy.

Theirs, like Peter the Great's, was a secular view of the state, a secular faith in the future. Against them the slavophils opposed what was essentially a religious conception of Russian life and civilization—one from which Peter, they argued, had deviated with ruinous consequences. Vaguer and more protean in doctrine than the westerners, the slavophils dwelt upon the unique inheritance which had been confided to Russia. The Orthodox Church was, for them, a leaven of spiritual unity in the life of the nation beyond the experience of the materialist west; it had so far preserved Russia, as one of them put it, from 'the crimes of Europe'. They discovered in the Orthodox faith a pervading sense of fraternity which might heal all divisions in society. They saw in the village commune, the *mir* or *obshchina*, and in the *artel*, a small co-operative association in industry and agriculture, the basic types of economic organization in Russia which would permit her to avoid the evils of exploitation in the west. They retained firm faith in the supreme attributes of the throne. The slavophil view, in brief, was that Russia must follow her own star. In a sense, indeed, her separate path of destiny implied nothing less than a mission to Europe.

It was the westerners who captured the mind of the student generations of the forties and afterwards. The slavophils, though their historical arguments were hopelessly confused, were more original as thinkers, but they claimed few converts among the young. Yet it may well appear to-day that their ultimate influence was the more profound, that in the Russian Communist synthesis of westernizing and slavophil attitudes it is the slavophils' missionary urge which has predominated. 'The messianism of backwardness' was Trotsky's phrase for it, and, like other brilliant phrases of his, it was nearly but not quite just. The slavophils idealized the Russian past, they were romantically wide of the mark on the origins of the *mir*, but their idealism was as genuine, their rejection of 'official' Russia as whole-hearted, as that of their opponents; the accretions of mystical and nationalist-conservative fantasy came later, in the sixties and afterwards, degenerating into the extravagances of pan-slavism. It was Herzen, indeed, who recognized in westerners and slavophils the two faces of a Janus figure of Russian idealism. And, more particularly after 1848, it was slavophil distrust of the bourgeois values of Europe which infected the westerners themselves, as the classic instance of Herzen proves. From Herzen's dawning faith in the Russian peasant as the vessel of socialism came the Narodnik, or populist, movement of later decades which was the repository of Russian socialism before Marxism. Almost from the start, indeed, socialist sentiment in Russia was inimical to the west.

For both parties to the literary and historical debate serfdom was the immediate crux of the matter. The emperor's secret committees toiled in vain. Yet Russia's need was so patent, the peasants' own expectation so unwavering, that rumours of emancipation were constantly in the air. Though he denied them as constantly, Nicholas had every reason to know that it was insufficient to urge the landowners, as he had done, to remember their obligations to their peasants. For a new and aggravating factor in serfdom was at work: the population was growing fast and 'land hunger' in some areas was already an ominous portent. It was the real cause of perhaps most of the six or seven hundred peasant risings in the reign, their number increasing from year to year, half of which were put down only with the aid of military force. In the relatively populous central black-earth regions the landowners lived in growing anxiety, often in fear of arson and murder.

Relatively populous; for neither then nor afterwards were the vast spaces of rural Russia in any strict sense over-populated. But it was in the central regions that Russian methods of cultivation which were still for the most part primitive pressed hardest upon the growing numbers of the serf peasantry. The landowners, great and small, formed a nobility, not a farming class. Few had any knowledge of nineteenth-century agricultural technique. Nor had the great majority the resources of capital for better cultivation of the land; as a rule, their capital consisted of serfs only. This, in point of fact, appeared the insurmountable obstacle to any scheme of emancipation, all the more insurmountable because so many landowners possessed a handful of peasant households only. It is estimated that more than three-quarters of the total number of private estates at this time comprised fewer than a hundred male serfs.

What further defeated the good intentions of some of Nicholas's advisers was the economic diversity of the conditions of serfdom. Emancipation, when it came, was crippled at the outset by the need to reconcile different and competing claims for compensation. Where the soil was most productive it was ownership of land that mattered most; where the soil was infertile it was the ownership of serfs. For a domestic economy and a mercantile economy existed cheek by jowl in Russia in the middle of the nineteenth century. In the new fertile regions of the south, for instance, the owner farmed to an increasing extent on his own account for the market and his peasants' labour dues were reflected in the rapid growth during the reign of Russian grain exports* from Odessa and other Black Sea ports. He would have been prepared to consent to liberating his serfs on condition that he retained possession of the whole of the land, thus assuring himself of a supply of dependent cheap labour. But on the poor clay soil of the 'consuming' provinces of Moscow and the north, where the estate owners lived chiefly on rent and the payment made by their peasants for permission to work in the towns and factories, liberation would have entailed ruin for their masters, willing though they might be to surrender part of their land on terms.

This, however, is to anticipate the prolonged bargaining on the eve of emancipation. In Nicholas's reign only patchwork measures of peasant reform were attempted. In 1833 the sale of serfs without land by private auction was prohibited. In 1838 the Ministry of State Domains, formed out of Section Five of the imperial chancellery set up two years earlier, put in hand a scheme for peasants on state land which was designed to increase the holdings of the poorest categories and to alleviate conditions generally. Not a great deal was accomplished by this and similar means, and it has even been argued that they worsened rather than eased the lot of the state peasants. Finally, by a law of 1842 a peasant was enabled to purchase a holding of land from his master on agreed terms of payment or service or both, thus securing for himself 'personal' freedom while continuing to be bound by the obligations he had assumed. Thousands of richer peasants seized their opportunity, but few landowners of their own accord availed themselves of the law. The emperor was urged in some quarters to specify the sum required for liberation and the amount of land to go with it; but, except in the case of the provinces of the south-west, where the squires were mainly Polish and their interests of no great concern to him, he refused to commit the landowners. The most he would do in strictly Russian territory was to extend the serf's right of purchasing both freedom and land in the circumstances of the sale of an estate to pay the owner's debts.

Such sales, in the end, provided a clue to the solution, or the attempted solution, of an intractable problem. The landowning class as a whole had acquired tastes and habits which money alone could buy. A great many had thus mortgaged their estates: it is estimated that in 1843 more than half of all the private estates had been mortgaged, often at heavy rates of interest. A considerable

* By 1850 they had risen to almost one-third of the total of Russian exports.

number of owners could thus contemplate parting with some of their land to their peasants if the latter would in effect assume responsibility for their debts. Here was a possible means of release from both material and moral obligations.

Not every landowner sought to evade his obligations to the serfs for whom he could no longer find adequate employment on the land. Some attempted to divert this superfluous labour to industry, themselves setting up factories of various kinds. But the economic attachment of the peasant to the village commune proved a formidable obstacle to the growth of new enterprise. In industry, moreover, as in agriculture, the productivity of serf labour was low, and a crowning economic argument for emancipation was the dearth of free labour for industrial development. In 1840, indeed, the possessional factories had been enabled by law to free their serfs. But so long as rights of serf ownership otherwise belonged exclusively to the nobility the expansion of trade and industry was restricted to the narrow limits of the free labour market. Yet from the thirties onwards Russian industry did in fact begin to show a marked advance. Cotton, metallurgy and sugar refining developed most notably under the stimulus of protective tariffs. Factories slowly multiplied, sometimes through the enterprise of peasants of serf status (ownership was nominally vested in their master), and by the end of the reign the number of factory workers was over half a million, a threefold increase in forty years. Railway construction made a start with the short line between St Petersburg and Tsarskoe Selo ('the tsar's village'), opened in 1837; the line—inflexibly straight by Nicholas's wish—between St Petersburg and Moscow was begun in 1842. And foreign enterprise and foreign capital began to appear on the scene. All this brought the liberation of the serfs nearer.

The will to end serfdom, however, came only after the disaster of the Crimean War, which shattered all illusions of imperial power and stability even in conservative quarters. The war itself was one of the most absurd in European history and one of the most sacrificial in conduct. In the diplomacy that led up to it Nicholas's obstinate conceit was matched by bellicose stupidity on the British and French side. Nicholas would not abandon his designs on the sick man of Europe. He visited England in 1844 and convinced himself that there would be no effective opposition from that quarter. His knight-errant legitimism blinded him to the resurgence of French power. The quarrel, begun in 1851, over Orthodox and Catholic claims to the guardianship of the holy places in Jerusalem was trivial. It smouldered for two years. In July 1853 Nicholas invoked the terms of the treaty of Kuchuk-Kainardji, the Russian army marched into Moldavia and Wallachia, and the British and

French navies sailed for the Straits. With this support the sultan demanded that Russia evacuate the provinces. Diplomacy still continued in a fever of injured sentiment, and it was only at the end of the following March, some five months after Russia and Turkey were already at war, that Britain and France entered the struggle at Turkey's side.

The defection of Austria was a bitter blow to Nicholas, though it was something he might well have foreseen. He could not have foreseen the punitive allied decision, after their attacks by sea had ranged from the Baltic and the White Sea to Kamchatka, to embark upon the invasion of the Crimea. For with the Russian withdrawal from the Danubian principalities Britain and France had virtually gained their ends. Yet in September came the landings at Eupatoria, on the Black Sea, the battle on the Alma, and the beginning of the siege of Sevastopol.

On March 2, 1855, six months before the shattered city of Sevastopol fell, Nicholas died, exhausted and unnerved by failure. It was widely believed at the time that he had committed suicide by taking poison, and the belief is shared by some historians to-day. His death marked the collapse of the portentous system of authoritarian rule which he had built for the salvation of Russia amidst the perils of universal revolution.

CHAPTER XIV

REFORM AND THE AFTERMATH

CATASTROPHIC REVERSES in war have often provoked a radical transformation of the existing structure of state and society. The Crimean War is commonly linked with the Russo-Japanese war in 1904 and the first world war to illustrate a sequence of military defeat and revolution in Russian history. The link is, in one respect, tenuous; not because in 1905 and in 1917 the midwife of revolution, in the cant phrase, was violence, while the 'great reforms' which followed the Crimean War were set in train only by the fear of violence, but because those reforms amounted to something appreciably less than revolution. If the emancipation of the serfs entailed a drastic revision of the legal and administrative order of society, it left the basic pattern of the state unchanged. It was precisely because emancipation in 1861 was too little and too late that violence attended the successive phases of revolution in the next century.

The process of reform inaugurated by the act of emancipation was begun on the initiative of the most conservative until then of Russian emperors. Alexander II, the 'tsar-liberator', came to the throne at the age of thirty-seven with the habit of a military disciplinarian as exacting as his father's and the deserved reputation of an even more unrepentant diehard. Drawn closely by Nicholas into the tasks of government, he had proved the friend of reaction and the faithful ally of the landed nobility. Yet as autocrat he alone was capable of setting in motion a scheme of peasant liberation. Not a strong character in spite of his drill-sergeant habit of mind, in the first flush of resolution Alexander uneasily combined with his unthinking conservatism a stubborn support for new measures.

In the six months between his accession and the fall of Sevastopol after a heroically borne siege there could never have been any doubt that the war was lost. The emperor had not hesitated to try to restore peace, but in the course of diplomatic negotiations while hostilities continued he had to reckon with an obdurate war party. Only the Austrian threat to join the allies finally drove home the lesson of the country's exhaustion, the crippling Russian losses, the financial drain, the reverberating anger of all sections of the population.

By the terms of the treaty of Paris concluded on March 30, 1856 Britain, France and Austria guaranteed the integrity of Turkey and the Christian subjects of the Porte were placed under the protection of all the powers, not of Russia alone. The Straits convention of 1841 was reaffirmed and the Black Sea neutralized—that is, closed to Russian warships. Russia restored to Turkey the Caucasian fortress of Kars, whose capture had represented her solitary gain in the fighting, together with Batum. And the smart of Russia's retreat from the principalities was made more wounding by her exclusion from the mouth of the Danube through the surrender of part of Bessarabia to Moldavia, which together with Wallachia formed the virtually independent state of Rumania three years afterwards.

The humiliation of the Crimean War went deep. What the war had demonstrated in the first place was that Russia's military power was a sham. Paradoxically, the demonstration struck hardest on liberal susceptibilities; it was an assured military ascendancy in Europe, after all, which had been invoked to justify a system of police tyranny at home. Against an Anglo-French expedition of no more than seventy thousand, Nicholas should have been able to mobilize an army at least ten times as large. Yet the vast war machine of the empire had all but fallen apart at a touch. Indecision and intrigue at the top had been matched by official incompetence or venality at almost every level; supplies had broken down, Russian equipment had proved lamentably inferior, even less provision than on the allied side had been made for medical services, and neither the blunders of the enemy on the one hand nor the stoicism of the Russian peasant soldier on the other had saved Russian arms from catastrophe. Even in hitherto conservative quarters the moral had seemed plain while the war still continued. If defeat could serve any useful purpose, it would be to compel recognition of the need for reform. After the fall of Sevastopol the conviction grew that defeat was indeed to be desired, since it seemed certain that the bonds which imprisoned the Russian people would not be loosened otherwise.

For the crux of reform was still the abolition of serfdom. If any doubt existed on that score it was dissipated in the slightly freer atmosphere of opinion at the start of the reign, when the censorship regulations were relaxed. The language of opposition to the regime was still aesopian. The Russian radicals in exile—most notably Herzen, whose periodical *Kolokol* (*The Bell*), published in London, was by devious ways smuggled into Russia and even laid at times on a high official's desk—could give free rein to their passion of indignation, but in the press of Moscow it was necessary to disguise the plea for the emancipation of the serfs by a demand for 'the rational distribution of economic forces'. Not until the end of 1857 was the ban lifted on the open discussion of the problem of serfdom.

By that time the militant idealists had been carried forward on a great surge of hope by the emperor's announcement of his intentions. Diehard though he was, Alexander could not misread the prevailing anxiety for a fresh start. Nor did he lack advisers—they were to prove the real agents of emancipation—who pointed to the abyss that had opened before the regime. It was in April 1856, after the peace treaty had been signed, that in addressing an assembly of the nobility of Moscow he used the famous words, 'It is better to abolish serfdom from above than wait until it begins to abolish itself from below', and bade his audience think the matter over. The remark kindled radical sentiment to a blaze of fervour, in which Alexander was acclaimed as the saviour of Russia. The emperor himself had no specific plan of reform in mind. Emancipation, he was persuaded, could in no way affect the sacred principle of autocracy, nor need it seriously damage the interests of the nobility. What was essential was to give a lead and then to secure the support of the landowners themselves. The lead was given in the imperial rescript issued towards the end of 1857 which promised the serfs with their freedom the right to buy land from their landlord, and which provided for the setting up of committees in every province to consider the method of applying the principle. It was at this point that the temperature of radical hopes fell.

The long and involved story of the compromise of 1861 reflects the victorious rearguard action of the nobility and the eclipse of the forces of conciliation in Russian society. Reform was achieved through the tenacity of the reformers, but the spirit of reform was largely extinguished by the resistance of the ranks of privilege. Freedom for the peasantry was won only on terms which substituted a new form of economic servitude for the old and perpetuated their isolation from the rest of society.

The emperor had given his pledge, but it remained to strike a bargain with a quarter of a million landowners and their representatives at court and among the bureaucracy. The private committee of servants of the state appointed by Alexander had originally recommended liberation of the peasants without land, and, having thus raised the spectre of revolution, had been instructed to think again on the lines of the imperial rescript. It was against this background that delegates of the landowners in each province conferred in committee with representatives of the government. At the beginning of 1858 the whole debate was referred back to the private committee, now re-named the main committee. Though many of the landowners, particularly the backwoodsmen in the south, had been unyielding in the claim to retain the whole of their land, gradually the main practical issues took shape. They precluded any uniform scheme for the whole of Russia, but everywhere the problem was reduced to three essentials: the amount of land to be allotted to the freed peasant, the conditions of allotment, and the form and extent of compensation, guaranteed by the state, to be paid to the landowner. A separate committee was appointed to draft the law of emancipation, and a further committee was required to work out the financial terms.

The whole scheme was thrown into the melting-pot in the following year with the arrival in St Petersburg of landowning delegates from every part of the empire. Their demands were not lost upon the drafting committee, the fruit of whose labours passed to the main committee, who whittled the scheme down still further before the draft passed to the State Council, who hesitated, were pressed by the emperor to hasten their deliberations and who finally incorporated small modifications of their own. These completed, the document was delivered to the emperor for signature and promulgated on February 19/March 4.

'Serf law (*krepostnoe pravo*) for the peasants settled on the estate of landowners and for the people of the *dvor* [that is, the household serfs] is for ever abolished.' This was the governing clause of the imperial edict of 1861, which brought the curtain up on a laborious drama of twenty years of deepening anti-climax. Sixteen government decrees in all were necessary to secure the complete abolition of serfdom for some forty million or more peasants (the 'free' peasants at this time numbered seven or eight million), divided almost equally between those on private estates and those on state lands and on the estates of the imperial family. And even then for the majority the end of the settlement was all but worse than the beginning. The general principle adopted in 1861 enabled the freed peasant (other than the household serf, who on being liberated was left to his own devices) to purchase by credit an allotment of land. For the land thus surrendered the owner was compensated by the government in state bonds on a generous valuation, the cost being recovered from the peasants by annual instalments, known as redemption payments, which were determined by somewhat abstruse calculations. These payments were to be spread over a period of forty-nine years.

It should be borne in mind, first, that the land allocation was, in a legal sense, only permissive. The peasant purchased his holding by agreement with the landowner, and with the aid of government agents, known as arbitrators, who prepared the relevant deeds. Within the next twenty years, it is true, 85 per cent. of the landowners did in fact part with land to their peasants. But for those peasants who declined the responsibility of purchase the law offered with liberation a free holding of about one quarter of the normal allotment. Such holdings later became known, significantly, as 'beggars' allotments'. Not until 1882 was redemption made obligatory for the 15 per cent. who had contracted out of the main scheme.

For the peasantry as a whole the terms of settlement were cankered at the start. Through over-valuation of the land they imposed a crushing burden of indebtedness, through concessions to the landowners' property claims they reduced peasant holdings to a disastrously uneconomic size. In theory, compensation was restricted to the value of the land; the loss of serf dues or serf labour was expressly omitted from the reckoning. Yet in the thinly populated forest areas of the north, where alone the peasant's allotment was maintained at the size he had worked before gaining his liberty, the value of the land was flagrantly swollen to include the landowner's share of his serf's earnings. Everywhere else holdings were cut down to an average of half of what the peasant had formerly cultivated—even less than that in the central and southern black-earth regions, where the landowners produced for the market. It was precisely where pressure on the land was already most acute, indeed, that the terms of emancipation worked to the peasant's greatest disadvantage.

With all this, moreover, his holding of land did not become his private property. Emancipation established nothing resembling a system of peasant proprietorship in Russia. The land released by the owner ostensibly remained his property, with possession formally vested not in the individual peasant but in the peasant commune. While continuing to observe the old methods of partitioning the land among the peasant households and enforcing a crop cycle and general methods of cultivation the commune now also assumed collective responsibility for the payment of taxes. Ruled by its *starosta* (elder) and an elected assembly, it thus stepped into the place of the landowner as the peasant's master and a basic unit of local administration.

Liberty for the emancipated peasant, in brief, was only half-liberty. True, he now enjoyed the right to marry as he pleased, to own property, to go to law. But freedom did not confer upon him equality of civil rights with the rest of the community; he was still a world apart from those who had never known serfdom. He continued to pay the poll-tax, which for another quarter of a century was added to his yearly redemption payments. He, and he alone, was still subject to corporal punishment. And he was still bound to the commune by the old interior passport system, unable to leave the locality and look for employment elsewhere save by consent of the assembly, which would commonly exact in return the regular payment of his contribution to the collective dues of the community. What he gained with his liberty was—more than all else, perhaps—a sharpened class consciousness, a more vivid sense of the gulf which divided him from the landowner and the bureaucracy, and possibly a heightened capacity also for collective action.

On the eve of emancipation the radical intelligentsia had apparently been prepared for the worst. Their fever of hope had long passed; they had followed with increasing apprehension the landowners' tactics and seen the substance of liberation, already threatened by the principle of peasant purchase, steadily eroded. Even so, the actual terms brought a shock of dismay. The whole temper of the tsar-liberator's offering was all too faithfully reflected for them in the dismissal immediately afterwards of Lanskoy and Miliutin, the Minister of the Interior and his chief assistant, through whose tenacity of purpose the scheme had been saved from ship-wreck. Among the peasantry themselves, only half-comprehending as they were in face of so involved and qualified a statute, there was smouldering discontent, and with it the suspicion that their masters had forged a document in the name of the tsar, the people's protector. The proclamation was followed, as the government had indeed expected, by peasant riots and disturbances in all parts of the land. In the next few months hundreds were suppressed by military force.

The turn of the peasants on the estates of the imperial family came in 1863; that of the state peasants, of which there were about thirty categories, in 1866. Their conditions of tenure had almost always been easier than those of the serfs on private estates, more especially in latter years, and they were now granted correspondingly better terms of land purchase. But for them, too, annual payments represented a great deal more than was consistent with the size of their holdings. Throughout the country peasant arrears accumulated. They were written off in later years, the payments were scaled down, fresh arrears accumulated, and the outstanding redemption debt, after it had been revised so as to permit payments to be continued until 1950, was finally cancelled in the year of revolution 1905. But the whole economic scheme of peasant emancipation had foundered before then.

There were three main reasons for failure. First and foremost, in circumstances of a rapid natural increase in population in the second half of the century, the original halving of the peasant's holding was sheer catastrophe. In the years immediately after 1861 the amount of land worked by a peasant household in European Russia probably averaged between thirty and thirty-five acres; for the individual male in each household the corresponding figure was about eight acres. The size of this holding was hopelessly uneconomic because Russian peasant agriculture was still for the most part as backward as it had been a couple of centuries before, and because the peasant had neither the capital nor the knowledge to improve his methods of cultivation. Capitalist agriculture in the south brought with it here and there a relatively advanced technique and higher yields, but peasant farming itself, still conducted on the strip system, remained stagnant and unproductive. Next, the conservative weight of the commune left little opportunity for individual initiative. The periodical redistribution of land among the village households was by itself an effective brake upon peasant enterprise, which then as now thrived upon a sense of property: it has been all too common an error, indeed, to assume that the Russian peasant lacked a sense of private ownership. And, finally, in the face of increasing peasant numbers, shrinking allotments, growing impoverishment and the emergence of a large landless or almost landless proletariat in the villages, the government lacked both the will and the means to assuage land hunger.

The aggravation of peasant difficulties after 1861, it may be repeated, provides the principal clue to the popular mood in 1917. His allotment of land seldom occupied the peasant for more than two or three days in the week; in many instances the retention by the landowner, in spite of the services of the arbitrator, of all the good pasture and of access to water and woodland, was a source of constant friction; in the most fertile central regions winter brought the recurring threat of starvation. The expansion of industry until the 1880s was still too small and too slow to permit the diversion on any considerable scale of idle labour in the villages to urban centres of manufacture. Yet in order to pay his taxes and to maintain his family the peasant, burdened though he was, frequently had no choice but to acquire more land, however exorbitant the rent, however close to serfdom the conditions under which he acquired it.

For land, up to a point, was available. The landlords who had at last given consent to the liberation of their serfs still retained for the most part half or more of their private estates. Most resumed their habit of life as agricultural squires with free labour. But many of the nobility, having paid off their debts, were well content to abandon farming, lease the remaining part of their estate and go off to live in St Petersburg or Moscow. The peasants' need was often enough a heaven-sent opportunity for them. The law, it should be noted, allowed both the communal lease of further land and the purchase of land by an individual peasant in complete independence of the commune and in full ownership. Here, in the spectacle of the untapped resources of the private estates, was all the evidence which the peasantry required that emancipation was as yet incomplete. The popular belief in a 'second emancipation' persisted in spite of Alexander's continued warnings, and even gained momentum. The belief had not been extinguished in 1917.

Restricted though it was, the personal freedom that the peasant had acquired changed the face of society. The change, when all is said, went not very much deeper than that. The reforms that followed shattered a structure built on semi-feudal law, but much of the old system of peasant-landlord relations survived, and with it the psychology of serfdom. And the mode of village life and the everyday habit of the peasant family at work in the fields, or in the earthen or wooden hut with its brick stove and lamp-lit icon on the wall in which three generations were crowded in what were often the most brutalizing conditions, were not greatly altered. Nevertheless, the formal liberation of the great mass of the population from the arbitrary power of the landowner had uprooted the whole administrative and judicial order of things. Emancipation could not stand alone. It was essential in the first place to fill the empty place left by the squirearchy of Russia with a reconstructed system of local self-government.

On January 13, 1864 the new Zemstvo law was introduced to Russia. It allowed for the creation of elected zemstvos (local councils) at the district and provincial level which, existing side by side with the machinery of central government, assumed responsibility for functions and services hitherto largely ignored by the latter. The councils were empowered to levy a tax for such local requirements as the repair of roads and bridges (hitherto a recognized part of serf obligations) and for poor relief, and to these were soon added elementary schools and public health services. A district zemstvo assembly was elected for three years, met for ten days in the year, chose from among its members a permanent governing board and sent representatives to the provincial zemstvo, which functioned under similar conditions. The scheme was bold and progressive in conception. But in its statutory form it was emasculated by the same forces which had whittled down the terms of emancipation. Though a bias in favour of the propertied classes would have been no more remarkable in Russia than in the west, the original plan of giving equal rights of representation to the peasants, the townspeople and the peasants' former masters was completely scrapped in favour of a system of indirect voting in three separate categories which ensured for the gentry a heavy predominance on the councils.

The work of the zemstvos, which were set up only in European Russia, touched rural conditions of life at many points. It engaged the sincere enthusiasm of men of liberal mind in the provincial wilds. Almost from the first their activities were hedged round by every sort of official obstruction. Towards the end of 1866, when the forces of reaction were firmly enthroned in the capital, the zemstvos' power of taxation was severely circumscribed. Their independence was constantly challenged, not least by the district or provincial marshal of the nobility, who by right presided over their annual meetings. Yet a great deal was accomplished in these circumstances by the more enterprising councils. Primary education, technical aid in farming, hospital and first-aid services were tentatively established with the aid of a paid staff, and, though the effect in most areas was merely to scratch the surface of peasant want and ignorance, a new technique of administration was un-doubtedly being learned during the reign. Official obstruction evoked, too—though motives here, as will be seen, were mixed—a temper of political opposition. It was above all the gentry in the zemstvos who conceived of them as a preliminary stage on the road to constitutional government. The zemstvos were elected; the principle of government at the centre was still an unqualified absolutism. When, in the accepted phrase of the time, 'would the building be crowned?'

In December 1864 came the reform of the law courts. This, in some ways, effected as notable a change as any of the great reforms. To replace the landowner in his function of local magistrate it was necessary to institute new lower courts. But it was no less essential to undertake the task, which for so long had been shelved, of reconstituting the notoriously corrupt and inefficient higher courts. The reform, put into operation in the following year in St Petersburg and Moscow and then extended to other parts of the empire, was closely modelled upon western—chiefly French— practice. It established the independence of the courts and the principle of equal justice for all. Judges were to be irremovable; court proceedings, governed by a strict system of prosecution and defence, were to be held in public; trial by jury was introduced in criminal cases, in which preliminary investigation was taken out of the hands of the police and entrusted to an examining magistrate. In the rural districts justices of the peace were elected by the zemstvo assembly.

That the principle of equality before the law was denied to the peasant population by the special jurisdiction of the commune (or of the canton, a grouping of communes) was always evident. More significant were the prompt encroachments upon the independence of the courts by arbitrary police action. In the climate of repression within a year or two of the enactment of reform administrative justice made steady inroads into the due processes of law, while the reform when it reached outlying areas was drastically reduced in scope. Nevertheless the doctrine of the independence of the courts was henceforth accepted and was often to be vindicated in later years with dramatic effect. A signal result of the reform was the rise in Russia of a legal profession conspicuous for its intellectual and forensic abilities.

Two more reforms remain to be noted, though these were introduced at a time when the original impulse of innovation was wholly spent. One was the reconstitution in 1870, after protracted hesitations, of Catherine the Great's town councils, which had been moribund at birth. Once again, a system of separate voting groups weighted election to the town duma in favour of the largest property-owners. Flagrantly unrepresentative in character, the power of rating withheld from them and their funds drawn largely from voluntary contributions, the town dumas were at best perfunctory in the seventies in promoting education and public health, though they developed rapidly in the next reign. In the largest cities they were headed by a commandant, equal in rank to the governor of a province, who worked in close association with the police authorities.

L

The other reform was of much greater consequence. The conscription law of 1874 followed a series of army reforms in earlier years carried through by an exceptionally able and humane Minister of War, Dmitry Miliutin, a brother of Nicholas Miliutin, the driving force behind emancipation. The law brought Russia into line with European practice in establishing a principle of uniform obligation for military service, which was tempered by an enlightened system of exemptions. The period of service was reduced from the former 'life sentence' of twenty-five years to six in regular service and nine in the reserve; educational qualifications earned a reduction in length of service. Training was revised, the cruellest forms of corporal punishment were abolished and a broad system of army education was established. It has frequently been observed that before 1917 it was chiefly in the army that the Russian peasant learned to read and write.

The compromises of Alexander's early reforms had reduced extreme radical opinion to despair. Plots and conspiracies, though of an amateurish kind, were in the making when revolt once more flared up in Poland in 1863. The immediate occasion was an attempt to put down the Polish secret societies which had been organizing disturbances in Warsaw and elsewhere; the cause—fostered by Polish émigrés—was, as always, the dream of independence and the frontiers of 1772. The war was a guerrilla war, waged on the Polish side by students and the urban middle classes and fought largely in the forests; the peasantry stood aside and were not to be won over to the nationalist cause by promises of land reform. Polish resistance was broken by the Russian army after eighteen months and an era of savage repression and russification followed. Henceforth the very name of Poland was abandoned for the official designation of 'the Vistula provinces'. The Polish peasants were emancipated on terms which paid much less regard to the claims of their Polish masters than the Russian nobility had won three years earlier, but for the rest St Petersburg entered upon a sweeping campaign against every manifestation of Polish nationalist sentiment.

What was specially significant during the Polish insurrection, which stirred no little sympathy in the west, was the sharp division of opinion it evoked between Russian liberals and the radical minority. Leading liberals, caught up in a wave of popular patriotic feeling, turned conservative; radicals who, like Herzen, put the cause of Polish revolt before Russian patriotism, appeared to lose their following overnight. Herzen himself suffered a decline in influence which nothing he did afterwards could arrest. The early secret society of Land and Liberty (*Zemlia i Volia*),* which had attempted

* The phrase was Herzen's own.

to make common cause with the Polish rebels, collapsed ignomini-
ously. Anti-Russian insurrection, it seemed, had only converted
the opposition as a whole to support of conservative Russia.

Yet this was a brief aberration only: the intellectuals of the
1860s were not to be so lightly dismissed. They were a new breed.
The quarrel of westerners and slavophils—the 'idealists of the
forties'—had lost significance for the generation reared in the
heady and emotional atmosphere of student debate in Moscow and
St Petersburg during the years before 1861. In their disillusionment
they had discovered more adventurous horizons. It was to socialist
doctrine—a faith in peasant socialism in Russia and the will to
achieve it by revolution—that they were led by new teachers. The
intelligentsia stood on the threshold of *narodnichestvo*, the cult of
the *narod*, the people.

The Narodniks first spoke to the educated youth of Russia
in the voice of Nicholas Chernyshevsky, the son of a priest, a
revered name in their martyrology of imprisonment in Siberia.
With him are habitually associated the names of Dobroliubov and
Pisarev. As in Belinsky's time, the principal medium of opposition
was still literary criticism, and it was in the 'thick' magazines of
the period that they conducted their disguised propaganda.
Dobroliubov and Pisarev, the one bitter in invective against the
liberals, the other—most of whose critical essays were written in
prison—the type and pattern of revolutionary iconoclasm, both
died young. Pisarev's 'nihilism', projected in the half-prophetic
figure of Bazarov in Turgenev's *Fathers and Sons*, his puritan
materialism ('boots matter more than all your madonnas and all
your cultivated talk of Shakespeare') and his exclusive belief in
the social utility of science worked strongly upon his generation.
But the seminal Narodnik influence, itself largely derived from
Herzen, was Chernyshevsky's. His propagandist novel, *What is
to be Done?* was the bible of the era before Marxism. He saw in the
peasant commune the foundation of an egalitarian order of society
and in the peasant himself the means of achieving it. The 'instinctive
socialism', as Herzen had called it, of the Russian peasant would
enable Russia to pursue a separate path of progress of her own and
so evade the horrors of capitalist development.

The goal was revolution, not reform of a more genuine character
and not constitutional government. In the sixties and afterwards
the plea for a national assembly, whether on the lines of the old
zemsky sobor or on more up-to-date principles, came above all
from those liberal-conservative elements among the nobility who
dreamed of retrieving their former class ascendancy. The true
radicals of the era were content to ask only for full civil liberties
and most of all for freedom of speech and of the press. They were

still at the utopian stage of believing that the common will must prevail, that the socialist ideal could be achieved by 'spontaneous' revolution.

Their propaganda could not fail to stimulate official reaction, which in turn evoked more uncompromising forms of opposition. 'Underground' literature circulated more and more widely. University students, so many of them of the needy kind and with little prospect of finding employment after their own heart, were a natural prey to extreme ideas. Their protests and demonstrations, a portent of the next half-century, were met by police action, by Cossack force, by mass arrests, by expulsion, exile or imprisonment. The terms on which this trial of strength was conducted, including as they did the restoration in 1863 of a large degree of university autonomy, could not remain unchanged. The crisis broke in the capital in April 1866, when a young student named Karakozov fired a revolver in public at Alexander. The shot missed, but its echo reverberated until the last day of the reign. Karakozov, though a member of a revolutionary group, had acted entirely alone. But his attempt precipitated a sweeping campaign against the entire student body. It was signalized by the appointment of the procurator of the Holy Synod, the notorious Dmitry Tolstoy, as Minister of Education, a post he held for the next fourteen years.

The schools and universities experienced a swift change of climate. Discipline became increasingly rigid, closer supervision was exercised through a reconstituted inspectorate. Expulsions multiplied, though disturbances did not cease. The temper of radical opinion in these years was curiously illustrated by the passion of resentment aroused by Dmitry Tolstoy's revision in 1871 of the curriculum of the *gymnasia* (grammar schools)—which alone gave right of entry to the university—in favour of larger doses of Greek and Latin. This was construed, no doubt accurately enough, as an attempt to maintain a class bias in higher education, but even more wounding to the student generation reared on Pisarev was the blow thus aimed at their faith in the natural sciences. Tolstoy made every effort to deprive the zemstvos of control of the primary schools they had set up and failed only because they alone would bear the cost of maintenance. One special aspect of his educational policy deserves notice. Since the universities were closed to women, a considerable number proceeded to Germany and Switzerland to study medicine. They were not merely students of medicine when they were recalled at a critical phase of revolutionary agitation in Russia.

The press and publishing were similarly chastened. The new censorship regulations introduced as a temporary measure a year before Tolstoy took office easily outlasted the new minister himself.

Books were still subject to inspection before publication, but the preliminary censorship of newspapers and periodicals in the two capitals was replaced by a system of punitive censorship. Here was the opportunity for persecution, crippling fines, the imprisonment of editors and outright suppression. The radical magazines, naturally enough, suffered worst.

In spite of all that authority could do to stifle thought and imagination, the reign of Alexander II is lit by a great glow of intellectual, artistic and scientific achievement. The roll-call of great names in the procession of nineteenth-century Russian novelists includes Turgenev, Tolstoy, Dostoevsky, Goncharov, Pisemsky, Saltykov-Shchedrin and Leskov. In poetry, though the golden age was beyond recall, there are the later Tiutchev and Fet, Maikov, Alexis Tolstoy and Nekrasov. Russian science attains sudden and spectacular maturity in the biological studies of Mechnikov, the achievement in chemistry of Mendeleyev, the physiological research of Pavlov. Russian music comes into its own with 'the five'—Balakirev, Cui, Mussorgsky, Borodin and Rimsky-Korsakov —and Tchaikovsky. In history there is the incomparable Kliuchevsky. And always there are the social theorists, the political prophets and teachers, the apostles of revolution.

For there was no power in Russia to command the advancing waves of revolutionary agitation to turn back. The intellectual leaders of the seventies were for the most part exiles from their own land, but exile enabled them to preach revolution all the more persuasively. Though rival doctrines were soon to appear, the gospel of the Narodniks possessed the most generous minds in Russian society. It is customary nowadays to dismiss their agrarian socialism as sentimental and nebulous, but it was they who nurtured the impulse of mass revolution in 1917.

The first of the two shaping influences of the decade was the erudite P. L. Lavrov, a former colonel of artillery, whose *Historical Letters*, in which he urged the need for a long preparation for social revolution, the obligation of the educated class to serve the dark masses and the creative force of the 'critically thinking individual', touched a deep chord in youth. The other was N. K. Mikhailovsky, another 'conscience-stricken noble' (his own phrase) seeking to expiate the sins of serfdom. Zürich, where Lavrov lived in exile and where so many Russian students had congregated, became known in the seventies as the Mecca of Russian youth.

From Michael Bakunin, the pilgrim of insurrection in half the countries of Europe, came a gustier wind of doctrine. The revolution he awaited was one which would establish a free society only by destroying the state and with it religion, property and the family. From Geneva in his *Cause of the People* Bakunin preached revolutionary anarchism and a strategy of local insurrection in Russia. It was a disciple of his, Sergey Nechayev, author of a 'catechism of a revolutionary', who in the exercise of dictatorial power over the small revolutionary groups he had organized forged a classic Russian instrument of conspiracy and terror. From the murder in 1871 of a fellow conspirator on his instructions sprang a developed technique of implicating revolutionary groups or parties in a common guilt.

Though Lavrov was an admirer of Marx and was not unaffected by him, though the echoes of Bakunin's duel with Marx in the First International had reached the intelligentsia and a Russian translation of *Capital*—dynamite which the censor failed to recognize—was published in 1872, Marxism did not in effect appear on the Russian scene until the close of the decade. What gained a hearing for it was the evidence of the growth of a native industrial capitalism. From the first industrial capitalism in Russia was state-aided. Under the direction of Reutern, Finance Minister from 1862 to 1878, financial assistance on a lavish scale was extended to the promoters and contractors of private railway companies. The great era of railway construction came in the closing decade and a half of the century, but between 1866 and 1876 more than ten thousand miles of railway were built. Perhaps it should be added that a large part of the enormous state funds invested was lost in speculators' profits. This railway boom nourished trade, already fostered by a low tariff policy, and quickened the general expansion of industry. The investment of foreign capital—French, British, Belgian and German—was facilitated by an overhaul of the administration of the Russian state bank and by the introduction of private banking institutions.

The Narodnik faith had still to flower into a political movement, but since it gained support from the popular reaction to Russian diplomacy and war in the seventies a brief glance at foreign policy during the reign may be helpful at this stage. Under Gorchakov, the most professional and perhaps the vainest Foreign Minister Russia as yet had had, the first aim of policy was to undo the worst consequences of the treaty which had ended the Crimean War and which had left Russia isolated in Europe. This brought her once more, especially after the Polish rebellion of 1863, into close relations with Bismarck's Prussia and then with Bismarck's Germany.

Her power temporarily halted in the west, Russia continued to advance, following what both before and since has appeared a historic law of alternation, in the east: in the Far East and in central Asia. In the Far East China formally surrendered in 1860 the entire lower course of the Amur and the whole of the right bank of the

Russia and the Balkans

Ussuri where it meets the Amur and stretches to the Pacific. On that southern extremity arose in the following year the port and naval base of Vladivostok (Lord of the East). Far to the north, however, across the Bering straits, a virtually uncolonized and defenceless Alaska was sold to the United States in 1867 for 7,200,000 dollars— a proceeding of no great interest at the time.

Expansion in central Asia was on an even vaster scale than in the Far East. It had little in common with earlier movements of colonization in Russian history. The 'civilizing mission' of the Russian people among the Kazakh nomads of the desert steppe was deliberately extended by war to the frontiers of India and Chinese Turkestan. This was imperial adventure, whatever pretext for war could be found in the raids of the Uzbek, Tadjik and Turcoman peoples inhabiting the historic lands of Tamerlane's empire.

Tashkent was captured in 1865, the fabled city of Samarkand in 1868, and within a few years the incorporation into the Russian empire of the khanates of Khiva, Bokhara and Kokand was completed. It was the all but final victory of the forest over the steppe. But the price was paid in an exacerbation of imperial rivalries and in deepening British hostility to Russian designs elsewhere.

Russia's war with Turkey in 1877 originated in support of Slav nationalist risings in the Balkans. But the diplomatic prelude to war echoed with the entire history of the eastern question. A postscript to the treaty of Paris had been written in 1870, when with Bismarck's support in return for her neutrality in the Franco-German war Russia denounced the clauses barring her warships from the Black Sea. Here was the access of strength which touched off her forward policy in the Balkans. It was a policy backed by both rational and irrational forces. The dream of planting the Cross once more on Santa Sophia—of possessing herself of Constantinople and the Straits—was now prompted by economic interest and the quest for security; protection for Russia's foreign trade embraced not only her constantly rising exports of wheat from Odessa but the heavy industry of the Don basin and the oil of Baku. The dream was also fostered by the extravagances of pan-slav doctrine. It was a protean doctrine, in which blurred distinctions separated the intangible unity of the Orthodox world from a more tangible unity of Slavdom and which with sharpened emphasis laid upon Russia a mission of empire in the Balkans embracing all Slav and Orthodox peoples.

Revolt in Bosnia and Herzegovina in 1875 agitated every cross-current of Balkan politics. The Serbian and Montenegrin declaration of war on Turkey, the stream of Russian volunteers in aid of the Serbs, Serbian failure, crisis in Bulgaria, the Turkish Bulgarian atrocities and the vain efforts by the powers at mediation had brought an inflamed Russian opinion to fever point by the time war was declared in April 1877. Once more the story of Russian muddle and incapacity was repeated: this was Moltke's 'war between the one-eyed and the blind'. But once more also the obedient courage of the Russian soldier was demonstrated in the successive assaults, with appalling casualties, on the Turkish fortress of Plevna, which fell towards the end of the year. In the following January the Russians had advanced from Adrianople to the Sea of Marmora and Constantinople was almost within their grasp. Their hand was stayed only by the presence in the Sea of Marmora of the British fleet.

In what followed the balance of power in Europe was at stake. The treaty of San Stefano between Russia and Turkey, signed in March 1878, completely transformed the map of the Balkans and

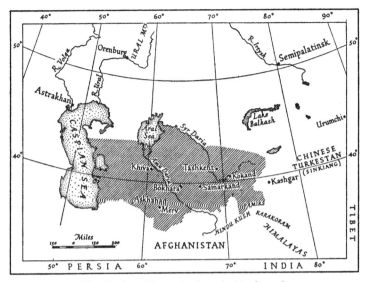

The Russian Advance in Central Asia from the
1860s to the 1890s

left Turkey at Russia's mercy. Among much else, it created, between the Danube and the Aegean, a greater Bulgaria wholly dependent upon Russia and under Russian tutelage. The next and clearly indicated objective was the Straits. But all this was forbidden fruit. Short of war with Britain and Austria in alliance, Russia could not but consent to the re-writing of the treaty, with the aid of Bismarck as honest broker, at the Congress of Berlin in June. The Russian gains were still very considerable, including as they did Batum and the restoration of the part of Bessarabia lost thirty years earlier, but Russia's prestige in the Balkans had slumped, Bulgaria and Serbia had evaded the pan-slav grasp, Turkey was not driven from Europe, and Constantinople and the Straits were as far off as ever. Gorchakov signed the treaty with bitter disappointment. He could not fail to realize the shock in store for Russian nationalist sentiment, though neither he nor anyone else was prepared for the stimulus which it perversely gave to the revolutionary movement.

Narodnik idealism had borne astonishing fruit in 1874 in a naïve and romantic crusade *v narod*—to the people. As though collectively driven by a force of nature, a large company of men and women, perhaps some two thousand in all—students (many of them newly returned from abroad by government order), teachers, repentant nobles, officials—went out in all directions to preach a gospel of revolution to the peasantry. It was an exalted venture of mixed comedy and tragedy, in which the crusaders met only with peasant incomprehension or distrust and were often betrayed to the police when they did not betray themselves. The movement vanished almost without trace, but the lesson had been learned that a coherent programme and a strategy of insurrection were necessary. Three years later a reborn secret organization of *Zemlia i Volia* came into being. The aim of this new and more formidable society of Land and Freedom was social revolution, but its immediate tactics were propaganda and terrorism. Its famous 'administrative section' undertook the provision of forged passports and the like, its no less famous 'disorganizing section' was responsible for assassination and prison raids. The campaign of assassination of high police officials and others—it is studded with historic incidents —and the no less ruthless campaign of government reprisals finally split the revolutionaries. In the summer of 1879 they broke into two groups. One, known as *Cherny Peredel* (Black Partition), whose central figure was Plekhanov, not yet the father of Russian Marxism, made a stand for peaceful and non-political propaganda among the peasants. The other, *Narodnaya Volia* (The People's Will), demanded still more disciplined methods of conspiracy and was pledged to the assassination of the tsar.

In an atmosphere of strange tension, in which popular Russian sympathies, always streaked by a native anarchy of temperament, were closer to the handful of men and women armed with bombs than to those who fought them with powers of administrative arrest, summary trial by court-martial and execution, the underground war drew to a climax. The fanaticism, devotion and ingenuity of the conspirators survived every defeat. Something of true nobility falls on the figures of Alexander Mikhailov, the most resourceful of them all, and the worker Andrey Zheliabov, an intrepid spirit, whose leadership in the plot eventually passed to his mistress Sofia Perovsky, the daughter of a governor-general of St Petersburg. But few of the conspirators failed in desperate heroism. Their leading figures were trapped, but vengeance was taken and spies were shot. Mines which were laid on the railway track failed to explode or blew up the train which preceded the imperial train. A conspirator obtained employment in the Winter Palace in St Petersburg, for weeks smuggled in small sticks of dynamite and blew up the dining-room, with dreadful loss of life, only just too soon to achieve his purpose—the emperor had been delayed by a guest. It was after this episode in February 1880 that the Third Section was incorporated in the police department of the Ministry of the Interior. This was the work of the new 'dictator', a trusted servant of the state of vaguely liberal reputation, General Loris-Melikov, who had been called in as head of a supreme commission to effect desperate remedies. Dmitry Tolstoy was dismissed, the press censorship moderated, and overtures were made to the zemstvos to assist in creating a more hopeful order of things.

This 'dictatorship of the heart' concluded, Loris-Melikov as Minister of the Interior drew up a project for associating elected representatives with the tasks of legislation. It was not a constitution that he thus proposed, not a scheme of representative government, though the method of imperial consultation with an elected body which he favoured might well have served as an approach to it. But on March 1/13, 1881, the very day on which Alexander had appended his signature to the project, the People's Will struck again. Its principal leaders were dead or under arrest, but there was a surviving remnant to throw two bombs at the tsar-liberator on the way back from a military parade in the capital. The second of the two bombs did its appointed work.

CHAPTER XV

RETURN TO THE PAST

IT SHOULD NOT have been difficult to forecast with some accuracy the effect of the assassination of Alexander II. The emotional shock was profound. For the vast majority of the nation, perhaps in some degree for all but the terrorists themselves, something of sacrosanctity still clung to the person of the throne. Conservative Russia was aghast. But liberal opinion, too, shared no less sincerely in the expression of horror at the deed and hastened to dissociate itself from any suspicion of sympathy with the revolutionary cause. The peasantry, whatever admiration they may have felt for terrorist daring at the expense of police officials, mourned the death of their 'little father'. During the next few years only a handful of revolutionaries of a new type, who for their own part had abjured terror, preserved an untarnished image of the heroism and sacrifice of the People's Will.

As always at the beginning of a new reign, much seemed to depend upon the personal disposition of the sovereign. For the thinking part of the population, convinced in spite of the need for stern measures that a policy of conciliation had still to be sought, the omens were far from favourable. In his middle thirties, of powerful physique, simple in habit and of strongly marked domestic tastes, Alexander III was all of a piece in the strength of his conservatism. Unlike his father, in whose reign he had always thrown his weight against reform, he was a formidable character, narrow but clear in mind and capable of a brutal directness of speech. The immediate question was whether, in filial piety—which his father's murder had in no way shaken—the new sovereign would accept as an obligation the plan of legislative reform which Alexander II had endorsed.

The question was soon answered. Though he had been taught history by Soloviev, a conservative but humane scholar, his chief tutor had been Constantine Pobedonostsev. And Pobedonostsev's philosophy of authoritarian reaction was the principal ideological influence upon the throne for the whole of the reign—and for the formative part of the next and last reign. A former professor of civil law in Moscow University, translator of Thomas à Kempis, appointed procurator of the Holy Synod in 1880, his was a strange mind, brilliantly gifted but steeped in a cold, hard bigotry, its integrity subtly qualified by a vein of studied flattery. The mainspring of his pessimistic thought was distrust of the west, of liberal institutions and ideas, of parliaments and civil liberties. Against these dangerous seductions he set the divine principle of Russian autocracy and the devotion to the throne of the Orthodox Russian peasantry. This was Uvarov's doctrine of Orthodoxy, autocracy and nationality in new and more sinister dress.

It was Pobedonostsev who drafted the accession manifesto, in which Alexander proclaimed his faith in 'the power and right of autocracy'. The temper of government from now onwards was not in doubt, though as yet the wind was tempered to liberal and quasi-liberal ministers. Loris-Melikov, his project abandoned, and Miliutin and another minister resigned; Ignatiev, the former's successor, made a bid for conciliation on even more modest lines and similarly fell. Not only a new temper but a new policy could henceforth be distinguished. The purpose of the regime was to put the clock back. Since reform had ended in treason, the time had come to undo reform, at least as far as possible, and to return in spirit to the years before 1861. It was this nostalgia for the *ancien régime* which shaped the alliance between autocracy and the nobility. Together with the forward drive of industrial capitalism in Russia it constituted the principal source of policy in the reign.

No marriage of forces could have been more tempting than that between the crown and the nobility, and none could have been less realistic. For although the revolutionaries, who had dreamed of terrorizing the government into surrender, had gained nothing, this reversal to the order of Catherine the Great was suicidal for both parties. It could not fail to dig deeper springs of popular revolution than those Pugachev had tapped. There was little difficulty in wiping out the last traces of the terrorist organization, a task confidently executed by Viacheslav Plehve, the chief of police; execution and *katorga* in Siberia completely shattered the revolutionary movement for the time being. And there was fairly general support for the emergency decree of August 1881, which enabled the ordinary machinery of law to be suspended in any province in favour of one of three types of administrative security, ascending in order of severity to martial law. Yet the fact remains that between 1881 and 1905 there were few parts of Russia where one or other of these types of emergency regulation was not in force. Even Alexander's iron hand, moreover, did not stay terrorist plots against him. Among those who suffered execution in 1887 as the result of one such plot was Alexander Ulianov, whose younger brother assumed the name of Lenin.

Repression left room for a policy of controlled economic concessions to the peasantry. Their numbers rose from fifty million in 1860 to seventy-nine million in 1897, and in the interval the average size of holdings was steadily shrinking. The peasantry contributed about five-sixths of the state revenue in indirect taxation and poll-tax. A class of relatively prosperous peasants, it is true, grew more prosperous through the purchase of land* and the exploitation of hired labour, but for the less fortunate either no extra land was available for renting or the burden of rent was crippling. To crown all difficulties, harvests throughout the eighties were bad, though it was only in the early years of the next decade that famine conditions developed.

Attempts to remedy a constantly deteriorating state of affairs were put in hand by the new Finance Minister, the able and methodical Bunge. Redemption of holdings was made obligatory in 1882 and redemption payments were reduced in the same year. Two years later a Peasants' Bank was established to assist peasants to buy more land on credit. It appeared at first to be of limited use, since the original funds at its disposal were small and the terms of repayment beyond the capacity of all but the richer peasants. But it did in fact assist peasant land purchase on an increasing scale. In 1886 the poll-tax, which now represented a declining part of the revenue, was abolished. A year later Bunge was dismissed from office.

He had given aid not only to peasant agriculture. In 1885, after

* Of the total amount of land sold privately by the landowners between 1861 and 1905 by far the greater part went to buyers from the towns.

a note of alarm had been sounded at the operations of the Peasants' Bank, a Nobles' Land Bank was founded with the object of enabling harassed or improvident members of the nobility to retain their estates for the benefit of generations of nobility to come. The credit terms offered were generous, and the number of estates thus mortgaged to the state grew rapidly in succeeding years. This was a notable means of cementing the alliance of crown and nobility.

Not agriculture, however, but the expansion of industry held the chief place in the economic preoccupations of the government. From now onwards direct state investment was liberally supplemented by a policy of loans and subsidies and of concessions and special privileges to foreign capital. Except for heavy machinery, which Russia was as yet unable to produce, a mounting tariff protected the growth of native industry. The directing force behind railway construction in the later years of the reign was Sergius Witte, who from local stationmaster had risen to be Minister of Communications and who in 1892 was appointed Minister of Finance. Coarse and astute, immensely energetic, a clear-headed and resourceful opportunist in politics, Witte's most impressive achievements belong to the next reign. But it was he who carried through the building of the Trans-Siberian railway, begun in 1891, by laying a track from Cheliabinsk, already linked to Moscow, to the Pacific.

There are two aspects of the development of industry during these years that merit special notice. One was the virtual abandonment, after Bunge's dismissal on suspicion of 'socialist' leanings, of the rudimentary factory legislation which he had introduced in the textile industries and elsewhere. The centres of Russian manufacture were belatedly experiencing all those commonplace evils of an industrial revolution which western Europe had largely outgrown: wages paid perhaps twice a year, a system of truck, the all but total absence of living accommodation for factory workers and dangerously insanitary conditions of labour. In the textile industries in particular Bunge had established a system of factory inspection and had attempted to reduce hours and improve conditions of employment for women and children. But with his departure from office almost all regulations were ignored. It was not, in fact, until the next reign that a maximum working day of eleven and a half hours for adult males was established.

Even more significant was the peculiar concentration of industry in an otherwise backward agricultural country. It has been calculated that from 1881 to 1893, when the total number of factories in Russia declined by almost a quarter, the number of factory workers all but doubled, reaching a figure of nearly one and a half million. Concentrated in a relatively small number of giant plants—

metallurgy in St Petersburg and in half a dozen centres in the south, textiles in St Petersburg, Moscow and Lodz, oil in Baku, naval construction and merchant shipping in the Black Sea ports, the new industrial proletariat grew conscious of its potential strength. In St Petersburg above all, precisely because conditions on the whole were better there than elsewhere owing to the shortage of labour in the surrounding countryside, the opportunities for some form of workers' organization grew more favourable from year to year.

Throughout the reign political repression grew in severity. Pobedonostsev's influence had been capped by the return of Dmitry Tolstoy, this time to the Ministry of the Interior, where he remained until his death in 1889. Once more the tsar's government commanded the tide to turn back. In 1884 the last vestiges of university autonomy were abolished and rectors, deans of faculties and the holders of the principal chairs were henceforth appointed by the minister. The struggle to take over control of the zemstvo schools was renewed. The press was tied and gagged by a system of ministerial warnings, by restrictions on sale in the street, restrictions on advertisement and a ban on the employment of the politically suspect. And the policy of russification was stretched to the extreme of persecution of national and religious minorities.

It was only now, indeed, that its full rigours were felt in Poland. From there it was extended to the historic enclaves of Polish sentiment in the Ukraine and to the Ukrainians themselves, among whom a cultural separatism had begun to acquire a nationalist colouring. For the first time, too, the autonomous institutions of Finland came under direct attack. In the Caucasus the Armenians suffered the worst discrimination. The religious minorities subjected to ruthless pressure included the Stundists (who had affinities with the Baptist Church) and other Russian dissenting sects, the Lutherans in the Baltic states, the Moslems in Transcaucasia, the semi-Tolstoyan Dukhobors (fighters of the spirit), who refused military service. The harshest persecution of all was aimed at the Jews. The Jewish pale of settlement in Russia, a legacy of the partitions of Poland, was still further restricted, Jewish peasants were driven from their commune and simultaneously forbidden to acquire land, and their entry to the grammar school and university and to the professions, already beset by many forms of discrimination, was regulated by quota restrictions. An official antisemitism, plainly revealed in the connivance of the police in the pogroms which followed the assassination of Alexander II, gained momentum in Russia until 1917, and has perhaps not yet been wholly spent.

No single act of government during the reign stirred more

passionate resentment than the law of 1889 which established land captains (*zemskie nachalniki*) in the rural districts. For all practical purposes, this was a restoration of the arbitrary power over the life and affairs of the peasantry which had formerly been exercised by the landowner under serfdom. It seemed to bring back the breath and being of serf law. Under the guise of countering peasant disorder, the land captains, who were generally chosen from members of the minor nobility and who took their instructions directly from the Ministry of the Interior, were given wide authority in the whole field of local administration and at the same time were installed in the place of the locally elected justices of the peace. This all too often implied a return to the judicial despotism of an earlier day.

Only a degree less bitter was the feeling aroused in the following year by the introduction of a new zemstvo law. The system of indirect election, already flagrantly inequitable, was now drastically modified to ensure an absolute majority for the representatives of the gentry, and zemstvo activities were curbed in all directions. The provincial governor was given an absolute right of veto over all new proposals. The effects of the new law, which sprang from blind suspicion of all local initiative, were tragically evident in the years of famine and epidemic in 1891 and 1892, when measures of relief by the zemstvo authorities in the stricken provinces were obstructed at every turn, regardless of the cost in death and suffering, by a government which was itself incapable of organizing assistance.

Repression, together with the pervasive influence of Leo Tolstoy's doctrine of non-resistance, had taken its toll of the revolutionary movement within Russia, where it began to revive only in the closing years of the reign. But the exiles abroad had not been idle. The old controversy between westerners and slavophils was revived in a new form. Was the belief in a unique Russian path of development still tenable? Russian Marxism originated in the studies of Plekhanov, who in 1883 founded in Geneva a group known as *Osvobozhdenie Truda* (Liberation of Labour), which gave a fresh and 'scientific' orientation to socialist dreams at home. For Plekhanov the Narodnik faith in a socialist system of society based upon the peasant commune was a chimera because Russia, in his view, must inevitably pass through an advanced stage of industrial capitalism. She could not but tread the same road of economic development as Europe. The social revolution would be created not by a backward peasantry but by the industrial proletariat; not terror but political struggle was the means to this end. Here, eventually, was the guiding light of a new generation of Russian revolutionaries.

It remains to indicate the principal aspect of foreign policy during the period. The conflict of interest with Britain in central Asia was renewed by Russian pressure on the Afghanistan frontier and once more brought the prospect of war very near. At the same time the Russian position as mentor and guardian of the Balkan Slavs was strained by Bulgaria's assertion of a will of her own. But these developments were both subsidiary to the substitution of France for Germany as Russia's ally in Europe. This was, in effect, a turning point in Russian foreign relations and in the balance of European power. Although a German-Russian 'reinsurance treaty' had been concluded in 1887, the memory of Bismarck's part in the Congress of Berlin still rankled in St Petersburg, and a tariff war with Germany was fought with little ceremony. In 1890, after Bismarck had been dismissed, the reinsurance treaty was permitted to lapse. It was the alliance with Austria on which Germany after Bismarck set most store, though for another fifteen years she continued to court Russia's favour also. The road to the latter's new alliance was paved with French loans. Secret negotiations were set on foot in the summer of 1891 and were supplemented by a military agreement next year; the terms of the treaty of alliance —a secret, though in broad outline an open one, until 1918— were finally ratified in December 1894.

Alexander III had died on the previous November 1, exhausted by the ordeal of sustaining the full weight of Russian autocracy in what was virtually protective custody in his own palaces.

CHAPTER XVI

REAPING THE WHIRLWIND

THE HINDSIGHT OF history is a distorting mirror, but nemesis visibly stalks the twenty-three years of the reign of the last of the Romanov tsars. Neither for this nor for any other period of the past will a determinist reading of history satisfy the imagination. But the workings of fate are most strangely illustrated in the reign of Nicholas II by the momentum of events. From beginning to end the pattern of these agitated and ghost-ridden years is shaped

M

by the accelerating rhythm with which fortuitous and unrelated happenings converge upon a single current of affairs. The principle of autocracy he had inherited was for Nicholas II an inviolable trust. Through every mischance or portent of crisis his first rule of conduct was to preserve it. The fateful thing above all others was that no man was by character less fitted to assume the obligations of autocrat of all the Russias. Nicholas shared his father's tastes, his father's exemplary family devotions; though of still narrower intelligence, he had the Romanov charm in an exceptional degree—even those he used worst always remembered it. But where as a ruler Alexander III was all strength of purpose his son was all weakness. Nicholas was incapable, except in the perverse obstinacy of the weak, of a mind or will of his own. This made him as autocrat at once unteachable and treacherous, particularly in his dealings with his ministers. In his pathetic ineffectualness, as Trotsky noted with virulent and somewhat vulgar wit, he recalls Louis XVI; in his duplicity and obstinacy, as in the ingratitude with which he cast off those who might have saved him and set himself instead to digging his own grave, the likeness with Charles I is unmistakable. And in the empress Alexandra, who had been Princess Alix of Hesse-Darmstadt, granddaughter of Queen Victoria, a resemblance to both Henrietta Maria and Marie Antoinette is no less striking. More than anybody else it was emperor and empress who brought with ruin to themselves a scourge of revolution to the Russian people more calamitous in suffering than any other in history.

Though in 1905 Nicholas was driven by the extremity of events to confer a semi-parliamentary constitution upon Russia, at no time between his accession and abdication was he prepared to concede that his autocratic prerogatives could be in any way diminished. A loyal address on the occasion of his marriage at the outset of the reign from the liberal zemstvo of Tver presumed to speak of the hope that 'the voice of the people would be heard'. Under Pobedonostsev's tuition Nicholas in reply affirmed his inflexible resolve to rule as autocrat and swept aside all 'senseless dreams' that the zemstvos would be permitted to engage in the administration of state affairs. From that height of personal absolutism he never looked back, even after he had ostensibly yielded to the voice of the people.

Between his accession and the revolution of 1905 each of the constituent elements of Russian society had its own distinctive preoccupation. For the peasants, or for the vast majority among them, it was land hunger. Precisely how far the differentiation between rich, middling and poor peasants had gone by this time it is hard to discover; but of the ever more intense pressure upon the masses of rural over-population there is no question. Russia owed an increasing agricultural production to the higher technical level of farming on the large estates, not to the peasant allotments, where the wooden plough still predominated. But peasant yields, small though they were, contributed to the huge exports of grain with which Russia paid for her foreign loans. If the peasant regularly sold part of his harvest, it was seldom because it was surplus to the needs of the household but because there were taxes to be paid, because he had accumulated debts and arrears of redemption dues and because the price of the barest manufactured necessities was inflated by high tariffs and was otherwise beyond his means. Without an increase in the size of their holdings the majority were condemned to sharpening want. And yet there could be no such increase while great estates remained in private hands. It was in these conditions that migration to the empty lands of Siberia, hitherto illegal, was sanctioned in the nineties. The scale of transfer, however, could never keep pace with the rise in population.

At the summit of the economic structure of society was a new class of industrialists and entrepreneurs growing steadily in numbers. With the adoption of the gold standard in 1897 Witte's policy of attracting investment capital from the west was powerfully strengthened. The proportion of foreign to Russian investment was particularly high in the metal, engineering and oil industries. There was a small sector of industry which was relatively enlightened in self-interest, but it was of negligible weight on the side of political moderation.

The court, often active in the formulation of economic policy, and higher officialdom were both deeply involved in the financial speculation of these years. Nicholas was always vulnerable to the intrigues of members of the numerous imperial family, who enveloped the court in an atmosphere of chicanery and corruption. It was they who bore heavy responsibility for the war with Japan in 1904. As for the bureaucracy as a whole, its strongest instinct was inertia. There were energetic officials at the centre among a legion of the inert, but all too often it was the highly-placed local functionary who stood in the way of zemstvo or town duma plans of local development. Among the liberal or liberal-conservative zemstvo leaders were men of conspicuous ability. Together with those professionally engaged in the zemstvo service as doctors, agricultural experts, statisticians and the like, they vainly attempted to form a mediating influence between official reaction and the potential forces of revolution.

The chief underground opposition to the regime came from the Socialist-Revolutionary Party, the heirs of the Narodnik tradition.

Formed as a secret political party during 1900–2, they stood for the common ownership of all the land, which was to be distributed on 'just' principles, though not as private property, among the peasants, and for a federal state structure based on the right of self-determination of all the national minorities. They advocated terror as an integral function of propaganda and possessed a special 'fighting organization' to direct it. The mode of existence of these conspirators of the underground was a melodrama of disguise and false identity, of pursuit and retribution, of police provocation and double-dealing. Yevno Azev, for years the head of the Socialist-Revolutionary fighting organization and the planner-in-chief of its boldest outrages, was also a paid police spy and informer, and which was uppermost in him it is to this day impossible to tell.

Though they were essentially spokesmen for the peasantry, the Socialist-Revolutionaries could expect little organized support in the villages of Russia. They had their active following in the towns and particularly among university students. They maintained close links with revolutionary groups among the national minorities—Jews, Poles, Finns, the Baltic, Caucasian and other peoples. But among the intelligentsia in the larger cities and the better educated workers in the factories illegal Marxist groups, who shared the perils of the underground, were gaining in strength. Under the pseudonym of Lenin (the adoption of a pseudonym was a common revolutionary practice for purposes of protection), Vladimir Ulianov, born in 1870, the son of an inspector of schools who had risen to a minor rank of nobility, had been prominent in a Marxist group in St Petersburg in 1895, and had been sentenced for his propagandist activities to a term of three years' exile in Siberia. His was only one of many small bodies engaged in Marxist study and agitation in different parts of Russia. In February 1898 a handful of representatives of various such groups met in Minsk and formed the Russian Social-Democratic Labour Party. Though the delegates promptly fell into the hands of the police and the party itself was for the next five years reduced to an illusory existence in Russia itself, this marks the formal beginning of the organized movement from which Bolshevism emerged.

The niceties of scholastic disputation between the various Russian Marxist schools and sects, though they bore directly on practical issues of revolutionary ends and means, do not belong to this narrative of events. Personal differences played their part in a vehement and habitually offensive style of controversy, but the central divergence of opinion was always on questions of organization and strategy. For all but a short fraction of the period from the beginning of the century until 1917 the principal Social-Democratic leaders were in exile. In 1901 copies of a Marxist journal, *Iskra* (*The Spark*), directed chiefly by Plekhanov, Lenin and Julius Martov, which was originally published in Munich, began to reach Russia by underground means. In the following year Lenin published a pamphlet under the title (taken from Chernyshevsky) of *What is to be Done?* which sign-posted a road to proletarian revolution. In it he urged the formation of a compact and strongly centralized party, membership of which should be strictly confined to active revolutionaries.

It was chiefly on this proposal of restricting membership of the party to a dedicated and professional body of revolutionaries that the Russian Social-Democratic movement was split at its congress, interrupted by the police in Brussels and resumed in London, in the summer of 1903. What was involved in the character of the membership was the entire strategy of victory. For Lenin, as for those who similarly laid claim to the authority of Marx but nevertheless rejected the proposal, there were necessarily two distinct phases of revolution. The first phase, in a country in which capitalism was not yet fully developed, could only produce a 'bourgeois-democratic' regime. The question at issue was by what means, and after how long an interval, the transition from bourgeois democracy to proletarian revolution could be made. There was no way to proletarian victory, Lenin argued, other than by ensuring that leadership in the bourgeois revolution was retained by a disciplined vanguard of the industrial proletariat. The immediate function of the party was thus to foster the revolutionary class consciousness of the workers in alliance with the poorer peasantry. Only a party of professional agitators and organizers, in fact, could guide the second phase of revolution from bourgeois democracy, through the dictatorship of the proletariat, to a socialist order of society.

Lenin's opponents accepted only part of this analysis and prescription. They doubted the wisdom of rejecting all aid from radical and socialist sympathizers; they entertained no hope of revolutionary support from the peasantry, who by Marxist definition were petty-bourgeois; and, most of all, they had grave doubts about the length of time, left unspecified by Lenin, which would be required to transform a bourgeois revolution into a socialist revolution. Perhaps the majority were in doubt also about the dictatorship of the proletariat as an instrument of socialism. The opposition was not united; the young L. D. Bronstein, for instance, whose revolutionary pseudonym was Trotsky, condemned the proposed party organization as too narrow but was at no great distance from Lenin in expounding the notion of an accelerating pace of revolutionary transition—a doctrine which two years later developed into the theory of permanent revolution. A vote taken on the specific issue of the editorial policy of *Iskra* formally determined a great historic issue. The majority (*bolshinstvo*) sided with Lenin, and took the name of Bolsheviks, the minority (*menshinstvo*) of Mensheviks: both rather ridiculous names for movements which have made so much history. It is an oddly ironic circumstance that the majority was only temporary and that, the voting being reversed shortly afterwards, *Iskra* fell to the opposing camp. But the factions had been formed and the momentous rift between them grew into a devouring abyss.

Echoes of the earliest of these disputes reached Russia at a time of agrarian riots, industrial slump, sharpened reaction and renewed terrorism—and of a fantastic venture in 'police socialism'. Strikes, like labour unions, were forbidden, but from the early nineties they had grown more frequent in the two capitals and in the industrial regions of the south. Increasingly, too, they were characterized by political demands. The idea of organizing 'illegal' unions under police protection in order to divert the strike movement to purely economic ends originated in the mind of Sergey Zubatov, chief of the *Okhrana* (security department) of the Moscow police. There could be no clearer indication of the arbitrariness of the Russian police system or of its power of inspired miscalculation. The Zubatov experiment did in fact procure some gains for textile and metallurgical workers, but it was abandoned after his agents had been responsible for a wave of strikes in Odessa, Baku and other centres in the south in the summer of 1903 in which the leadership had passed to revolutionary elements.

By that time Socialist-Revolutionary terrorists had numbered among their victims the Minister of Education and the Minister of the Interior. Into the latter post stepped Plehve, who had liquidated the remnants of the People's Will. Strikes, peasant riots and student demonstrations were punished by flogging and imprisonment, and spies and informers abounded everywhere. The hand of the police was heaviest, much to the emperor's satisfaction—Nicholas was rabidly anti-semitic—on the Jews. It was the Ministry of the Interior which instigated the hideous pogrom of the Jewish population of Kishinev, in Bessarabia, and it was in a department of the ministry that the *Protocols of the Elders of Zion* were forged. Even the most extreme of Plehve's measures, however, did not by themselves promise a return to order. What was required, in his view, in order to remove the menace of revolution was 'a successful little war'.

The war with Japan sprang from the policy of expansion in the Far East which Nicholas inherited with much else from the previous reign. But it was directly provoked by more adventitious aids. The far-fetched ambitions of empire in which Nicholas was encouraged during his travels as heir to the throne in 1890–91, when he laid the foundation-stone of the terminus of the Trans-Siberian railway at Vladivostok (and also narrowly escaped death at the hands of a member of a Japanese secret society), turned to licence for the most reckless greed. In pursuit of the wealth of China ventures in Manchuria were supplemented by a forward policy in Korea. The Russian guards who protected the Chinese Eastern railway running through northern Manchuria to the coast— a concession wrested from the Chinese in 1896—soon constituted an army; the lease from the Chinese of Port Arthur in the south was similarly translated into virtual annexation after the Boxer rebellion in 1900; and Japanese penetration of Korea was countered, first, by diplomatic pressure, next by the grant of timber concessions on the Yalu to a clique of grand-ducal associates, finally by undisguised political adventure. In these affairs Nicholas chose to exercise sovereign rights of policy-making. His Foreign Minister was generally left in ignorance of each new forward move in the Far East; Japanese proposals for a division of spoils were slighted, compromise agreements repeatedly evaded; and Witte who, commercial empire-builder though he was, read the danger signals, was dismissed from office in August 1903. The Japanese had been very patient before they embarked upon war without a formal declaration in the following February.

On the Russian side, a faint stir of popular enthusiasm soon died down and a facile confidence at the highest official level was soon dissipated. The Russian disasters piled up: defeat on the Yalu, the siege and then the surrender of Port Arthur, retreat after the slaughter at Mukden, the annihilation of the Baltic fleet (which had very nearly precipitated war with Britain in the famous Dogger Bank incident, when Russian vessels fired on English fishing boats in the belief that they were Japanese warships), at the end of a round-the-world voyage, in the straits of Tsushima. Only Japanese exhaustion after so considerable an effort and anxiety in face of the signs of Russian recovery gave American mediation its opportunity. The treaty of Portsmouth (New Hampshire), signed on August 29, 1905, ceded Korea to Japan as a sphere of influence together with the southern half of the island of Sakhalin, but otherwise Russia lost little more than the southern Manchurian peninsula with the ice-free facilities of Port Arthur at its tip.

Long before hostilities were ended Russia had been gripped by revolution. The scale and the strength of this challenge in 1905 to the whole order of state went beyond even revolutionary hopes at the time. It had mixed origins, bourgeois, proletarian and peasant. The hated Plehve had been struck down by a bomb in July 1904, and his successor, a bureaucrat of more accommodating temper named Sviatopolk-Mirsky, had set himself the task of winning the support of the moderates among the zemstvo representatives. The latter's meeting in Moscow in November 1904, in the midst of catastrophic news from the war front, kindled a torch for every professional group in the country. Everywhere the demand arose at banquets and conferences for freedom of speech and assembly, agrarian reform, new industrial legislation and, most of all, for an elected national assembly.

It was not the spate of liberal resolutions which touched off the revolution, however, but Bloody Sunday, January 9/22, 1905, when the priest Gapon, a histrionic and ambiguous figure who had been associated with Zubatov's experiment in police socialism, led a vast crowd to the Winter Palace in St Petersburg to lay their humble requests before the tsar in person. The plan was dangerous and was recognized as such, for among the processions carrying icons and singing the national anthem were almost certainly some with less innocent intent. Military precautions had been taken in the capital, but the authorities nevertheless panicked. In circumstances of cold-blooded brutality the separate processions were dispersed by fire as they approached the centre of the city. The number of casualties is not known, but there were possibly as many as a thousand.

In the revulsion that followed all the forces of opposition were temporarily united and the established order of authority was turned upside.down. Amid demonstrations and riots, amid a prolonged turmoil of strikes, terrorism and mutinies which culminated in a general strike and the open challenge to the government of the newly formed St Petersburg soviet, autocracy sounded the retreat. In one respect at least the decisive factor was the peasantry. It was the violence of peasant risings and the methodical seizure of the private estates in the autumn months of 1905 which turned the scale, shattering the confidence of the bureaucracy in their power to restore order without making political concessions and winning from the emperor the reluctant promise of an imperial duma or parliament. Not the industrial proletariat—certainly not the middle-class liberals—but the peasants forced the hands of the regime and in so doing brought the beginnings of constitutional government to Russia.

The immediate course of events after Bloody Sunday was marked by the dismissal of Sviatopolk-Mirsky, a great rash of strikes, the assassination of the grand-duke Sergey, governor-general of Moscow, and an evasive pledge by the emperor in March to consult with elected representatives of the nation. This was the signal for a renewed orgy of conferences, the formation in May of a union of professional unions under the leadership of the historian Paul

Miliukov, the mutiny next month of the crew of the battleship
Potemkin of the Black Sea fleet and a growing temper of mutiny
among the troops in the Far Eastern rear. On August 19 proposals
were published for a heavily class-weighted system of election to
an imperial duma with purely consultative functions; they met
with open derision. On August 29 peace was concluded with
Japan, and Witte, who had conducted the Russian negotiations with
great adroitness, proceeded to return home. He arrived at a time
when rural Russia had burst into flame. The peasants had taken
the law into their own hands. If the industrial workers represented
the most active revolutionary force, it was the peasantry who inspired the greatest fear.

There was, to begin with, a curious and almost uniform orderli-
ness in the methods adopted by the peasants to possess themselves
of the local landowner's estate. He was driven from his manor
house but was otherwise unmolested, grain and livestock were
distributed among the members of the village assembly and the
land was formally transferred to the commune for partition in the
spring. But this relatively peaceful terror soon turned in many
areas to methodical arson and brigandage, and appalling cruelties
were committed as 'the red cock crowed' on great manor houses
and police headquarters. Peasant hatreds were given free rein, and
the worst horrors, particularly in the Baltic provinces, occurred
after the terror had already had its political effect. For it was not
a parliament that the peasants looked for but the distribution
among themselves of the private estates.

The revolution itself ended in defeat. It reached its climax in
October in a general strike in St Petersburg and a nation-wide
strike on the railways and among other groups of workers for
which the active revolutionary elements were themselves wholly
unprepared. Within a few days the affairs of the country were
almost at a standstill. It was amid the general breakdown that on
October 26 a soviet (council) of workers' deputies, originally consisting of some thirty or so elected representatives of strike committees led by picked members of the revolutionary parties, was
improvised in the capital. Similar soviets were formed soon afterwards in other cities. The St Petersburg soviet, predominantly
Menshevik in complexion, with the semi-Menshevik Trotsky as its
most dynamic personality, immediately assumed the character of
an organized revolutionary authority. In the popular influence it
exerted, indeed, it bore the likeness of a rival power of government.
Its immediate revolutionary tactic was to press the demand for a
constituent assembly.

The crisis in the capital lasted four days, during which the man
of destiny near the throne was Witte. He had never doubted that

autocracy was better suited than any other principle of government to the vast, disparate and backward empire, but in the climate of universal hostility to the regime which had been created by the emperor's total incapacity the sole alternative, in his view, to a military dictatorship to put down sedition was a representative system. On October 17/30 an imperial manifesto was issued which, while proclaiming the inviolability of the principle of autocracy, announced the summoning in the near future of a legislative duma elected by popular franchise. All new laws would require the consent of the duma. The government would be reconstituted as a council of ministers headed by a chairman in the virtual capacity of Prime Minister—a post to which Witte was appointed a few days later. In the meantime full civil liberties were granted to all.

The manifesto was shrewdly devised. It succeeded in its primary aim of drawing away the liberals and moderates of every shade from support of the revolutionaries to the side of an apparently chastened and yielding government. Though liberal hopes had outdistanced this pledge of a qualified constitutionalism, in default of a constituent assembly the gain seemed real enough. For the majority it was indeed victory. For the vanguard of revolution it was defeat; the tactical alliance with the bourgeois parties thus broken, the socialist groups were no longer the spearhead of a developing bourgeois revolution. Witte sought to press home his advantage by inviting the active collaboration of the liberals. In face of their refusal he fell back upon the normal procedure of bureaucratic government.

Failure though it was, the revolution of 1905 was described by Lenin years afterwards as the 'general rehearsal'. It marks in effect the close of the era of autocracy. For in spite of all restraints upon the legislative power of the duma, in spite of the restrictions and the eventual drastic manipulation of the franchise on the one hand, of the reserved powers of the crown and the technique of emergency legislation on the other, a principle of representative government had been conceded which could not afterwards be completely revoked. The significance of the transformation was not lost upon either revolutionaries or reactionaries. The Social-Democrats would not as yet confess themselves beaten. Amid continued strikes, riots and mutinies, the St Petersburg soviet engaged in a renewed trial of strength, but its call for a second general strike met with a notably weaker response. And for their part the Union of the Russian People, a newly formed league of extreme and viciously anti-semitic conservatives, who were supplied with ample funds and who commanded the services of criminal 'black hundred' gangs, rallied to the side of autocracy.

Though visibly weakened, the St Petersburg soviet, which had begun to issue arms secretly to its supporters, had still to be disposed of. During the weeks that followed the publication of the manifesto it was widely asked whether Khrustalev (its titular leader) would arrest Witte or Witte arrest Khrustalev. The government struck in the middle of December and was able to arrest the great majority of the members of the soviet; an attempted third general strike and scattered risings by way of reply petered out in confusion. The end came a fortnight later, not in St Petersburg but in Moscow, where a soviet had been formed on December 5 and where the barricades went up in the workers' quarter in response to the summons from Lenin, who had returned in haste to Russia. The armed insurrection there, a desperate venture by a couple of thousand men, lasted for an entire week and was finally suppressed by artillery fire. It had cost in all more than a thousand lives.

The insurrection finally severed all links between the revolutionary parties and the liberal opposition. Its suppression was a signal for the restoration of law and order throughout the empire. Punitive expeditions executed methodical vengeance in the countryside, sedition in the urban and industrial centres was countered by sentences of death and imprisonment. The harshest phase of repression was still to come, but, having regained confidence, the government set to work to harry the political parties in the approaching campaign of election to the duma. There were four main bodies of opinion. In the centre were the Constitutional Democrats (Cadets), who were led by Miliukov and whose programme of winning a more substantial form of parliamentary government ran to measures of liberal compromise in social policy and the alienation of the land, with compensation for the owners, to the peasantry. To the right of the Cadets were the Octobrists, who were content with the gains achieved by the October manifesto, from which they took their name. Farther to the right were various monarchists, nationalist and reactionary groups. And to the left of the Cadets were the Socialist-Revolutionaries and both Social-Democratic factions. All three socialist groups formally agreed to boycott the election, though in the event there were Social-Democratic candidates in some areas and Socialist-Revolutionary opinion was strongly represented in the composite Trudovik (Labour) group.

The elections were held in March 1906. Conducted on an indirect and far from universal suffrage, with candidates grouped in separate electoral colleges according to social class, they gave an enormous majority to the parties in opposition to the government. Precise figures are difficult to determine because of the absence of close party affiliations in some instances and uncertain allegiances among various peasant groups, but the Cadets formed by far the largest party with some 178 seats out of a total of 524. The Trudoviks gained 94 seats and 19 Social-Democrats were elected. This opposition strength of the centre and left was reinforced by almost all the deputies elected for the non-Russian nationalities of the empire, the Poles more particularly. For the liberals it was, once more, a famous victory.

Less than two months before the duma was to meet an event occurred which prepared the ground for a decisive stroke of government policy. On April 3, 1906 agreement was reached on the terms of a French loan of more than 2,000 million francs— the largest foreign loan which Russia had ever contracted. Negotiated at the price of Russian support for French diplomacy, it ensured the government's financial independence of the duma and all its works for some time to come. It represented the last but one of Witte's services to his imperial master; the last was acknowledged only after he had already fallen. On the morning of May 23, when Nicholas opened the first session of the imperial duma in the Winter Palace, the fundamental laws of the empire were published. In their revised and final draft they represented, to a considerable extent, Witte's own work. He had earned, as he knew, the everlasting ingratitude of the emperor for his part in the October manifesto, and he had since tried to insinuate himself back into Nicholas's favour. Coarse-fibred and in some ways unprincipled, he was nevertheless a realist of uncommon ability and resource. Could he have saved the dynasty? It is a question that cannot be answered since he was not permitted to try. Under heavy pressure from the reactionary camarilla of the court, he offered his resignation as chairman of the council of ministers and experienced the mortification of having it accepted. His resignation was announced five days before the new fundamental laws were made known.

They made great rents in the fabric of the proffered representative system. Ministers were appointed by the emperor and were responsible to the emperor alone. The conduct of foreign affairs was reserved exclusively to the crown. The largest items in the budget, the estimates for the army and the navy, together with the cost of upkeep of the court, were outside the competence of the duma. A renovated State Council, half of whose members were nominated by the crown and the other half chosen by the zemstvos and by corporations of the higher elements in society, shared equal legislative rights with the duma; the consent of both chambers was required for all new laws. And, under the celebrated article 87, the government enjoyed rights of emergency legislation by imperial decree at any time during which the duma was not in session.

In this carefully prepared situation the proceedings of the duma, resumed in the Tauride Palace (built by Catherine the Great for Potemkin), were largely a formal and empty ceremony. The Cadets, who took the lead, modelled themselves closely upon English parliamentary procedure, and perhaps for that reason among others there was immediate deadlock. The government declared that the prosposals placed before it were inadmissible, the duma having rights of interpellation only; the parties nevertheless continued their debate and innocently thought to bring matters to a head by the device of a vote of censure. On July 21 the doors of the palace were closed in intimation that the duma had been dissolved.

There followed, in the same innocent fashion, an appeal to the nation, from Viborg, just across the frontier in Finland, of some two hundred Cadet and Trudovik members. The appeal called for civil resistance—refusal to pay taxes or to furnish recruits for the army—until the rights of the duma had been restored. The gesture was without effect, though disturbances continued for other reasons. And meanwhile there appeared on the scene as Premier the impressive and half-tragic figure of Peter Stolypin, a Volga provincial governor who by firm measures had held his own during the fierce disorders of 1905 and who had been appointed Minister of the Interior in the previous government. Intelligent and courageous, strongly conservative and often ruthless but always to be respected for his convictions, Stolypin lacked only political breadth and something of flexibility in the arts of the politician. Of him also it may be asked whether he could not have saved the dynasty if Nicholas had permitted him to try.

Elections were announced for another duma to meet in the following year, and meanwhile Stolypin applied himself to the sternest repression. He was remembered ever afterwards by the peasantry (whom he went on to placate as they had never been placated before) for the field courts-martial which were set up in the areas of greatest disturbance in 1905; hundreds of death sentences were summarily executed upon those who had instigated riot. Not only peasants, however, came under sentence of the field courts-martial; the government's terror was also directed against those suspected of complicity in the so-called partisan actions of Bolshevik and Socialist-Revolutionary groups, who in the quest of funds for the revolutionary leaders abroad resorted at this time to open banditry. Among the moving spirits in this field was a Georgian with the revolutionary pseudonym, among others, of Koba, which concealed the identity of Josef Djugashvili, who took the name of Stalin.

But with repression in the countryside went a truly revolutionary scheme of transformation of the structure of peasant society. Though the scheme had been foreshadowed a few years earlier, it was Stolypin who broke with the tradition and customary law of centuries in attempting to dissolve the commune in a system of peasant proprietorship. The commune, it has well been said, was the sacred cow of Russian nationalist sentiment: from opposite poles radicals and conservatives alike had discovered in it the emblem of a unique Russian destiny among the nations. Now this basic pattern in the life of the Russian masses, rigorously preserved in the settlement of 1861, was discarded in the interests of creating a class of individual proprietors in the villages on which social stability could be built. For it was still peasant unrest that was feared most of all by the ruling elements in society and the support of a conservative peasant sector that was most desired.

The continued expansion of industry and commerce entered into this dramatic reversal of principle, but Stolypin's chief concern in this wager on 'the sober and the strong' was to turn to political advantage the peasant's desire, in Russia as elsewhere, to own his land. In November 1905, when all redemption dues were virtually cancelled, the collective responsibility of the commune for the payment of taxes, which in certain forms of peasant tenure had been annulled two years earlier, had finally been terminated. The decree enabling peasants to leave the village commune of their own accord came in the following October. A month later, on November 22, 1906, the essential part of the scheme was given legislative form in the peasant's right, wherever two-thirds of the village assembly were in favour, of consolidating his scattered strips in the common fields into a single holding which would henceforth be his permanent and personal property.

The peasant commune was by no means destroyed by this legislation. In 1917 it still ruled the life of the great majority. But over an ever widening area Stolypin's agrarian reform was changing the face and form of peasant society. In village after village the transition was being made—often with the aid of the purchase of crown and private land—to a new social economy. At the outbreak of war in 1914 one in every four peasant households in European Russia had converted their holdings into personal property, and one out of every ten had already consolidated them. Only time, it seemed, was needed to extend the principle to the whole of rural Russia. But already the psychological transformation that Stolypin had originally looked for was visible—partly, it should be said, in a sharpening social antagonism in the villages between the relatively well-to-do and the poor.

Outside the villages, however, the political struggle took precedence of everything else. In the elections to the second duma the

scales were heavily weighted on the government side by manipulation of the electoral law and other discriminatory devices. The
remarkable thing in the circumstances is that a more extreme
opposition was returned with an even larger majority. Cadet
representation declined, but, although party allegiances were again
sometimes confused, the Trudoviks and the Socialist-Revolutionaries standing in their own right had between them gained ground,
more than 50 Social-Democrats of both factions had been elected,
and the forces of both the extreme and the moderate right were
sharply reduced. Once more, dissolution proved the only remedy.
It was engineered in the first place by inflammatory accusations by
the extreme right that members of the duma were plotting against
the emperor's life and was followed by an attempt to exclude the
revolutionary parties from a special sitting.

This time the decree of dissolution did not stand alone. It was
accompanied by a thoroughgoing revision of the electoral law
which, since it was in flagrant violation of the fundamental laws,
was accurately described as a *coup d'état*. The peasantry, it was
plain, were the key to the electoral problem; it was essential to
reduce their representation. The rigging of the indirect procedure
hitherto adopted was carefully prepared. Apart from merging the
urban votes in those of the provinces and reducing the number of
deputies for the non-Russian nationalities, the weight of the
revision fell upon an involved scheme of class differentiation by
which the rural gentry predominated in the lists from which the
members of the duma were actually chosen. The election results
for the third duma were at last favourable from the government's
point of view; the balance had tilted sharply to the right. The
Octobrists now formed the largest single party in the duma with a
third or so of the total membership. They were flanked on their
right by various strong groups of unabashed reactionary temper;
while the socialist parties were very nearly wiped out.

In the interval before the duma met in November 1907 Stolypin
stamped out the dying embers of revolution. The effect of court-
martial sentences of death and of a new crop of trials for crimes
committed in 1905 was supplemented by severe restrictions on the
press. It was repression with a purpose, a prelude to some degree of
conservative reform. Under Stolypin, who did not hesitate to
resort to the powers conferred by article 87 and to ignore the
statutory provision that emergency legislation should afterwards
be ratified by the duma, the government knew its own mind.
Tenacious and unafraid, he carried weaker ministers with him
in developing his agrarian experiment. He had to reckon not only
with the Octobrists, who stayed in formal opposition and in the
process undoubtedly acquired something of parliamentary

experience, but with the blind forces of revenge both in the duma and at court. These brought him down at last. The third duma sat almost for the full term of five years, but Stolypin's premiership was cut short before the end. He had incurred together with the distrust of grand-ducal circles the jealousy of Nicholas. In September 1911, at a special performance in a theatre in Kiev attended by the emperor, he was killed by a Socialist-Revolutionary who was also a police agent. It is not improbable that there was deliberate official connivance in the murder.

The fourth duma, elected in 1912, showed a further swing to the right. It continued more or less where Stolypin had left off, though the government had less grip on the course of affairs and bolder and uglier forms of pressure came from the court. Kokovtsev, the new Prime Minister, was dismissed in January 1914, partly for his share in voicing a widespread concern at the favour enjoyed in imperial circles by a Siberian peasant of notoriously dissolute habit named Grigory Rasputin.

War in 1914 brought to an abrupt halt the constructive achievement and the promise which had been won in the short space of the previous eight years. The achievement was much more considerable than the foreigner has been taught to think, the promise more hopeful. A foundation had been laid for constitutional government, a more stable order of rural society had begun to take shape, industry was still gaining in strength and the pace of liberal social legislation was quickening. The tide of revolution was indeed fast running out, chiefly because the peasant masses, who at last enjoyed equal civil rights with the rest of the population, had been given new incentives. The peasants now owned three-quarters of all the arable land in European Russia. Their standards of living, thanks to the work of the zemstvos and perhaps even more to the rapid growth of rural co-operative associations, were rising. True, the distinction between the comparatively prosperous—the kulaks —and the poor was becoming more marked, and this was a principal cause of the peasant riots of 1911. But over the country as a whole agrarian reform had by 1914 undoubtedly eased the fundamental problem of Russian society since the act of emancipation. A solution, it seemed, was in sight.

The case of the industrial workers was different, though in spite of the continued restrictions upon trade unions they also had made notable if smaller gains. Rising wage levels in some industries apart, a beginning had been made in 1912, for example, in health and accident insurance. Perhaps the most striking illustration of improved conditions in the industrial centres of population is provided by the advance in education. In picturing the liquidation of illiteracy after the revolution as a task in which the Bolsheviks started from scratch Soviet propaganda has constantly ignored the record of the government, the zemstvos and more especially the town councils in the years from 1908 onwards. The number of primary schools rose rapidly from year to year, and it is estimated that in 1914 half the number of children of school age in Russia were in fact at school.

It is true, once more, that industrial unrest was again becoming marked towards the close of this period. After the grim affair of the shooting of the strikers on the British-owned Lena goldfields in the spring of 1912 a resurgent strike movement throughout the country reached a point of crisis in St Petersburg in the summer of 1914. But the disputes were primarily economic. The revolutionary parties themselves seemed almost to have faded away. Their leaders, Socialist-Revolutionary and Social-Democrat alike, were in prison or Siberian exile or in exile abroad, where they were engaged in virulent controversy and manoeuvre. The most obdurate factionalism was that maintained by Lenin. At a congress in Prague in 1912 which was directed without scruple against Menshevik influence, Lenin conferred upon his Bolshevik following the title of the true, the only, the whole Russian Social-Democratic party. The tactical gain was not to be despised, though two years later the Bolsheviks might still have appeared no more potent a revolutionary force than scores of earlier Russian revolutionary groups in quarrelsome exile.

The truth is that a new and less political mood had settled upon educated society at home. The old verities of revolutionary struggle had lost their power; the political intelligentsia had been visited by lassitude. Exotic doctrines of one kind or another had their place, but at the same time fresh and invigorating influences were at work. There was a genuine spiritual revival in these years of Orthodoxy, in which ex-Marxist intellectuals were prominent. After 1905, when Pobedonostsev's rigid hand had been removed from affairs, a desire for Church reform, even for the liberation of Orthodoxy from the fetters of the state, steadily gained ground. For the rest, the movement away from politics was towards commerce, the professions, technology, the arts and sciences. The temper of literature had almost wholly changed since the beginning of the century. The autumnal glory of Russian prose was over with the death of Chekhov in 1904. Gorky in exile pursued his somewhat leaden mission of realism, Bunin remained faithful to an older and more lyrical convention, Kuprin, Andreyev and others dabbled in high-pitched success, but the truly creative impulse came from the Symbolist poets—Briusov, Bely, Blok—and their successors, all of them in revolt against 'civic' and utilitarian ideals of literature. Art and revolutionary politics met only in the muddier reaches of fiction.

N

War alone revived the practical prospect of revolution. With another decade of peace a successful Russian revolution is perhaps not easily conceived; attempted revolution, yes, but not success. That hypothetical decade of peace is met, of course, by the appeal to the dialectic of history and the argument that war was inevitable, the fruit of the contradictions of capitalism in its final phase of imperialism, and that the developing Bolshevik strategy of revolution was in fact based precisely upon that prophetic analysis. Yet imperialism did not prove to be the final phase of capitalism, and there are no inevitabilities in history. War in Europe was averted half a dozen times between 1905 and 1914.

Russia's part in the diplomatic origins of the first world war need not detain us long. The final parting of the ways of Russia and Germany came after the exorbitant German bid for an alliance between the two countries in the treaty of Björkö in 1905 while Russia was bound to France and Germany to Austria. The Triple Entente followed two years later. The rivalry of Russia and Austria in the Balkans culminated in the Austrian annexation of Bosnia next year, and, after the confusion of the Balkan wars of 1911–13, the powder magazine was fired with the assassination of the Archduke Franz Ferdinand at Sarajevo on June 28, 1914. Strategic necessity was invoked on the Russian side to justify full instead of partial mobilization, after which Germany declared war.

Russia's course in the war during the two and a half years before revolution broke out in February/March 1917 can be plotted only briefly here. The outbreak of war literally brought the nation to its knees in a religious fervour of patriotism; even the socialist parties—with the sole exception of the Bolsheviks*—were swept unresistingly by a tide of popular emotion. St Petersburg promptly acquired the more Russian style of Petrograd. From the first, however, the forces of government were divided in sympathy. Among ministers, though after the early months they came and went rapidly, there were always some who were moved by a lingering sentiment of affinity with imperial Germany, while pro-German connexions at court exercised a covert influence upon affairs. Yet within a fortnight the Russian offensive in East Prussia, mounted in haste in fulfilment of treaty pledges, bore witness to the fidelity to her allies with which Russia trod the road to destruction almost to the end. It was the Russian disaster at Tannenberg, in face of the German reinforcements withdrawn from the western front, which saved the allies on the Marne.

Russia waged war at appalling odds and with native fortitude.

* The five Bolshevik deputies in the duma—a sixth member, incidentally, had been a police spy—were arrested in November 1914 and imprisoned in the following February in Siberia.

In spite of the reorganization of the army during the years before 1914, she suffered from glaring deficiencies in arms and shortages of equipment and from technical inferiority in every sphere. Military leadership, which was for the most part as inferior, was sapped, as so often, by intrigue. The great Russian spaces and the superiority of Russian manpower offered real enough advantages, but the one was neutralized by a reckless policy of enforced civil evacuation in retreat and the other as recklessly expended. After the first winter, crisis was at hand in an acute shortage of munitions and in the total inadequacy of medical and auxiliary services.

In this situation the crowning irresponsibility of the government was to reject all concerted forms of voluntary aid in prosecuting the war. At all costs the principle of autocracy must in substance be preserved. The duma, the zemstvos, the town councils were all suspect as potential instruments of democracy and were firmly excluded from the task of organizing the resources of the country. Yet the spectre of defeat had become visible by the spring of 1915, when depleted units at the front were being brought up to strength by men without rifles. The duma met for the briefest of sessions and was then dissolved, after which the government fell back on the extended use of article 87. In government circles nationalist sentiment had been intoxicated by the secret allied pledges* in March and April to support Russian claims—after victory had been won—to the possession of Constantinople, but the supply position had meanwhile gone from bad to worse. In the summer came the shattering German and Austrian offensive along almost the entire front, and with it the loss of the whole of Poland, the greater part of the Baltic states and immense areas of the Ukraine and White Russia. In August the centre and right-centre groups in the duma united in opposition to the government in a progressive bloc, which pleaded for the formation of a ministry enjoying 'the confidence of the country'; the war could only be won, it was urged, by the co-operation of goverment and people.

The emperor's reply in the following month was nothing less than to assume the title and function of commander-in-chief of the Russian armies. It was a rash and unconsidered step, though its most fateful consequences could not have been foreseen. In removing himself to military headquarters Nicholas delivered the government and the country into the hands of the empress. Ignorant, hysterically strong-willed, driven by a superstitious religiosity from the moment of her conversion to Orthodoxy, Alexandra had always set herself the duty of fortifying her husband's prerogatives as autocrat. There was no more positive treachery in

* These were announced in the duma in December 1916. At the stage of dissolution Russia had then reached they made virtually no impression.

her than in *l'autrichienne*, but behind her stood the figure of Rasputin, who had indeed urged Nicholas to proclaim himself commander-in-chief and who in the end probably served as an instrument for others.

A wanderer from his Siberian village, a frequenter of a common Russian sort of shrines and monasteries who had acquired a no less common reputation for holiness (he was never a monk), illiterate, inordinately coarse and yet of commanding personality, Rasputin may well have had hypnotic powers. The heir to the throne suffered from haemophilia, and it was Rasputin alone who, after the doctors had failed, appeared able to arrest the bleeding which from time to time threatened the boy's life. For the imperial pair he thus became 'a man of God'. More than that, he became 'our Friend', the incarnation of the virtue and saving loyalty of the Russian peasant masses. Of prodigious lusts (his name derives from the word *rasputnik*, a profligate) and much peasant shrewdness, he propounded the familiar doctrine that sin is necessary to salvation. The empress had always refused to believe a word against him and had nourished an implacable hatred of the duma for its revelations concerning him before the war. Now Rasputin helped to guide the destinies of the empire.

Increasingly, from September 1915 onwards, it was on his indirect instructions that ministers were made and unmade and civil policies modified or abandoned; even the military conduct of the war may in some degree have been influenced by him. His tenure of power reflected an accelerating process of decomposition of the whole regime under the ordeal of war. And the irony of the situation was that as Russia approached political breakdown its military strength was being restored by the un-official labours of industrial committees and the united efforts of zemstvos and town councils. The total figure of Russian casualties was enormous; when the end of the fighting had been reached the number of dead was possibly two and a half million. But the remarkable improvement in military supplies in the summer of 1916 was shown by the striking power of Brusilov's offensive in Galicia. Though short-lived, the victory demonstrated once more the astonishing Russian power of recovery.

In the end, however, it was mounting economic strain which brought political breakdown. The enemy blockade had wiped out Russian foreign trade; through the loss of the greater part of the strategic railway network in the west and south-west all communications and transport were hopelessly overburdened; fuel was perilously short; and, worst of all, growing food shortages in the towns exacerbated the effect of the steep rise in the cost of living. By 1916 Russia had mobilized no fewer than thirteen million men, far more than the military machine could absorb, and both agriculture and the consumer industries were under acute strain. Problems of distribution apart, the peasants were either producing less or were holding back their grain because of the scarcity of manufactured goods in return. The position in Petrograd in particular deteriorated from week to week. As yet there was little revolutionary propaganda. But by the autumn strikes were spreading from factory to factory and food queues in the capital were a commonplace.

Now came the first mutterings of revolution. The government, the duma, the educated classes all sensed the wrath to come. From the autumn of 1916 ministers had succeeded ministers at a farcical pace, each more incompetent or of more dubious character than the last, and not a single figure of note was left to whom those of good will in the duma could rally. The emperor was beyond the reach of counsels of prudence and plots of every kind were being hatched at court. Brusilov's campaign had collapsed in a dreadful toll of lives, and, though the front as a whole was still intact and plans had been laid for a spring offensive to coincide with an allied offensive in the west, a trickle of desertions had begun and was increasing daily. In the rear, in barracks and in factories revolutionary propaganda was making headway; at court the hope of averting revolution by concluding a separate peace with Germany grew visibly. On December 30, after cyanide of potassium in his wine had failed to kill him, Rasputin was disposed of by several revolver shots, the chief murderer being a member of an aristocratic family who was related by marriage to the emperor. There was much relief in the capital, the imperial pair were stricken by grief, but otherwise all was as it had been before.

When the end seemed very near and the grand-dukes were playing with the idea of a palace revolution, clear warnings were addressed to the emperor from various quarters. Perhaps the least conventional and most outspoken warning came from the British ambassador. But Nicholas was deaf, blind, trivially preoccupied, at one and the same time unperturbed and fatalistic. The duma met once more in the Tauride Palace in an atmosphere of foreboding; police and troops were standing by to meet the threat of disturbances. In the event all was relatively orderly in the streets. Then, abruptly, in the midst of a wage dispute at the vast Putilov works in the capital, the revolution broke.

On March 8* the queues at the bakers' shops in the capital seemed less amenable to control than usual. On the following day strikes

* The first of the two revolutions in 1917 is still commonly designated, in accordance with the Russian calendar at the time, the February revolution; the second —the Bolshevik *coup d'état* in November—the October revolution.

broke out everywhere in the city, strike processions formed, almost the entire population came out on the streets and the first shots were exchanged with the police. The movement became at last irresistible. This was revolution—elemental and unorganized, it is true—but indubitable revolution: meetings, speeches, protests, violent clashes with the police, the mounted Cossacks mere spectators, the crowds joined by soldiers from the garrison, then by entire garrison units consisting largely of raw peasant recruits. March 12 was the crucial day, when two regiments of the Guards came over to the side of the demonstrators, the arsenal was seized, weapons distributed, the prisons opened, police headquarters fired. A soviet of workers' and soldiers' deputies, elected in haste from the factories and barracks of the capital, took possession as though by right of a wing of the Tauride Palace while the duma conferred in another wing.

The duma, never a genuinely representative body, was the only one which could now step into the breach. On March 14 it sanctioned the formation of a provisional government under Prince Lvov, leader of the union of zemstvos. The only socialist member of the government was Alexander Kerensky, who headed the Trudovik group in the duma. That same day the Petrograd soviet gave provisional support to the provisional government. All was as yet provisional. But nowhere was there a moment's doubt that the monarchy and the whole order on which it rested had been swept away. Planless, aimless, chaotic, the March revolution of 1917 had been achieved at the cost of a few hundred lives and of injuries to perhaps a thousand people. The Bolsheviks had next to nothing to do with the fall of tsarism.

The literature on the course of events in Russia between March and November, when the Bolshevik faction seized power, is formidable. It is also extremely varied in interpretation. Those decisive eight months are not easily contained in a nutshell, and the bare recital of events that is attempted here is meant only to list key circumstances.

On March 15 Nicholas II, emperor of Russia, who from military headquarters had given orders some days before for the suppression of all disturbances in the capital, was persuaded to abdicate. He did so in favour of his brother Michael (who declined the immediate risk of acceptance), and for his own protection was placed under arrest shortly afterwards. The provisional government thus appeared to have stepped into the seat of supreme power. But where, in point of fact, was the source of power? From the first day of the overthrow of the tsarist regime the answer could admit of no doubt. A government had been formed which had no roots in the life of the masses, no popular movement or force of coercion

behind it; the sole source of power was in the revolution itself.
Authority was exercised in the name of the popular revolutionary
will, of which the newly formed soviets in the capital and throughout the rest of the country were the guardians. The Petrograd
soviet had extended support to the provisional government only
on the condition that a constituent assembly to be elected by
universal franchise would be summoned in the near future to
establish a permanent form of government for Russia.

The Bolsheviks were still a mere handful in the Petrograd soviet,
in which Mensheviks and Socialist-Revolutionaries predominated.
The very names of the Bolshevik leaders were as yet unknown to
the vast majority of the population of the capital. But for both
Social-Democratic factions the moment of decision had arrived.
This was the bourgeois-democratic revolution: where did they go
from here? For a time not even the Bolsheviks recognized the
peculiar opportunity which sprang from the dual power of government and soviets; the realities of the situation were not apparent
to them until the return of Lenin from exile a month later. Even
the famous Order No. 1 of the Petrograd soviet, issued on the very
day the provisional government was formed, did not immediately
give them their cue. Addressed to the Petrograd garrison, it called
on the soldiers, while urging them to maintain discipline, to form
committees of their own in every unit to control the distribution
of arms, to superintend part at least of the authority hitherto
exercised by their officers and to obey no order from the government which was inconsistent with the instructions of the soviet.
Order No. 1 was observed by almost every unit in the army
and the entire system of military discipline was thus destroyed
at a blow.

All through the war Lenin had waited in impatient anxiety in
Switzerland. He had taken his stand in characteristic terms against
the blood lust of imperialism, raging against the heathen socialist
parties in the Second International which supported their respective
governments and urging upon all true socialists in the belligerent
countries the duty of transforming the war into a civil war against
their own government: revolution in any one country, he
maintained, would be the signal for revolution elsewhere. This
revolutionary defeatism was proclaimed at a conference of like-
minded socialists from various European countries held at Zimmer-
wald, in Switzerland, in September 1915 and again at Kienthal in
the following April. As the slaughter continued and war-weariness
developed Lenin's excitement grew. The news from Russia in
March 1917 worked like a fever upon him. Since there was no
other way of reaching Russia immediately, it was a sealed train
which bore him through Germany to the scene of revolution, an

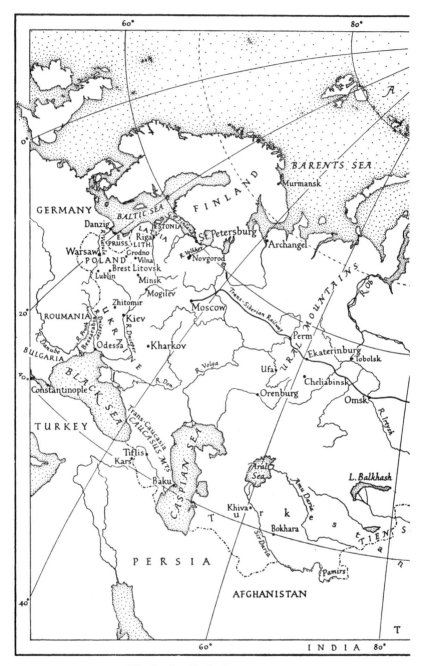

The Russian Empire in 1914

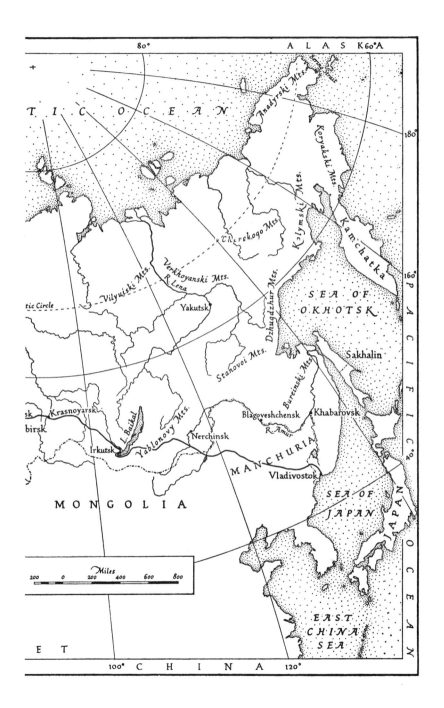

80°   A L A S K 60°A

T I C   O C E A N   180°

Anadyrski Mts.

Koryakski Mts.

Cherskogo Mts.

Kolymski Mts.

Kamchatka

Vilyuiski Mts.   Verkhoyanski Mts.
                        R. Lena   Dzhugdzhur Mts.   S E A   O F
tic Circle   O K H O T S K .   160°

Yakutsk   P

                        Stanovoi Mts.   A
                                                                                                C
                                              Bureinski Mts.   Sakhalin   I
sk   Krasnoyarsk   F
birsk   L. Baikal   Blagoveshchensk   Khabarovsk   I
          Irkutsk   Yablonovy Mts.   Nerchinsk   R. Amur   C
                                                                                                ·
                                              M A N C H U R I A   o
                                                        Vladivostok   ·
     M O N G O L I A   S E A   O F
                                                              J A P A N   J
                                                                               A
                                                                               P
                                                                               A   O
                                                                               N   C
                                                                                        E
                    Miles   A
200   0   200   400   600   800   N

                                                          E A S T
                                                          C H I N A
                                                          S E A
E   T

100° C H I N A 120°

unknown but evidently dangerous agitator who might assist the German cause there.

Even before his arrival the dilemma of the provisional government was plain at a glance. However deep the longing of the Russian people for peace, what would be left of either Russia or revolution in the event of defeat and occupation by the German armies? Yet in continuing the war in the midst of revolution how was the provisional government simultaneously to re-establish order, restore a shattered economy and satisfy the immediate demands of the revolutionary masses?

The dialectic of history may have been on Lenin's side, but there were two cardinal errors which the provisional government committed and which with courage and realism might have been avoided. Both sprang from toying in the midst of revolution with parliamentary pretensions which were alien to Russian thought and habit. One was to delay consideration of what was still called the agrarian question, which could only mean the distribution among the peasantry of the land still in private ownership, until the constituent assembly had been summoned. The landowning interest, it is true, was strongly represented in the government; but, in face of the avidity with which of their own accord the peasants soon began to take possession of the private estates, in face also of intensified food difficulties in the towns, there was no real alternative to sanctioning the complete transfer of land. The other fundamental error of the provisional government was to allow itself to be paralysed by legalistic niceties into 'democratic' tolerance of the forces which were openly seeking to destroy it.

Lenin arrived at the Finland station in Petrograd on April 16. He had been preceded in the capital by Stalin and other Siberian exiles and was followed next month by Trotsky. He was forty-seven years old and at the climax of his faith and his career. He acknowledged in startling fashion the welcome that awaited him from his followers and from socialists of a different persuasion. He had come, he said, to bring not unity but division, not the tactical support of bourgeois revolution but the immediate promise of proletarian revolution. Until Lenin's arrival socialists of every brand had taken it for granted that the second stage of revolution was still distant, and that a coalition of forces in aid of the first was imperative. Now the astonishing summons to his followers was to refuse recognition of the provisional government and demand the transfer of power to the soviets. That, Lenin urged, was the path to socialist victory: all power to the soviets. The goal in sight, he announced, was peace, bread, freedom. The appeal of the first item was addressed to the army, of the second to the peasants, of the third to the class-conscious industrial proletariat, the appeal of all three to the country at large. All power to the soviets: the transition in Russia from a bourgeois revolution to a socialist revolution would be the signal for revolution in other lands and the eventual triumph of world socialism.

It was a breath-taking programme, which did not at once win acceptance even from Lenin's disciplined following. Yet the argument and the force of will of his leadership soon prevailed among them. And, from the moment his strategy of war against the provisional government had been endorsed, the drama of 1917 unfolded at dizzy speed. Peace and bread: among all other party slogans this alone made sense to the masses. Bolshevik agitation was tireless, impassioned, brilliantly organized. At the front and in the rear, in the capital and in all the industrial and provincial centres the propaganda of peace and the proletarian conquest of power gathered momentum. In Petrograd and elsewhere factories were seized and 'workers' control' established. In the countryside the seizure of the private estates was begun in earnest. It was now that desertion and fraternization at the front spread widely and the last vestiges of military discipline began to disappear; the first thought of the peasant-soldier was to return to his village to share in the distribution of the *barin's* land. There has been vehement and interminable argument whether the Russian armies had already disintegrated before the March revolution or whether disintegration came only with Order No. 1, but what is certain is that complete anarchy sprang from the soldiers' soviets in the months after Lenin's return to Russia.

The growing strength of the soviets did not as yet imply that they were under Lenin's leadership. The Bolsheviks fought tooth and nail for control, waging war as implacably against Mensheviks and Socialist-Revolutionaries, both represented in a reconstituted provisional government, as against the government itself. Yet at the all-Russian congress of soviets which met in Petrograd in the middle of June there were still only 105 Bolshevik delegates against 248 Mensheviks and 285 Socialist-Revolutionaries. Faith in the provisional government was fast fading, but even in the capital the Bolshevik leaders were obliged to wait on events before they could weaken popular allegiance to the rival socialist parties. Then came the 'July days', in which they deliberately tested their strength by heading a half-spontaneous armed demonstration in the capital in support of the transfer of power to the soviets. The demonstration petered out, in part through the provisional government's eventual show of force; the story was spread abroad that Lenin was a German spy; and Kerensky felt himself strong enough to issue an order for the arrest of the Bolshevik leaders. Lenin went into hiding across the frontier in Finland. But the trial of strength had not been wasted. In hiding Lenin prepared for the seizure of power, not by the soviets, but by the Bolshevik party.

The Russian offensive in the south-west early in July, the last fighting that was seriously attempted, had collapsed in foregone failure. From that point the moderate socialists who were in the majority in the Petrograd soviet and its central executive committee abandoned their earlier resolve to continue the war. In August the provisional government was once more reconstituted as a coalition of liberals and moderate socialist parties with Kerensky as Prime Minister. In September General Kornilov, the newly appointed commander-in-chief, headed an attempt to restore military and civil order by dismissing the Petrograd soviet and, if need be, overthrowing Kerensky's government. It was to the soviet that Kerensky turned to defeat Kornilov's threatened march on the capital. The attempted counter-revolutionary *coup* dissolved into thin air, but the revolutionary legality of the soviet now masked the complete ascendancy of the Bolshevik faction. Its party membership had risen to more than 200,000. The directing spirit of the soviet, as in 1905, was Trotsky, who had definitely assumed the title of Bolshevik in July. In the last days of October it was he who controlled the soviet's newly established military revolutionary committee, which itself controlled the entire body of garrison troops.

Was this the historic hour? Lenin himself had no doubts. Early in October he had returned in disguise to Petrograd. His was the dominating mind and will in the fevered debates in Smolny, the school for daughters of the nobility which the Bolsheviks had taken over as their headquarters. His was the decision to seize power by an armed uprising. For some weeks before the event the planned insurrection was an open secret; only the chosen date was as yet unknown. It might have been guessed. The elections to the constituent assembly were in sight, but they were to be preceded by the meeting of a new all-Russian congress of soviets on November 7 (October 25).

The Bolsheviks struck in the early hours of that day. The principal buildings in the capital were seized by garrison troops and detachments of armed factory guards, the Winter Palace—which served as Kerensky's headquarters—was under siege, ministers were under arrest. What transpired in Petrograd was simultaneously enacted in other large cities and communication centres. There was little resistance anywhere save in Moscow, where the Kremlin twice changed hands and a body of three thousand military cadets fought the insurgents for a week. Except in the greater part of the Ukraine, the Cossack lands and most of Transcaucasia, and in the Russian countryside, the Bolsheviks had instantly won power. In the evening of November 8 a new government took shape in the *Soviet Narodnykh Commissarov*, the soviet of people's commissars, to be known as Sovnarkom, of which Lenin was chairman and in which Trotsky was commissar of foreign affairs and Stalin commissar of nationalities. It issued two decrees. The first was an appeal to all peoples at war and to their governments to begin immediate negotiations for a just and democratic peace without annexations or indemnities. The other, lifted without hesitation from the Socialist-Revolutionary programme for the peasantry, announced the abolition of all private ownership of land and its transfer to the charge of peasant soviets pending the decision of the constituent assembly. In point of fact, the Bolshevik land decree merely acknowledged the situation which the peasants had themselves created between the two phases of revolution in 1917.

CHAPTER XVII

AFTER 1917:
BETWEEN WEST AND EAST

IN 1917 THE BOLSHEVIKS mastered an inchoate mass impulse of revolution whose roots stretched deep into the Russian past. This impulse they proceeded to direct or to divert—the verbal distinction is pregnant with controversy—to ends of their own. Their seizure of power is at one and the same time a spectacular episode in the continuity of Russian historical development and a giant landmark in world history.

In the teaching of Marx and Engels, Lenin and his followers had both a comprehensive philosophy and an all-embracing plan of action. The philosophy projected the goal of a classless society, in which, when productive forces had been sufficiently developed to enable all to receive according to their needs, the state would wither away; the plan of action required the assistance of a dictatorship of the proletariat for the achievement of a completely socialist order. Yet since Marxist doctrine unfolded no mechanical law but had always to be applied to concrete situations, it was essential at every stage to extract policy from an analysis of Russian conditions. Here, then, was the dilemma. In Russia the proletarian revolution had come first and the broad industrial base on which to build socialism had still to follow; Marx had predicted the opposite sequence of events. Thus embarked upon a form of Marxism turned upside down, Lenin imposed upon the Russian revolution the peculiarly Russian scheme of Communism of which the theory is known as Marxism-Leninism.

Into this scheme there entered a great surge of idealism. The Bolsheviks, the Russian contingent in the army of international socialism, were heirs to the revolutionary faith and struggle of generations. In the task of creating a new and egalitarian order of society they could count not only on the discipline and devotion in their own ranks but on the still undirected energies which the fall of tsarism had released in the masses. The hope of sloughing off the semi-Asiatic backwardness and tyranny of the past filled millions of people throughout the length and breadth of Russia with heroic ardour and profound willingness for sacrifice.

The distinguishing tragedy of the Bolshevik regime springs from its traditional Russian character as a revolution 'from above', a revolution which denied the basic concept of political liberty. It did not assume that character at once; Bolshevism was carried to victory on the tide of a revolution from below. But Lenin and his followers represented a minority of extremists within a socialist minority. In March 1917 they numbered less than 50,000, and eight months later, when they gained power by an armed *coup d'état*, their following was still only a fraction of that of the Mensheviks and Socialist-Revolutionaries combined. Yet from the first their method of establishing a socialist society implied the rejection of all other revolutionary forces; revolutionary rule was for them Bolshevik rule. Even in the central committee of the party the members who looked for an 'all-socialist' government were soon left with no alternative to resignation. The virtually complete elimination by terror of rival forms of representation of workers and peasants came only with the civil war, but the initial Bolshevik claim to one-party rule was itself a principal cause of the civil war. The claim supported an otherwise vague and ambiguous doctrine of the dictatorship of the proletariat, and was perhaps inherent in the psychology of professional revolutionaries. Under the stimulus of one-party rule, the dictatorship of the proletariat became, successively, the dictatorship of the Communist Party, of the central committee of the party, of the praesidium or Political Bureau (Politbureau) of the central committee, of the *vozhd* or leader. Bolshevik democracy became totalitarian, the Communist state monolithic.

On the evening of November 7, 1917 the all-Russian congress of soviets of workers' and soldiers' deputies voted their support, by 390 votes out of 650, for the successful insurrection earlier in the day; even so, the majority included an appreciable number who were not Bolsheviks. It should be made clear, perhaps, that there was little expectation in the country that the new regime would or could survive. Within a fortnight, it was confidently predicted, the Bolsheviks would have disappeared in a fresh turn of the revolutionary kaleidoscope. The staffs of the ministries, banks and public institutions in the capital held aloof from their temporary masters and were content to wait. Yet the first weeks were decisive. A month after the seizure of power a separate congress of soviets of peasants' deputies, overwhelmingly Socialist-Revolutionary in character*, united with the earlier congress on terms which included S.-R. representation in the central executive committee of the joint body and in Sovnarkom. It may be doubted whether, on the Bolshevik side, this was more than a tactical move to gain time for the extension of their power from the urban areas to the rural soviets. Six weeks later still, on January 18, 1918, after elections held in November for which the Bolsheviks themselves had originally pressed so loudly, the long-deferred constituent assembly met at last. The Bolsheviks had captured 175 seats only out of 707; the S.-R.s were dominant with 410. But Lenin's plans in face of this situation had been laid well in advance. On the following day the members of the constituent assembly were removed from their meeting-place in the Tauride Palace by the Bolshevik guards in attendance and the assembly was dissolved. It was as simple as that. In the Bolshevik reckoning, there was no place in revolutionary Russia for 'parliamentary illusions'; the authority of the congress of soviets was authority enough. And indeed the eclipse of the constituent assembly, though it caused consternation among the rival socialist and non-socialist parties, made little impression on the country as a whole. Constitutionalism and civil rights were far removed from the habit of mind of the masses.

The doctrine that sovereign power resided in the congress of soviets was not formally proclaimed until July 1918, when the Bolsheviks had secured their hold on the machinery of government and the congress itself ratified the newly prepared constitution of the Russian Socialist Federative Soviet Republic (R.S.F.S.R.). But it may be of advantage at this point to outpace events and glance at the constitutional principles on which the regime was built.

In theory the primary source of authority in the state was the elected local soviet. The village or urban soviet formed the base

* There was always a split in Socialist-Revolutionary policy. It was the left wing of the party which originally favoured co-operation with the Bolsheviks.

of a pyramidal structure reaching up through canton, district, provincial and regional soviets to the apex of the congress of soviets. Except for the formally disfranchised—who included clergy, ex-police agents and the former nobility—the right of electing members to the local soviet was conferred upon all of both sexes who had attained the age of eighteen; voting at the initial stage, and at every indirect stage afterwards, was open—that is, by show of hands—and thus afforded a simple means of controlling the primary elections and the choice of representatives from the village soviet to the canton soviet, from the canton soviet to the district soviet, and so on. Representation at the apex was heavily weighted in favour of the towns; equal representation was given to 25,000 urban dwellers and to 125,000 rural dwellers. When the congress was not in session its central executive committee took over; to this body of some three hundred persons, itself directed by a smaller inner praesidium, was delegated full legislative authority. In point of fact, there was no clear demarcation between its functions and the legislative functions which Sovnarkom, whose members formally constituted the Soviet Government, combined with executive power.

Where in this scheme of things was the Bolshevik faction? In March 1918 it had finally cut loose from all other Social-Democratic connexions, as Lenin from the moment of his return to Russia had wished it to do, and assumed the title of the Russian Communist Party (Bolsheviks). It had no place or mention in the constitution. Yet in fact it was the unyielding steel frame of government, the ubiquitous instrument of policy at every level. The congress of soviets was enthroned in nominal sovereignty, but to an increasing extent its function was to endorse decisions already taken. And these decisions were taken in the course of Communist Party debate. The Communist Party was not, of course, a political party in the conventional western sense but a hierarchy of leadership. Admittance to the party, now confined almost entirely to those of proletarian or 'poor' peasant origin, carried with it a missionary obedience to the social task; the party member was a servant of the historical process, and as such executed whatever charge was laid upon him. While at the top, therefore, the membership of both Sovnarkom and the praesidium of the central executive committee of the congress of soviets consisted of an inner ring of the central committee of the party, at all other levels Communists filled key positions in civil administration, in the trade unions, in the armed services and everywhere else. From December 1919 every unit of the machinery of state and society had its party 'cell' or 'fraction', which guided all policy decisions. The secret of Bolshevik power, in brief, was the close interlocking of the party with all organs of authority. The Russian Communist Party (Bolsheviks) was the reality behind the façade of 'Soviet' Russia. Almost from the outset, indeed, the title of 'Soviet Government' was a deliberate misnomer.

This, however, was not fully evident while the Bolsheviks were still engaged in consolidating their power and while the civil war had still to be fought and won. Among all their initial preoccupations not the least absorbing was the problem of how to bring the imperialist war to an end. The German armies, preparing for their massive spring offensive in the west, had been largely content to hold their hand in the east. But until peace was restored the success of the revolution was precarious, and unless revolution elsewhere came to Russia's aid revolution in Russia appeared to be doomed. In grappling with the problem the Bolsheviks had proclaimed the right of self-determination of the border nationalities—Poles, Finns, Baltic peoples, Ukrainians, the peoples of Transcaucasia, all of them wholly or partly occupied by the enemy or seized by a popular movement for independence—and had simultaneously sought an armistice. Negotiations with the central powers opened in December at Brest-Litovsk*, where the terms of an armistice were agreed. But the German terms of peace outraged the Russian sensibilities even of Bolshevik internationalists. Negotiations were suspended, Trotsky fell back upon the desperate expedient of 'no peace, no war' (Russia, that is, would neither make peace nor resume fighting), the period of armistice came to an end and the German armies were ordered to advance. There was strong feeling in the Bolshevik ranks in favour of a 'revolutionary war' of resistance, but the danger in that event was that power would slip from their hands into the hands of military and other representatives of the old regime. It was left to Lenin, convinced that a social revolution in Germany was in sight—a revolution in his view more momentous than the Russian—to argue the tactical necessity of accepting the German terms.

The treaty of Brest-Litovsk was signed on March 3. It proclaimed what was in effect German annexation of eastern Poland, the Baltic states and the whole of the Ukraine, reaffirmed the independence of Finland and awarded the areas of Kars and Batum to Turkey. It thus deprived what was formerly the Russian empire of more than a quarter of its population and of its total arable land, three-quarters of its iron and coal and half of its industrial plant. This was a staggering price to pay for peace. Revolution or no revolution in Germany—and there were perhaps few who shared Lenin's confidence—it horrified Russian opinion of every shade. The rumour spread widely once more that Lenin was a German spy. The Socialist-Revolutionaries, increasingly at odds with the

* Now Brest.

O

Bolsheviks on almost every issue, were as inflamed as any section of political opinion, and their representatives withdrew from Sovnarkom. Events were moving towards attempted counter-revolution, civil war and foreign intervention.

The causes of the civil war were complex and tangled. The anti-Bolshevik sentiment of the former ruling classes apart, there was the wounded patriotism of those officers in the disbanded imperial army who planned to rescue Russia from the humiliation of Brest-Litovsk and disloyalty to her allies. Headed by a number of leading generals, the small 'volunteer army' in the south at first found only a negligible measure of support in the Cossack country of the Don and the Kuban, but from their initiative and the rising tide of disillusionment with the Bolshevik regime grew the movement led by General Denikin, who commanded the most dangerous by far of the anti-Bolshevik armies.

Then, in the strangest of all the strange episodes of the civil war, there was the unsought adventure of the Czech troops in Russia, numbering about 35,000 and consisting of prisoners of war and deserters from the Austro-Hungarian armies, who claimed the right to fight for Czech independence on the side of the western allies and who had been granted permission to proceed to the western front by way of Vladivostok. The Bolsheviks attempted to disarm the Czechs and then to intern them, and found themselves confronted by a Czech army in revolt and in control of all the principal cities along the Trans-Siberian railway from the Urals to the Pacific. Simultaneously, in a 'democratic counter-revolution', the Socialist-Revolutionaries seized power from the hierarchy of soviets on the Volga and in western Siberia, where the Bolshevik writ was as yet insecure. These were the origins of the Siberian White Government headed by Admiral Kolchak. Possibly the Bolshevik murder on July 16, 1918 of the imperial family in Ekaterinburg* was for conservative elements a stimulus to counter-revolution, though in fact not a single White leader sought to restore the monarchy.

As for allied intervention, anxiety at Russia's withdrawal from the war (and at Bolshevik repudiation of all Russian foreign debts) was sharpened by alarm that the large quantities of arms and military stores which had been dispatched to Murmansk in the north and Vladivostok in the east to aid the Russian armies might fall into German hands. Fear of Bolshevism as such had not yet fully ripened when relatively small allied expeditionary forces landed in the spring at Murmansk, Archangel and Vladivostok. The policy of active intervention was fostered above all by the hopes built upon the preliminary Czech successes.

* Now Sverdlovsk.

All these were major factors in the civil war. But another and no less significant factor was the Bolshevik policy of class struggle in the countryside. In the circumstances of party dictatorship, this sprang from sheer economic necessity. To extract grain from the recalcitrant peasants to feed the hungry towns the government resorted to forced requisitioning, and to assist in this process it deliberately fomented conflict between the richer and the poorer peasants. The campaign waged in the villages by 'committees of the poor' under official direction against the kulak and the middling peasant had all the advantage of doctrinaire expediency to recommend it, but its essential purpose was expropriation pure and simple. It was that, finally, which had brought the Socialist-Revolutionaries, traditionally the peasants' party, into open opposition.

What with dictatorial Bolshevik rule, the dissolution of the constituent assembly and the humiliation of Brest-Litovsk the S.-R.s had reason enough for disavowing the revolution which the Bolsheviks had made. Irreconcilable differences now drove them to desperate measures. In July they assassinated the German ambassador in Moscow in the hope of provoking Germany into military reprisals, thus outlawing themselves politically. But the crisis in their affairs came only after their murder of the chief of the Petrograd Cheka on August 30 and their simultaneous attempt on the life of Lenin. It was now that the red terror was unleashed and now that the dissident socialist elements in Russia coalesced with the conservative forces in counter-revolution.

For in the last resort the sanction of Communist dictatorship was terror. On December 20, 1917 Lenin had set up the *chrezvychainaya commissiya* (extraordinary commission) under Felix Dzerzhinsky for the suppression of counter-revolution. The Cheka, as it was called, which re-created in a new and more dreadful guise the old political police, was not provoked by violent opposition to the regime; it was rather considered indispensable for the wellbeing of the proletarian revolution. It claimed its victims from the outset, not all of them consisting of class enemies, and from the outset also it instituted the practice of taking hostages. But the full and appalling measure of its vengeance was not exercised until the summer of 1918. The immediate Cheka response to the attempt on Lenin's life was the shooting of five hundred class enemies in Petrograd.

Though admittedly it cost Russia fewer lives than the imperialist war, the Russian civil war was a chapter of unspeakable horror. It produced a chaos of competitive savagery on many fronts and inflicted a recurring ordeal of revenge and reprisals upon innocent sections of the population. Perhaps there were good reasons why this was so. The revolution itself, the product of ages of class antagonism, had been all but bloodless; only in an extremity of violence could the antagonism now find an outlet. The cruelty was in no way redeemed by the idealism on either side which now and then shone through it and no romantic view of proletarian revolution can conceal the inhumanity of those years. The most hideous excesses occurred in the Ukraine, where Reds and Whites and anarchist peasant guerrillas met in almost purposeless cruelty and the Jewish population experienced mass pogroms.

The periods of greatest danger to the Bolsheviks were, first, the summer and early autumn of 1918, when the pressure was heaviest upon the Red Guards and workers' detachments, who bore the brunt of the fighting while the newly formed Red Army militia was in training; and again, after the position had been retrieved as much as anything by the allied victory in the west, during the months from May to October 1919. At the beginning of the latter period Kolchak's army in western Siberia was poised for an advance into the heart of Russia, while at its close Denikin had reached a point 250 miles south of Moscow and Yudenich in the west was in the suburbs of Petrograd. But by that time the allied governments were pulling in different directions and the Red Army, tirelessly and brilliantly driven by Trotsky, had gained in resource and mobility. The civil war was all but over by the end of 1920, though the Japanese still occupied a position of some strength in the maritime provinces of the Far East.

With so much apparently in their favour the Whites failed more than all else because counter-revolutionaries are habitually blind to the lessons of revolution. The lack of unity among their leaders mattered less than their incapacity or refusal to enlist peasant support. Undeceived by the Bolsheviks, the strongest and most stable forces among the peasantry were prepared to support an alternative regime. But as the civil war progressed the reactionary elements, whose chief purpose was to undo what the peasants had achieved in 1917, gained ascendancy on the side of the Whites. In the last resort too many among the White officers fought for their estates. Caught between two fires, with little desire to fight on either side, peasant Russia fared equally disastrously at the hands of Reds and Whites.

Three events of lasting significance accompanied the civil war. One was the permanent transfer of the capital from imperial Petrograd to historic Moscow—a transfer which had been regarded as a temporary expedient in March 1918, when it seemed possible that the Germans would occupy Petrograd, and which now acquired symbolical meaning. The second was the formation in Moscow in March 1919 of the Third or Communist International (Comintern), designed to assist the proletariat of all lands in the overthrow of world capitalism. Lenin's faith in world revolution had so far failed him; revolution in Russia was working its own unaided passage, having gained nothing from the brief ardours of revolution in Germany or the transitory triumph of Bela Kun in Hungary. Yet the Bolsheviks still put their trust in the dialectic of history, and the Comintern, the unifying instrument in Moscow of the national Communist parties throughout the world and the source of so much Russian folly in the future, helped to sustain it.

The third event was war with Poland. In 1920 Soviet Russia formally recognized the independence of Finland and of the Baltic states. But amid the savage confusion of the civil war in the Ukraine agreement on the frontiers of an independent Poland was still to seek. The peacemakers at Versailles had drawn a boundary on the 'Curzon line'; the Poles had never ceased to dream of their greatness before the partitions or indeed even earlier. The war they began in the spring of 1920 brought astonishing fluctuations of fortune. The short-lived Polish gain of Kiev was followed by the sweeping advance of the Red Army upon Warsaw (the Bolshevik leaders went out confidently to meet revolution in Poland, as twenty years later they went out confidently to meet revolution in Finland) and then by headlong Russian retreat.The Soviet-Polish armistice in October was followed next March by the treaty of Riga, which advanced the eastern frontier of Poland well beyond the Curzon line—a settlement which, in the historic and perpetually unstable nature of Russian-Polish relations, settled nothing.

One item only in the legacy of the civil war brought comfort to Bolshevik Russia. By the time victory had been won the Red Army was a formidable fighting force and the centralized apparatus of Bolshevik power was proof against external shock. The Soviet Government headed by Lenin was unmistakably the government of Russia. But everywhere else was unrelieved disaster. First and foremost, the Russian economy had collapsed. For the Communist rank and file it had seemed simple enough on assuming power to proceed to the economic transformation of society through a state monopoly of foreign trade, the nationalization of the banks, the socialization of industry, the establishment of an eight-hour day and the principle of workers' control. But civil war had necessitated the introduction of 'war communism' with its ruthless system of confiscation, of universal labour service, of food priorities and differential rationing, all growing more stringent as official barter in every sector of the economy replaced a market in which money had lost all value. And even barter was threatened by the growth of a vast black market. After two and a half years of unimaginably destructive civil war almost the whole of industry lay in ruin, and agriculture, because all normal incentives were lacking, had shrunk to a perilously low level.

Realism is a native quality of mind. Though in the policies he pursued in power Lenin was always a strange compound of the doctrinaire and the opportunist, the realism he so often displayed in a crisis has about it the light of unequivocal genius. Amid warning outbursts of untamed peasant anarchy came the mutiny in March 1921 at the naval base of Kronstadt. No propagandist distortion of the event can conceal the disenchantment with Bolshevik rule to which it bore witness. The chief demands of the naval garrison of this historic centre of revolution were simple and unambiguous; this was a mutiny designed to end the ruthless dragooning of the peasants and to restore the effective power of the soviets. It may be going too far to describe these demands as a cry for the bourgeois-democratic realities of civil liberty, but without doubt they expressed a bitter sense of the Bolshevik abandonment of revolutionary ideals. The mutiny was violently suppressed, and with its suppression almost the last flicker of opposition to Communist dictatorship died out. But already Lenin had posed the basic political issue at a party congress and announced an abrupt *volte-face* in policy. The fruits of October were in jeopardy through the catastrophic fall in agricultural production and the exhaustion of industry. In the interests therefore of restoring the alliance of workers and peasants grain requisitioning would be abandoned for a system of taxation in kind. This would confer upon the peasant the right to dispose of his surplus on the open market.

The departure thus announced from a policy of theoretical socialism was a minimum concession to the peasantry. But the full implications of the New Economic Policy (N.E.P.) were drastic and far-reaching. The peasant's freedom to sell his surplus necessitated the revival of private trade and industry, and this in turn required the stimulus of a policy of concessions to private capital. N.E.P. signified, in fact, a sudden reversion to capitalism and the usages of capitalist society. There could have been no plainer indication that Russia was not ripe for proletarian revolution in 1917.

The retreat from socialism in Russia in 1921, at the time so widely misinterpreted abroad, was a strategic retreat. Neither Lenin nor anybody else in the Communist hierarchy had the least intention of abandoning the original Bolshevik aims; it was a 'breathing-space' only that they sought. The growth of a sector of private trading would not be permitted to interfere with the state monopoly of foreign trade nor with the state direction of large-scale industry. The immediate need was at all costs to increase the volume of production. Concessions to the peasants* were made all the more obligatory by the disastrous failure of the harvest in the Volga provinces in 1921 and the famine conditions of the following year, when only missions of relief by American and other foreign agencies reduced the number who died of starvation to what may have been something between four and five million. Peasants were now permitted by law to lease land left uncultivated by their neighbours, eventually even to hire labour. In industry a policy of decentralization took shape in a system of self-regulating 'trusts' controlling interdependent units of production. The stabilization of the currency, which had suffered fantastic depreciation, was taken in hand and completed in 1924, when the chief victims were the new flourishing class of private traders or Nepmen. By 1927, in a national economy of mixed private and state capitalism in which collectivist planning was already beginning to operate, production in some sectors had returned to the level of 1913.

It is hard to pick and choose among the salient features of these years between the introduction of N.E.P. and the inauguration of the first five-year-plan. In the indoctrination of the younger generation in Marxist and anti-religious or 'godless' principles (on coming to power the Bolsheviks had immediately abolished all religious instruction in the schools) the League of Communist Youth (Comsomol) took over where the schools left off. The emancipation of women was a genuine revolutionary achievement, though a leading motive for the equality of the sexes was the equal use of male and female labour, with little or nothing in the way of protective legislation for the latter. In 1922 the Cheka was transformed into the State Political Administration, *Gosudarstvennoe Politicheskoe Upravlenie* (G.P.U.), a distinction without a difference. In 1924 the Union of Socialist Soviet Republics (U.S.S.R.) was formed by the federal union of Russia proper, the Ukraine, White Russia and Transcaucasia (where a successful Menshevik regime in Georgia had been overturned by force in February 1921), and later in the year the union was extended to the Central Asian republics. In theory, the constituent republics always possessed the right to secede and enjoyed complete cultural autonomy. In point of fact, such autonomy was confined within the limits of a Marxist philosophy of culture and the centralization of power in Moscow was even stricter than it had been under the tsars.

A word is necessary on the course of Soviet foreign relations during the period of N.E.P. before summing up the crisis of domestic policy in which the personal and ideological clash between Stalin and Trotsky was resolved. Since world revolution had been deferred, the Soviet aim was to secure diplomatic recognition as

* The state tax in kind was eventually replaced by a money tax.

quickly as possible in a climate of what continued to be almost unabated hostility. Failing recognition, which was pursued through proposals for European disarmament and offers of non-aggression pacts, the practical need was to resume commercial relations with other countries. An Anglo-Soviet commercial agreement, the first in the series, was signed in March 1921 and diplomatic recognition was accorded three years afterwards. Many countries followed suit, though the United States, among others, abstained. The most important by far of these agreements was the Soviet-German treaty of Rapallo in April 1922. The ghosts of Peter the Great and of Bismarck presided jointly over it. Not recognition and trade only came with this realistic diplomatic venture at Rapallo but intensified mutual aid in the technical development of both the Soviet and the German armies. For the rest, Britain bore the brunt of Comintern propaganda and the Kuomintang in China was its principal beneficiary.

Soviet policy towards China entered into the conflict between Stalin and Trotsky. Originating in a clash of personality, which was specially in evidence during the civil war and which afterwards stood out from the entire play of ambition in the party hierarchy, the conflict, in the irrational mode of political behaviour from which even scientific Marxists are not immune, extended to almost every issue of Soviet policy. The ideological issue between these two strikingly antithetical figures was real enough; it did, in fact, correspond not only with personal rivalry but with the opposition of two main currents of Bolshevik opinion. How was the future of the revolution to be assured and by what practical stages was the transition to socialism to be made effective? On the one hand, the encircling enemy front of world capitalism was as yet unbroken; on the other, within Russia itself the growing class division in the villages endangered every principle of the socialist organization of society. The town or the country, more revolution or less, world-wide socialism or socialism in a single country—the U.S.S.R.: that, in substance, was the question.

In May 1922 Lenin suffered the first of the two seizures which, except for a period of some months before the second in March of the following year, disabled him from leadership for the remaining short period of his life. In that same month Stalin was appointed general secretary of the central committee of the party. The appointment marked the recognition of his exceptional abilities as an organizer, but was in no way intended to distinguish him from the other members of the Politbureau, among whom after Lenin himself Trotsky easily held pride of place. Yet within an astonishingly short time Stalin had won a remarkable measure of control of the party apparatus of power. The remorseless calculation displayed in the methods he employed became more familiar in later years, but it was sufficiently evident at the time to disturb Lenin. In December 1922 he expressed his concern at the Frankenstein he had conjured up in a letter which has become known as his will and testament. He found the general secretary 'too crude', was alarmed at the power Stalin had concentrated in his own hands, feared a party split and recommended that the general secretary be removed from office. Nothing had been done, however—or, rather, Stalin had taken his own measures—when on January 21, 1924 Lenin died.

Tempered though it had been by the fanaticism and the inhumanity which lurk in all revolutionary idealism, distorted in impulse by the rejection of liberty and the use of terror, the idealistic age of the Russian revolution, which while he lived retained a certain breath of incorruptibility, passed with him. He had been the supreme architect of Communist power in Russia. Peter the Great's city became Leningrad, Lenin's city. Lenin's tomb in the Red Square in Moscow became the shrine of Russian and world Communism. The new testament of Leninism was joined to the old testament of Marxism as the source and fount of revolutionary orthodoxy. But after Lenin, in hoary revolutionary metaphor, came the deluge.

With his death the forms of democracy hitherto reserved for internal party debate crumbled. While leadership was ostensibly shared by a triumvirate consisting of Stalin, Zinoviev and Kamenev the first of the triumvirs proceeded to establish undivided personal supremacy in party and state. Stalin's tactics in forming temporary alliances to strike down rivals and then striking at his allies were in a time-honoured tradition. Opposition leaders and opposition principles were conveniently identified as disruptive influences, and the majority Stalin secured at the party congress in December 1925 for what was in effect the policy of socialism in a single country was an endorsement of his own supreme authority. The charges levelled at him by a constantly shifting opposition of betraying Communist doctrine and of a tyrannical abuse of the party statutes left his control of the secretariat unimpaired. In 1926 first Zinoviev and then Trotsky were expelled from the Politbureau, and a year later from the party. Kamenev's expulsion followed. In January 1928, after the other two had recanted, Trotsky was exiled to Alma Ata, in central Asia, and a year later was deported. The struggle was all but over, though it remained to dismiss Bukharin, Rykov, Tomsky and others. Stalin had not merely succeeded to the mantle of Lenin. He had assumed a dictator's crown.

The five-year-plan for the development of the national economy arose out of the controversy between Stalin and Trotsky and the decision to proceed with the construction of socialism in a single country. Designed to transform Russia without further ado from an agrarian into an industrial country, it was a grandiose and startling conception, which remains the most original contribution of the Russian revolution to the history of our age. The idea of economic planning was by no means new. Nor did the comprehensive form it took in Russia in 1928, a form implied in Marxist economic doctrine, originate in an empirical void. The State Planning Commission (Gosplan), set up in 1920, had laboured for years at co-ordinating the researches of geologists and the blueprints of engineers in an integrated plan of industrial development. What was new in Soviet economic planning was its soaring ambition. The goal laid down—to overtake and surpass, by her own unaided energies, the most advanced countries of the capitalist west— seemed a flight of fantasy; the means proposed—the regulated adjustment of every aspect of life to an overall economic plan— the very pith of madness. And indeed there was more than a touch of the crudest megalomania in the progressive enlargement of the objectives of the plan. Yet the planned economy came to stay. The methods adopted in Russia to enforce it went beyond the most despotic authoritarianism of Peter the Great. The fearful cost of achievement, all the greater because the precise mechanism of planning had still to be learned and because there was only an army of unskilled and ignorant peasant labour to execute the plan, cannot be estimated either in lives or in human suffering. But in essentials the plan came off.

Since the volume of investment in industry which it called for could come only from production itself, notoriously low standards of living were reduced to the barest level of subsistence. The manufacture of consumer goods almost ceased. Strategic as well as economic ends dictated the eastward shift of heavy industry, the basis of armament manufacture, and in the vast new factory encampments in the Urals and beyond men and women from remote parts of Russia worked and starved and in winter half-froze. Labour discipline was maintained by stringent penalties. The integration of the educational machine with the labour demands of industry gave almost all forms of school education a vocational bias. Piece-work wages and a system in the plants and factories of socialist competition or emulation, another distinction without a difference, combined with a differential rationing system to support the drive for higher output. All the resources of propaganda served to stimulate a mood of heroic sacrifice and to obscure the harsh materialism of this essay in socialist construction. As in Peter the Great's time, the drive was merciless, the pace even more killing.

The five-year-plan, formally begun in October 1928, was completed in four years. The second five-year-plan duly began in 1932. Stakhanovism, all too often a crudely disguised form of 'speeding-up', came in 1935, and at the same time the award of honours and distinctions such as 'Hero of Socialist Labour' fell thick and fast. The basic tasks of socialist construction were achieved by the blood, toil and tears of peasant labour diverted to industry. It was in the wilds of peasant Russia that the real revolution effected by the first five-year-plan came with most shattering consequences. Not surprisingly; for the final argument for the policy of industrialization overnight sprang from the reduced deliveries of grain to the towns. The Russian revolution in the villages took the form of the collectivization of agriculture, a revolution still unfinished and perhaps as yet not entirely secure. It was inherent in a programme of capital construction in industry which demanded vast reserves of unskilled labour for the sinking of new mines, the erection of blast furnaces and steel mills, the construction of railways, the digging of canals. But at the same time it was both a practical and an ideological necessity of socialism in the villages. If the peasantry were the only available labour force for new industry, how could reduced numbers in agriculture maintain production, let alone increase it, in order to feed the towns? And how could the class war simultaneously be renewed in the villages in order that the political backwardness of the peasants might be overcome? The answer to these questions was the collective farm and the liquidation of the kulaks as a class.

For all who could read the signs the collectivization of agriculture was heralded long before the start of the five-year-plan by the experiment of the large-scale state farm (*sovkhoz*). Now the collective farm (*kolkhoz*), an enormous unit of socialized agriculture formed by the amalgamation of hundreds of individual small farms and reverting in principle in some degree to the village commune, was introduced as a means of establishing a classless society in the countryside. Collectivization was meant to wean the peasant from the petty-bourgeois backwardness of individualist habits of mind and from a sense of private property. At the same time it was intended to raise the technical level of farming by mechanization, and for this purpose a network of state machine-tractor stations was created, at least on paper, from which the *kolkhoz* would hire new types of agricultural machinery. The scheme, introduced on a voluntary basis, made a slow start; collective farming hung fire for every good reason but not least because the kulaks, the most efficient and successful peasants, would have nothing to do with it. The arts of persuasion were tried out by forcible seizures of grain and by incitements to violence. Then, in the early autumn of 1929 pressure was applied in earnest. When this proved unavailing the party missionaries and political police in charge of the operation declared uncompromising war against the kulak.

'The horrors of collectivization' is no empty phrase. This second and much greater Bolshevik revolution was waged with implacable cruelty and resisted with the extreme of desperation. The kulaks—and not the kulaks only but millions of peasants who possessed a couple of horses and a herd of half a dozen cows—were wiped out as a class. The killings, the rounding-up of groups of obdurate peasants by machine-gun squads, were warnings only. Droves of peasants—sometimes the population of entire villages—were packed off in thousands from all parts of Russia to forced labour and semi-starvation in the mines, timber camps and construction projects of the east or the Arctic north. But not, as a rule, until after they had made their stand in characteristic peasant fashion. They, too, could resort to murder or arson; most easily, to the slaughter of their horses and cattle rather than see them fall into the hands of others. It was the vast scale of this slaughter which inflicted an irreparable blow on Russian agriculture for two decades afterwards, which raised still higher the demands of mechanized farming upon industrial production, and which brought the drive for collectivization to a temporary halt. In March 1930, in his 'dizzy from success' remonstration, Stalin laid the blame for what had happened on the excesses of local party zealots. By that time not far short of three-fifths of the peasantry had been enrolled in a *kolkhoz*. The numbers declined sharply immediately afterwards, but then rose again in response to the incentives provided by the use of machinery and credit facilities and especially by the right extended to the *kolkhoznik* to retain a small individual plot of his own. But among the ghastly fruits of the campaign for collectivization was the 'man-made' famine of 1931–2 in the Ukraine and the northern Caucasus, where it had been resisted most fiercely and where the fields had lain almost totally neglected. There were millions of deaths from starvation in these regions.

From the accession of Hitler to power in Germany in 1933 the perspective of Russian history grows more obscure. Russia of the Byzantine and Asiatic age of Stalinism recedes into the seclusion of earlier centuries, sealed off from the west by an almost impenetrable curtain of security. For her people the hardships of forced industrialization are intensified by the needs of defence; for the Communist movements in all lands duty lies in supporting the foreign policy of the Soviet Union, the bastion of world socialism. Secretive and yet loud with the noise of propaganda, her principles of government are daylight clear. The law in all things—in industry and labour, in science and technology, in art and literature—

derives from the party line. The mortal offence is deviation from the party line. The next mortal offence is admiration of foreign example. For with Russian isolation goes a new brand of Russian— Great Russian—nationalism which is styled Soviet patriotism, from which all the familiar verities of international socialist faith have been discarded. Alexander Nevsky, Dmitry Donskoy, Ivan the Terrible, Minin and Pozharsky, Peter the Great, Suvorov and Kutuzov are the heroes of the new history primers. They shed their light upon the greatest in their line, for whom Russian history is indeed re-written. Stalin is heir to the Russian glory. He is the supreme world genius, the teacher of all peoples, the infallible leader of a monolithic state and party. The Stalin Constitution of the U.S.S.R. proclaimed in 1936 is the most democratic constitution in the world, indeed the only democratic constitution. In place of the congress of soviets it establishes a Supreme Soviet, which is elected by direct and secret ballot but from a single list of candidates, each of whom is in fact returned by a vote of 98 or 99 per cent. of the electorate. There is only one party in Russia, it is explained, because parties correspond to classes and in Russia there are now only two classes, workers and peasants, who are indissolubly united.

A monolithic state and party, and yet the melodrama and the mystery of the Moscow treason trials of the 1930s overhang the long night of Stalin's despotism. No more than the French revolution did the Russian revolution escape the fate of devouring its children. The road, however, was by different and more gradual stages. The terror had taken its toll of counter-revolutionaries and class enemies, but the dissident Bolshevik so far had suffered expulsion, disgrace or imprisonment but not judicial murder. The strange Communist technique of trial and confession had first been demonstrated with dramatic effect in the spring of 1928, when a group of highly-placed engineers were charged with sabotage. It had since become familiar in a crop of trials of saboteurs, spies, wreckers, diversionists and counter-revolutionaries, all accused of planning with foreign support to undermine or overthrow the Soviet regime and restore capitalism. But a new phase opened, a few months after the G.P.U. had been translated into the N.K.V.D. (*Narodny Commissariat Vnutrennykh Del*—the Commissariat of Internal Affairs), with the murder of Sergey Kirov, a member of the Politbureau and the party boss in Leningrad. The murder, like so much else in the prolonged spectacle of death and hallucination to which it was the prelude, remains a mystery. The orgy of speculation on the Moscow treason trials is not yet over, but it seems very probable that the murderer, a young party member named Nikolayev, was the sacrificial instrument of a group of disillusioned Communists of the younger generation. Whatever the motive, there begins at this point a nightmare of political persecution perhaps as dreadful as any in the annals of Russia.

In successive stages almost the entire Bolshevik Old Guard was liquidated. Outside Russia incredulity piled on incredulity as the drama unfolded. In August 1936 Zinoviev, Kamenev and fourteen others were brought to public trial on charges of conspiracy, in collusion with Trotsky and with German aid, to overthrow the Soviet Government, murder Stalin, sabotage industry, undermine collectivization and restore capitalism. All the accused pleaded guilty, made full confession and were duly executed. In January 1937 came the turn of Karl Radek, a close associate of Lenin's and the foremost Bolshevik journalist, and sixteen other prominent figures incriminated in a 'Trotskyist centre'. In June it was announced that Marshal Tukhachevsky and a group of other leading commanders of the Red Army had been tried as traitors, found guilty and summarily shot. At the close of the year seven more former pillars of the regime were put on trial and suffered the death penalty for treason. In March 1938 Nicholas Bukharin, the inflexible theorist of Communism, Alexis Rykov, ex-premier of the Soviet Government, and the brilliant Christian Rakovsky, a leading diplomat, stood in the dock with seventeen others beside Henrik Yagoda, the former chief of the N.K.V.D. who had superintended the earlier arrests and trials, and were dispatched as traitors.

The most gruesome aspect of this campaign of extermination,* which was conducted in an atmosphere of deliberately fomented hysteria and hate, was that the public trials represented an insignificantly tiny part of the whole. The scale of the purge in these two and a half years was monstrous. It extended throughout the length and breadth of the Soviet Union and played particular havoc in the constituent republics, where after the old leadership had been liquidated the new suffered in turn in precisely the same way. And not the leadership only. Everywhere the downfall of each party or government notability was the signal for the arrest of hundreds of people who at some time or other had been associated with him. The victims, condemned to death, imprisonment or concentration camp, were of all sorts and conditions, officials, managers in industry, authors and artists, foreign Communists in Russia, wholly insignificant men and women. Memories are never so short as when they are dulled by horror, but it should not be forgotten that vast numbers of people in Russia in these years simply vanished from sight. The purge in the army appears to have been as drastic as anywhere, and it is impossible not to conclude,

---

* In a few cases—for instance, that of Radek, who was sentenced to twenty years' imprisonment—the death sentence was waived.

in spite of conventional reassurances to the contrary, that the Russian forces in 1941 were perilously weakened by the virtual extinction of the experienced high command. The long ordeal came to an apparent end in March 1939, when the place at the head of the N.K.V.D. of the sinister Yezhov, who reigned only briefly and then disappeared without trace, was taken by the Georgian Lavrenty Beria. What more the purge had signified while it lasted than a psychosis of fear and blood lust, how much more was involved in the confessions than a half-incomprehensible morality of submission to the party will, it is impossible even now to tell. The great names among the victims had all been in opposition to Stalin at one time or other during his ascent to supreme power. That there was widespread opposition to his personal regime and policies is as beyond doubt as that all opposition was 'illegal'. That some of the victims represented, in his eyes, potential centres of resistance, or even pivotal agencies of an alternative government, is not impossible. The formal charges of treasonable conspiracy with Fascist and capitalist foreign governments were pure fantasy. Beyond that, however, all would be guesswork. But the palpable effect of the great purge was to isolate Russia still more completely from the rest of the world and to confine the Russian people more narrowly within the strait-jacket of Stalinism.

In spite of the Russian war psychosis of the decade before 1939, perhaps because of it, no people desired war less than the Russian. In 1939 they avoided it, though at the cost of making eventual war with Germany more certain. Inspired miscalculation on both the Russian and the Anglo-French side contributed to the Soviet-Nazi pact of August 23, 1939. The fatal Russian error went back to the doctrinaire folly of Moscow's instructions to the Communists in Germany to continue to wage war against the German Social-Democrats rather than against Hitler before the latter came to power —a folly which was not to be retrieved by entry into the League of Nations, the propaganda of collective security and the agitation for popular fronts in Europe. The failure of courage and realism in the Anglo-French policy of appeasement was crowned by the facile notion at Munich of a deal at anybody's expense, even Russia's, but their own. After Munich no diplomatic accommodation between Russia and the west was possible.

The chief events of the second world war from the Russian side are lit by brutal calculation and tragic grandeur. On September 17, 1939 the Red Army marched into eastern Poland and later in the month the formerly Polish areas of the western Ukraine and western White Russia were incorporated into Soviet territory. On November 3 the Red Army invaded Finland and in the following

March the Soviet-Finnish frontier was pushed back some seventy miles and an extensive strip of Finnish territory assimilated to the Soviet autonomous republic of Karelia. In June Bessarabia and northern Bukovina passed into Soviet hands. In August the Baltic states, in effect prisoners of Russia from the outbreak of war, were formally declared constituent republics of the Soviet Union. During all these months Russia was punctilious in observing the commercial clauses of the pact with Germany, but otherwise the diplomatic fencing with Hitler bore a remarkable resemblance to the tactics of evasion after Tilsit. All the more astonishing therefore, if the unpreparedness of the Red Army is any guide, is the apparent reluctance of the Soviet leaders to believe that war with Germany was imminent.

A strange and significant delay of eleven days, after the German invasion on June 22, 1941, attended Stalin's proclamation of 'a war of liberation' (the parallel with 1812 could scarcely have been emphasized with greater deliberation) and a strategy of guerrilla resistance in the rear of the advancing German armies. The pace of the Red Army retreat was catastrophic. In September the Germans were in the outskirts of Leningrad. In the following month began the battle for Moscow, the crisis of the war. The seat of government was moved to Kuibyshev, on the middle Volga, the trained Red Army divisions in the east were brought up to the Moscow front and in an early winter which was also the coldest in living memory the capital of the Soviet fatherland was saved. But in the south the dimensions of the retreat were ruinous. The vast losses in territory, in industrial plant and in human lives swelled the effect of the initial response to war in the western border regions. Though every attempt was made then and afterwards to disguise the facts, large sections among the Ukrainians and White Russians and the peoples of the northern Caucasus, together with almost the entire population of the Baltic states, were prepared to welcome the German armies. There was, indeed, active collaboration for a time. Only the German methods of conquest and exploitation of the 'inferior' Slav races disillusioned them and lent an extra ferocity to guerrilla reprisals.

In the spring of 1942 the prolonged drama of Stalingrad opened. It was the turning-point in the second world war. In the summer of the following year the Red Army moved forward through great areas of devastation towards unconditional surrender and the occupation of Berlin. Six days before war in the Far East ended the Soviet Government declared war on Japan. On the Russian side relations with the allies, both before and after the second front had been opened in the west, were marked by unvarying secretiveness and suspicion. These sprang not from Bolshevik doctrine only.

Russia had borne in overwhelming degree the brunt of the fighting. Her dead numbered anything from seven to eleven million, some twenty-five million people had been made homeless, hundreds of towns and thousands of villages and collective farms had been obliterated, mines, factories and power plants laid waste, the newly created wealth amassed by untold sacrifice destroyed by the invader. Perversely, it was this disproportion between Russian losses and the losses of the west which ruled out the prospect of collaboration in peace between the eastern and western allies in war.

'How many divisions has the Pope?' Stalin is reported to have asked on a famous occasion during the war. In the background of Soviet policy after the war were the divisions of the Red Army. The rulers in Moscow were content to cast away the goodwill and gratitude of the west in rebuilding Russia's strength and restoring Russia's isolation. A policy of systematic confiscation and of reparations in the eastern zone of Germany helped to tide Russia over the period of acutest want. The Balkans at last were brought under effective Russian tutelage through the creation of a ring of satellite Communist states. The iron curtain was lowered. After renewed privations and prodigies of effort Russia once more climbed the steep road to economic recovery, along which a new managerial aristocracy advanced by the side of the leading party cadres; while amid the tensions of the cold war the doctrine was sedulously propagated of Russia's unaided victory in the second world war and the superiority of Russian culture to all others. From end to end of the great Eurasian plain the energies of its drilled and indomitable peoples were turned to vast new projects of construction. Science was harnessed to the relentless expansion of Soviet military power. Through the continued exploitation of an impulse of idealism in ordinary men and women, above all in the young, the belief persisted that Russia was creating an order of life and society more desirable than any that had hitherto been attempted in history. From an all but completely socialist society Russia was now moving towards the infinite horizons of a Communist society. In waiting for history to prove them right the ominous shadow of the great purge of the 1930s fell for a moment upon the Russian people with Stalin's discovery of a 'doctors' plot'. But on March 5, 1953 Stalin died, the heir to all the ages of power in Russia.

Is it illusory, the hope of a more liberal regime in Russia since then? Only time will tell. But the question should be put in that form rather than directed in more conventional fashion to the prospect of friendlier relations between Communist Russia and the west. For continuous tension in one form or another between Russia and the west is perhaps unavoidable in our generation and even afterwards. In the terms of Chaadayev's historic analysis, Russia belongs neither to Europe nor to Asia. In the centuries of her history since the emergence of the state of Muscovy she has oscillated between the examples of Europe and Asia, finding in Asia rather than in Europe the contemporary principle of the absolute authority of the state. Now that her power straddles the world between east and west conflict on the periphery will always reach the nerve-centres of a rival and democratic system of power. What may detonate the conflict is the pressure upon an unchanged totalitarian despotism in Russia of the forces of internal discontent. These, after all, represent the dialectic of Communist rule. The peoples of Russia have known order; they have barely tasted liberty. Will the Communist rulers of Russia resist the necessity of liberty? That, rather than the possibility of a relaxation of tension between Russia and the west, is the question posed by Russian history since Stalin.

INDEX